Biology
of Suicide

Edited by
RONALD MARIS, PH.D.

© 1986 The Guilford Press
A Division of Guilford Publications, Inc.
200 Park Avenue South, New York, N.Y. 10003

PRINTED IN THE UNITED STATES OF AMERICA

Library of Congress Cataloging-in-Publication Data

Biology of suicide.

"A special issue of Suicide and life-threatening
behavior."
Includes index.
1. Suicide—Psysiolocial aspects. 2. Clinical
biochemistry. 3. Neurophysiology. 4. Biological
psychiatry. I. Maris, Ronald W. [DNLM: 1. Suicide.
HV 6545 B61]
RG569.B54 1986   616.85′8445   86-14207
ISBN 0-89862-578-5

Notes on Contributors

Gerald L. Brown, MD, psychiatrist-scientist, is at the National Institute of Mental Health (NIMH), Intramural Research Program. Research interests are biology and psychology of childhood mental illness, aggression and suicide. He directed the psychiatric residency, National Naval Medical Center, followed by Public Health Service research and administrative responsibilities at NIMH.

Denys de Catanzaro, PhD, was made Associate Professor of Psychology at McMaster University in 1985. Since 1981 he has held an NSERC University Research Fellowship. Much of his laboratory research has concerned effects of stress and pituitary-adrenal hormones upon reproductive behavior. He is author of *Suicide and Self-Damaging Behavior: A Sociobiological Perspective* (Academic Press, 1981) and in 1984 received the AAS Shneidman Award.

Frederick K. Goodwin, MD, psychiatrist-scientist, is Director, National Institute of Mental Health (NIMH), Intramural Research. His research has focused on manic-depressive illness, aggression, and suicide. He is the recipient of major research awards, and one of the five most frequently cited psychiatrists in the world.

David Lester, PhD, was Director of Research at the Suicide Prevention and Crisis Service of Buffalo, New York, from 1969 to 1971. Since then, he has been Professor of Psychology, Richard Stockton State College, Pomona, New Jersey.

Ronald Maris, PhD, recently published *Pathways to Suicide* (Johns Hopkins, 1981) and *Suicide and Ethics* (Human Sciences Press, 1983). He is Professor of Sociology and Preventive Medicine, University of South Carolina; Editor, *Suicide and Life-Threatening Behavior*, Director of the South Carolina Suicide Center.

Jerome A. Motto, MD, is Professor of Psychiatry, University of California at San Francisco School of Medicine, Associate Director, Psychiatric Consultation Service, University of California, San Francisco Medical Center. He was the President of the American Association of Suicidology 1972-73, Secretary-General, International Association for Suicide Prevention 1974-77. He received the Dublin Award from the American Association of Suicidology in 1979.

Charles L. Rich, MD, is Associate Professor of Psychiatry, University of California, San Diego and serves as chief of the Inpatient Psychiatry Service, San Diego VA Medical Center. He is currently involved in analyzing data from a large study of young suicides in the San Diego area.

Alec Roy, MD, for the last four years, has been a Visiting Associate, National Institute of Health in Bethesda, Maryland, carrying out biologic research in depression, schizophrenia, and alcoholism.

David H. Rubenstein, PhD, MPH, has recently completed a three-year NIMH-funded ethnographic study of suicide in Truk, Micronesia. Currently Rubenstein is Executive Director of the Centers for Asian and Pacific Studies at the University of Hawaii.

Michael Stanley, PhD, is Associate Professor of Clinical Psychopharmacology, Department of Psychiatry and Pharmacology, College of Physicians and Surgeons of Columbia University. He also holds the position of Research Scientist at New York State Psychiatric Institute. Dr. Stanley's research interests include biological research in suicide and suicidal behavior; neurochemistry of psychiatric and neurologic illness; mechanism of action of drugs used to treat mental illnesses; and ethical issues in psychiatric research.

Frederick A. Struve, PhD, is Professor of Psychiatry and Behaviorial Sciences, Eastern Virginia Medical School in Norfolk, Virginia. His overall broad research area is the electroencephalographic study of psychopathology. Current studies are exploring the complex relationships between the various subcortical dysrhythmias and stress induced psychophysiological reactions as well as clinical presentations in a behavioral medicine population.

Bryan L. Tanney, MD, is Associate Professor at the University of Calgary. He also acts as a consultant to the Suicide Information and Education Centre, and is actively involved in the development of training programs for caregivers of all expertises and disciplines in suicide intervention and prevention.

Herman van Praag, MD, PhD, founded in 1966, the first Department of Biological Psychiatry in Europe at the University of Groningen, the Netherlands. In 1977 he was appointed Professor and Chairman at the University of Utrecht and in 1982 he assumed the same position at the Albert Einstein College of Medicine/Montefiore Medical Center. His research on suicide focuses on biological correlates of suicidal behavior, interrelationship of suicide, hostility and depression, and measurement of disturbances in aggression and impulse regulation.

Preface

Rather than react passively to topics submitted to me as editor of *Suicide and Life-Threatening Behavior*—in other words, to let current author interest alone shape the development of suicidology—I have decided that it is occasionally necessary to actively solicit papers on selected special topics. The current volume represents one such proactive enterprise. (An earlier special issue was devoted to ethical issues related to suicide—viz., Volume 13, Number 4.) All papers in this volume were invited in an effort to secure the most highly competent scholars of the biology of suicide available in North America. I was fortunate to win the cooperation of so many basic scientists and research psychiatrists.

Why choose the biology of suicide as a special topic? The most obvious reason is the recent biomedical emphasis of the federal government and the National Institute of Mental Health (NIMH) on suicide research and funding. A second reason was a psychobiological conference in New York City in September 1985, cosponsored by the New York Academy of Sciences and the NIMH. The previous relative neglect of the biological aspects of suicide by *Suicide and Life-Threatening Behavior* and the American Association of Suicidology (AAS) was a third factor (i.e., there seemed to be a need to bridge professional isolation and to fill a suicidological lacuna). As a case in point, almost none of the New York City conference presenters were members of the AAS. Why not? One might reasonably argue that biomedical and basic science networks are simply different. But even the sociocultural and psychological presentations at the New York conference were by professionals most suicidologists had never heard of. Fourth, I desired to be as scientific and precise as possible in the study of suicide. And, finally, I wanted to increase communication between neurobiological researchers and clinicians.

The book before you implicitly addresses several fundamental questions (many of which are "nature–nurture" issues). For example, what is the relationship of biological variables to other factors in the etiology of suicide? Is suicide a biochemical event? Is biology suicidal destiny? How organic is suicide? Does brain or central nervous system (CNS) chemistry cause suicidal behaviors, or do external factors (e.g., stress) cause brain chemistry? What is the complex mix of social, personal, cultural, and biological factors in suicide? Of course, all of these questions are more complex and subtle than they are stated here to be.

We must remember that suicides are not all of one type. Suicide is a complex dependent variable, which implies (among other things) that biomedical or psychobiological factors are more a part of some suicides than they are of others (cf. Shneidman, *Definition of Suicide*, 1985). Just because all suicides die self-intended deaths clearly does not mean that there is any common (or set of common) physical precursors to suicide.

I need to comment on some psychobiological topics that have been left out of the present volume. A specific chapter on depression, antidepressant medications, and suicide was declined consecutively by four separate colleagues (viz., Drs. Klerman, Beck, Clayton, and Schuyler). Thus, when it was time to go to press, no suitable author had been found, and the topic unfortunately had to be omitted. In addition, I had intended to have a chapter by Dr. Lettieri on the drugs actually used to commit suicide and on drug automatism, but he did not have time to write the chapter. I also thought about reprinting an interesting paper on luteinizing hormones and violence by Drs. Mendelson, Dietz, and Ellingboe (*Pharmacology, Biochemistry, and Behavior*, (1982), but in the end decided against including any previously published research. Finally, Dr. Young (San Diego) worked on a chapter on suicide and the menstrual cycle, but was unable to complete it. Given the overlap of these 4 missing chapters with the 11 that have been included, I hope that the comprehensiveness of the book has not been seriously compromised.

It should also be noted that early in this project (viz., April–June 1984), about two dozen AAS members were surveyed concerning their views on the various aspects and relative importance of the biology of suicide. Most respondents felt that the biology of suicide (primarily a derivative of the psychobiology and psychopharmacology of depression) was in its infancy and only of very limited interest to AAS members. Respondents claimed that the biology of suicide was a highly technical subject of unknown and undemonstrated clinical relevance. They observed that biological research on completed suicides (i.e., postmortems) is extremely difficult to do. And, of course, *in vivo* procedures on suicide attempters are no substitute for postmortem procedures, because (obviously) some techniques cannot be used on living subjects, and only about 10–20% of suicide attempters ever complete suicide. Most of those surveyed felt that biological markers were not sufficient conditions for suicide, since some suicides have no biological abnormalities. The survey consensus was that biomedical indicators tend to identify subsets of populations containing those individuals who are at high risk for suicide, *if* personal, social, cultural, and other factors are also conducive to suicide.

Some of the major research findings of the book before you are now listed. I also provide citations (where applicable) that indicate the original authors of the research results, and I note which authors in the present volume discuss the topic. These findings are in no particular order, nor are any qualifications or subtleties provided. Please take them with the caveats intended. For more careful statements in proper contexts, the reader is (of course) referred to the full statements that follow.

1. Low levels (e.g., below 92.5 nmol/liter) of hydroxyindoleacetic acid (5-HIAA; a metabolite of the neurotransmittor serotonin, or 5-HT) in cerebrospinal fluid (CSF) is predictive of suicidal acts, especially of violent suicides (Asberg, 1973). (See chapters in this volume by van Praag; Brown & Goodwin; and Stanley *et al.*)

2. Low levels of 5-HT in the CNS are predictive of suicide. (See chapters by van Praag and Stanley *et al.*)

3. Elevated levels (viz., 9 mg/24 hours for women and 14 mg/24 hours for men) of urinary 17-hydroxycorticosterone (OHCS) are positively related to completed suicide (Bunney & Fawcett, 1965). (See chapters by Motto and Rich.)

4. A plasma cortisol level higher than 20 mcg% is related positively to suicide risk (Krieger, 1974). (See chapter by Stanley *et al.*)

5. A positive dexamethasone suppression test (DST) is related positively to suicide (Coryell & Schlesser, 1981). *See chapter by Stanley et al.*)

6. Blood platelets of suicides should show decreased binding sites for tritiated imipramine—an indirect indicator of 5-HT transmission activity in the brain (Stanley, 1982). (See chapters by Stanley *et al.* and van Praag.)

7. A blunted or absent response (<1 microunit/ml) of thyroid-stimulating hormone (TSH) to thyrotropin-releasing hormone (TRH) is predictive of suicide (Linkowski *et al.*, 1983). (See chapter by Rich.)

8. If the urinary norepinephrine–epinephrine ratio is low, then inward aggression (e.g., suicide) is likely; if the ratio is high, then outward aggression is likely (e.g., assault) (Ostroff, 1982). (See chapter by Motto.)

9. 3-methoxy-4-hydroxyphenolglycol (MHPG; a metabolite of norepinephrine) and homovanillic acid (HVA; a metabolite of dopamine) are positively related to suicide (Traskman, 1981). (See chapters by van Praag and Motto.)

10. Low levels o CSF magnesium are predictive of suicide attempts (Banki, 1985). (See chapter by van Praag.)

11. Suicide attempts are positively associated with paroxysmal EEG dysrhythmia (Struve, 1979). (See chapter by Struve.)

12. Monozygotic twin suicide concordance rates exceed those expected by chance alone (Rainer, 1984). (See chapter by Lester.)

13. Depressed patients treated with electroconvulsive therapy (ECT) are less likely to commit suicide than those treated with antidepressant medication alone (Avery & Winokur, 1978). (See chapter by Tanney.)

14. Patients with early symptomless autoimmune thyroiditis (SAT) often develop serious suicidal impulses (Gold, 1982). Such patients have an *exaggerated* TSH response to TRH. (See chapter by Rich.)

15. Suicide occurs in individuals experiencing severe coping impasses related to sex, health, and social production (de Catanzaro, 1981). (See chapters by de Catanzaro and Rubenstein.)

16. Some 15–20% of all alcoholics eventually die by suicide. (See chapter by Roy & Linnoila.)

17. Alcohol raises low brain 5-HT levels, but in the long run it lowers them. (See chapter by Roy & Linnoila.)

I wish to thank the authors for the considerable efforts that went into the preparation of this book. I also ask the reader's patience and indulgence. Much of what follows is highly technical and abstract. While the book may seem far removed from the clinical urgencies of the suicide's worlds, I remain convinced that an important dialogue has begun here. I hope you do, too.

Ronald W. Maris, Ph.D.
Center for the Study of Suicide
University of South Carolina
Columbia, South Carolina

BIOLOGY OF SUICIDE

CHAPTER 1

Clinical Considerations of Biological Correlates of Suicide

Jerome A. Motto, MD
University of California–San Francisco School of Medicine,
Department of Psychiatry

The search for biological characteristics of specific emotional disorders is a highly visible aspect of contemporary behavioral research. Spurred by remarkable advances in the technology of identifying and quantifying biological compounds, the focus on developing measurable chemical "markers" sometimes appears to challenge our time-honored dependence on psychosocial data for decision making.

The task presented to clinicians goes beyond finding time to keep up with new research reports. It has also been necessary to become familiar with a number of terms and concepts drawn from the languages of psychopharmacology, psychoimmunology, and neurochemistry. An understanding of neuroreceptors, neurotransmitters, neuromodulators, and neuroregulators; of up (or down) regulation; of various metabolites and their metabolic pathways, adrenergic, serotonergic, and dopaminergic systems; of agonists and antagonists; and of an array of biological test procedures and their quantification serves as a bare preparation for reviewing current behavioral research with any confidence of grasping its meaning. Neurobiological researchers generally assume that their readers have that understanding. One result of these developments is that over the past two decades psychiatry has given full recognition to the subspecialty of "biological psychiatry," which joins "dynamic" and "social" psychiatry to complete the foundation of the "biopsychosocial" approach to human behavior.

Many established clinicians have found it difficult to digest this new development at the rate that information has become available. This may not be difficult for those with a basic science background, or whose training was completed in the relatively recent past. For many mental health workers, however, the flood of new information presented in technical language poses formidable challenges. The most pertinent of these, shared by all clinicians, is determining the applicability of this burgeoning mass of biological information to their everyday work. A clinician's view of this question is the basis for the present discussion.

The field of suicide prevention is a relative newcomer to the biological arena, and it suffers from some of the same ills that have beset the field at large. As Carroll (1983) has observed regarding studies of depression, recent advances have outstripped the ability of our standard clinical concepts to integrate them in a coherent way. When Bunney and Fawcett (1965) first suggested increased urinary 17-hydroxycor-ticosteroids (17-OHCS) as an indicator of suicide risk, one could easily speculate as to the clinical implications of that observation. It would be consistent with Shneidman's (1985) pointing out "elevated perturbation" as an essential ingredient of suicide, and with the logical view that intense inner turmoil would stimulate adrenal cortical secretion, which would appear in the urine in the form of metabolic products. However, when the focus shifted to a succession of observations such as dexamethasone suppression, thyroid responsiveness, serotonin levels, and the binding of tritiated imipramine, this integrative process began to break down for many clinicians. In its place was a widening chasm between clinical workers and neurobiological researchers that is yet to be bridged. Though some persons are able to straddle both arenas, especially in research centers, communication between the two areas is largely limited to exchanging operational data and correlations.

One reason for the gap between biological research and clinical application regarding suicide is what Carroll (1983) refers to in depression research as a "crisis of paradigm." That is, what are we trying to recognize? A past history of suicide attempts? Future suicide attempts by means other than drug ingestion or a single wrist cut? Suicide in the indefinite future? A proclivity for violence? Until some clarity is introduced in the form of a conceptual model of what is being addressed, the application of biological research to the clinical management of suicidal persons is not likely to develop.

In the meantime, clinicians are keeping an interested if wary eye on what the neurobiologists are doing, and are even trying to assist in the formulation of the needed model. Suicide prevention workers are also finding much encouragement in the appearance of many new colleagues actively investigating suicide, drawn from such previously unrelated fields as clinical pharmacology and neurochemistry.

Candidates for Biological Markers of Suicide Risk

Urinary 17-Hydroxycorticosteroids

The idea of a measurable biological indicator of suicide risk first appeared in the literature in 1965; it was posed by Bunney and Fawcett, from the National Institute of Mental Health. When 3 of their 36 depressed research patients committed suicide during or shortly after inpatient care, those subjects were recognized as having shown some of the highest levels of urinary 17-OHCS of the entire sample. The possible clinical value of this observation was given added meaning by the fact that during the time they were inpatients, twice-daily clinical estimates of suicidal risk had placed all three of these patients below the mean for the entire group.

Bunney and Fawcett postulated that urinary 17-OHCS levels would reflect intensity of psychic pain in certain depressed patients, especially in those with limited psychological defenses. They cautioned that the contrary finding of a low 17-OHCS should offer no reassurance regarding suicide, as the implication of this compound for suicide risk might only apply to a specific type of patient.

This admonition was underscored by Levy and Hansen (1969), who subsequently reported two suicides of patients with consistently low urinary 17-OHCS as a "failure of the urinary test for suicide potential." They also pointed out that the excretion of 17-OHCS is very dependent on body size, and that the presence of psychotherapeutic drugs can interfere with the laboratory test. A similar caution was much later sounded by Fink and Carpenter (1976), who reported two suicides in patients whose mean urinary 17-OHCS levels were well below those suggested by Bunney and Fawcett as cause for concern (9 mg/24 hr for women and 14 mg/24 hr for men).

Meanwhile, Bunney and his group (Bunney, Fawcett, Davis, & Gifford, 1969) had retrospectively added 4 more suicides and 106 nonsuicides to their sample, and explored the pertinence of "long-term" and "short-term" patterns of elevated urinary 17-OHCS. This refinement was necessitated by the fact that 3 of the 5 suicides for whom data were available showed no elevation 10 days prior to their suicide, though 5 of the 7 suicides studied had long-term records of elevated 17-OHCS. The investigators reiterated their point that low 17-OHCS levels should not be considered indicative of low suicide risk, and summarized their data cautiously with the comment that "the future clinical significance of these findings remains to be fully determined" (p. 150).

Krieger (1970) uncovered a practical clinical issue when he reported that he was frustrated in his efforts to replicate Bunney and Fawcett's (1965) findings, because lack of patient cooperation and limitations of ward staff time prevented his obtaining complete 24-hour urine samples. This is a well-known problem in the absence of very strict patient supervision and compliance. Krieger thus abandoned his efforts to collect urine samples from "frequently confused, preoccupied and uncooperative psychiatric patients" (Krieger, 1975, p. 229), and turned his attention instead to measuring the precursor of 17-OHCS, plasma cortisol (Krieger, 1974). The lesson was clear, in any case, that some procedures may be routine in a fully equipped research setting, but less practical in other clinical areas or with other patient populations.

Little has been reported of urinary 17-OHCS determinations over the past 10 years, and current measures of cortisol secretion are using free cortisol rather than 17-OHCS. Yet the surface simplicity and logic of collecting urine to obtain a measure of psychic pain retains some of its early appeal. Even if restricted to well-staffed inpatient settings and very cooperative subjects, which would exclude most psychiatric settings, it might be considered in some problematic situations. Bunney (1984) still suggests a 17-OHCS determination, for example, when considering discharge or leave for a depressed patient with uncertain suicide risk. If it is seen to be elevated, he recommends repeating the test. If it is still elevated, it would imply that one should reconsider the discharge plan in view of the implied risk. It certainly sounds reasonable, and it is not very expensive (about $41), but at this stage of our knowledge, it is doubtful that such a sequence will be generally accepted in other than a research setting.

Cortisol Levels in Plasma and Cerebrospinal Fluid

Krieger (1974) suggested that the blood cortisol level was not only much simpler to determine than urinary 17-OHCS, but would more accurately reflect the intensity of emotional distress the patient was experiencing. He found that 13 patients who committed suicide within 2 years of the test had a significantly higher mean 8:30 A.M. serum cortisol level (21.08 µg%) than did 39 suicide-risk matched patients who did not suicide (16.5 µg%). On the basis of this finding, he recommended that if a patient who is recognized clinically to be at risk for suicide has a plasma cortisol level above 20µg%, "in the absence of other causes for such a high level ... [such a patient should] be recognized as having a high potential for suicide, be provided with more protective precautions, more frequent contact with his therapist, and prolonged after-care" (1975, p. 229).

Having given this unequivocal endorsement to use of the plasma cortisol level as a marker for suicide risk, Krieger postulated a higher than normal basal level of cortisol in some individuals, which could make such persons more vulnerable to suicide in the presence of added stress in their lives. This hypothesized elevated "set point" in the hypothalamus could result from genetic influence or from early emotional stress. He has pointed out further that depressive and suicidal states are seen in various clinical situations involving steroids, such as Cushing's disease, arthritis treatment with steroids, and certain contraceptive medications (Krieger, 1975). From a treatment perspective, the Sachar, Asnis, Nathan, Halbreich, Tabrizi, Halpern (1980) report that small doses of intravenous dextroamphetamine sulfate reduced the elevated plasma cortisol levels in depressed patients to normal in 90 minutes seems pertinent to these observations.

Another facet of this picture has been provided by Agren (1983), who determined "suicide scores" for patients with a major depressive disorder, based on past and current suicidal ideation and behavior. He found high plasma cortisol levels in subjects with a history of serious suicide attempts "earlier in life," and a correlation of the "suicide score" with the ratio of the pre–post dexamethasone suppression test (DST) plasma cortisol levels. Though not a generally usable procedure, such research findings support the suggestions for clinical application made earlier by Krieger (1974).

Recent studies of cerebrospinal fluid (CSF) have included CSF cortisol, which might be thought to reflect plasma levels. No clear relationship to suicidal behavior has been found. Both suicidal and nonsuicidal depressed patients show elevated levels, while nondepressed suicide attempters have levels only slightly above normal controls (Traskman, Tybring, Asberg, Bertilsson, Lantto, & Schalling, 1980). More recent results (Banki, Arato, Papp, & Kurcz, 1984) are even less encouraging, with no differences found in depressed "violent" suicide attempters, depressed "nonviolent" attempters (by drug ingestion or single wrist cut), or nonsuicidal subjects with varied diagnoses. The reason for the inconsistency between serum and CSF cortisol levels is not clear. From a clinical viewpoint, however, serum levels are so much simpler to obtain that this can comfortably remain a mystery for the researchers to wrestle with.

In spite of the logic and clarity of Krieger's suggestion and Agren's supporting data, measurement of the serum cortisol level to assess suicide risk has been utilized only infrequently outside the research area. The situation is unlikely to change unless clinicians are offered much more convincing evidence of the link between serum cortisol and subsequent suicide.

Dexamethasone Suppression Test

The DST is so simple, safe, inexpensive (about $45), and readily interpreted that in the past few years it has become the best-known biological measure of depression around the world. In those settings where such biological studies are done, it has generally replaced urinary 17-OHCS as a potential biological marker for affective disorders (Coryell & Schlesser, 1981).

Similar to the rationale for 17-OHCS and plasma cortisol determinations, the DST is based on the well-known observation of a hypersecretion of cortisol in persons with a major depressive disorder. Normally this hormone is regulated through interaction of the hypothalamus, pituitary, and adrenal glands. In nondepressed persons, the synthetic steroid dexamethasone will cause suppression of cortisol secretion for about 24 hours, while in about 50% of primary unipolar depressives this suppression does not occur. The test is most specific for endogenous depression.

The procedure typically involves drawing a pretest blood sample, giving the subject 1 mg of dexamethasone orally at 11 P.M., and drawing additional blood samples at 8 A.M., 4 P.M., and 11 P.M. the next day. If the level of serum cortisol exceeds 5 μg/dl in either the 4 P.M. or 11 P.M. sample, the test is positive, indicating nonsuppression, which may help in diagnosing a depressive state. The need for several blood specimens over a 24-hour period makes an inpatient setting most convenient. The test has been adapted to outpatient use by giving the patients the medication to take by mouth at 11 P.M., and having them return at 4 P.M. the next day for a single blood sample to determine their cortisol level (Peselow, Goldring, Fieve, & Wright, 1983). This method sacrifices some sensitivity, however.

In a retrospective report of DST data, Coryell and Schlesser (1981) noted that four suicides among their primary depressed patients had all shown abnormal DSTs when previously seen as inpatients. One suicide also occurred in a patient with secondary depression whose DST had been normal. They postulated from this a type of primary depression with an associated hypothalamic–pituitary–adrenal dysfunction that is more likely to involve suicide than are other types of depression.

At about the same time it was observed by Beck-Friis *et al.* (1981) and by Asberg *et al.* (1981) that several patients had made serious suicide attempts within 48 hours after the DST was administered. They raised the alarming question as to whether the DST might actually precipitate suicidal behavior by a process of "psychomotor activation." Nothing further was heard till over a year later, when two independent terms of investigators (Coryell, 1982; Kronfol, Greden, Gardner, and Carroll, 1982) reported that large-scale studies showed no relationship between administering the DST and subsequent suicidal behavior.

A flurry of reports followed, with a variety of observations about the association of the DST to prior or subsequent suicide attempts (Banki & Arato, 1983a, 1983b; Banki *et al.*, 1984; Targum, Rosen, & Capodanno, 1983) and to suicidal ideas or behavior (Agren, 1983). All but one found a closer association to suicide attempts in those persons who had a positive DST, especially when primary unipolar depression was considered. The exception was a study by van Wettere, Charles, and Wilmotte (1983), who found no predictive value when the test was given to a series of suicide attempters (with various diagnoses) on the day they were admitted to the hospital. Of special interest is Targum *et al.*'s (1983) report that in two suicide attempters with positive DSTs, follow-up revealed that repeated suicide attempts occurred after the DSTs reverted to normal. This fails to support the tentative idea of using the DST as a monitoring device, with an abnormal response signaling increased likelihood of suicidal acts. Reports of the DST with suicidal adolescents have also shown very mixed results (Chabrol, Claverie, & Moron, 1983; Crumley, 1983; Robbins & Alessi, 1985).

All of these reports have suffered from limited samples, varied populations, and differing criteria for suicidal manifestations. Even when positive findings are reported, some have reflected DST nonsuppression being "more frequent" in suicide attempters but not statistically significant (Banki & Arato, 1983a, 1983b); others have found significant correlation of a positive DST with suicidal behavior, with over half the nonsuicidal patients also having a positive test (Banki *et al.*, 1984).

Faced with such intriguing but not very clear relationships, clinicians have generally been inclined to take the conservative approach of watchful waiting. Notable exceptions exist, especially in hospital settings. For example, Babigian (1985) states that discharging a depressed patient whose DST is abnormal after treatment is to anticipate either an early relapse and readmission, or a suicide. In perplexing cases involving depression with questions of suicide risk, the DST is being used in some hospital settings in addition to outside consultation, simply to leave no stone unturned. As a general rule, however, questions about the low specificity of the test have made interpretation difficult, and most clinicians prefer to trust their own assessment.

The encouraging leads found thus far have been limited to certain depressive disorders. As Targum *et al.* (1983) put it, "The value of the DST (as a predictor of suicide attempts) in other (than primary unipolar depression) is yet to be demonstrated" (p. 879). Robbins and Alessi (1985) state the current clinical situation most clearly: "[B]ecause of the preliminary nature of all the reported associations of the DST with suicidal behavior, the clinical utility of these findings must be considered uncertain. They raise the possibility, however, that an abnormal DST may prove useful as a marker of increased potential for suicide" (p. 109). For the clinician, the DST remains in an investigational stage as regards determination of suicidal risk.

CSF 5-Hydroxyindoleacetic Acid

Since 1973, as a facet of their studies of the biology of depression, Asberg and her group in Stockholm have reported observations of CSF levels of 5-hydroxyindoleacetic acid (5-HIAA), a metabolite of the neurotransmitter serotonin. They observed that the distribution of levels of this compound in 68 depressed patients was bimodal, from which they postulated two separate biochemical subgroups of depression. Reminiscent of Bunney and Fawcett's earlier experience, when Asberg's group noted that the two patients in their sample who subsequently suicided were both in the lower-level mode, they decided to compare the high- and low-level patients for various kinds of suicidal behavior (Asberg, Traskman, & Thoren, 1976). When they found a significantly greater proportion and severity of suicidal behavior in the low-level group, they reported that, in their sample, a low level of 5-HIAA in the CSF was a "predictor of suicidal acts" (p. 1194). The actual numbers were eight suicidal acts (two of them lethal) among 20 low-level subjects, and seven (none lethal) among 48 high-level subjects. The investigators acknowledged the preliminary nature of the study and the small sample, granting that "the clinical value of 5-HIAA determinations as an indicator of suicidal potential remains to be proved" (p. 1196).

The subsequent report by this group (Traskman, Asberg, Bertilsson, & Sjostrand, 1981) generated much interest in the world press and gave considerable impetus to the idea of CSF 5-HIAA as a biological marker for suicide. The key finding was that in a complex sample of 119 subjects, 6 of the 7 suicides were included in a group of 30 subjects who had made a suicide attempt before admission, and who also had CSF 5-HIAA levels below the median for the entire sample (92.5 nmol/L). This prompted the statement that, while emphasizing the need for a larger study sample, "a 20% mortality from suicide within one year of the initial attempt among our patients with a low CSF 5-HIAA level is—quite alarming" (p. 635). The investigators reiterated, however, that routine 5-HIAA determinations to assist the evaluation of suicide risk would be premature.

Many reports followed, relating low CSF 5-HIAA levels to a variety of impulsive or disinhibited behavioral patterns—for example, of aggressiveness in borderline patients with a past history of suicide attempts (Brown, Ebert, Goyer, Jimerson, Klein, Bunney, & Goodwin, 1982); "violent" suicide attempts as distinguished from "nonviolent" attempts (Banki & Arato, 1983a, 1983b; Banki et al., 1984; Banki, Vojnik, Papp, Balla, & Arato, 1985); and suicidal schizophrenic patients in contrast to nonsuicidal schizophrenic patients (Ninan, van Kammen, Scheinen, Linnoila, Bunney, & Goodwin, 1984; van Praag, 1983). These findings were quite consistent, and cut across a number of diagnostic groups.

At the same time, research reports continued to involve small samples, and sometimes showed considerable overlap of values or ambiguity in the different risk groups. For example, Agren (1983) found, in considering current and past suicidal thinking and behavior, that current or recent suicidal ideation in depressed patients was associated with both low and high CSF 5-HIAA levels, while all past suicidal manifestations and current suicidal behavior (not ideation) were correlated with low levels. Other reports apparently contradicted earlier findings. Thus, Roy, Ninan, Mazonson, Pickar, van Kammen, Linnoila, and Paul (1985) postulated a lower CSF 5-HIAA level in schizophrenic patients who had a history of suicide attempts, but their data showed no significant difference among those with no attempts, nonviolent attempts, and violent attempts.

The widespread publicity that followed early reports of this potential marker stimulated a level of interest and enthusiasm that could scarcely be sustained. As we await replication studies, examination of larger samples, and considerations of age and treatment variables, the excitement is subsiding. It is unfortunate that obtaining CSF samples is neither easy nor entirely free of risk and discomfort. If the initial promise is realized, serious practical problems will still need solution before the CSF 5-HIAA levels can have general acceptance. For the present, the clinician's inclination is to wait and see.

Thyroid-Stimulating Hormone Response
to Thyrotropin-Releasing Hormone

The stage was set for exploration of the hypothalamic–pituitary–thyroid axis in suicidal behavior, just as it was in the hypothalamic–

pituitary–adrenal axis, by postulating dysregulation of that system as a marker for depression. Specifically, there is evidence of a suppressed response of thyroid-stimulating hormone (TSH) from the anterior pituitary to thyrotropin-releasing hormone (TRH) from the hypothalamus in depressive disorders. There are contradictory data as to whether this blunted response may be due to elevated serum cortisol, which would tie it in with the "stress" paradigm (Kierkegaard & Carroll, 1980; Loosen, Prange, & Wilson, 1978). The test is relatively simple and inexpensive (about $32). After a drug washout period and overnight fast, an indwelling needle is used to inject 0.5 mg TRH, with blood samples drawn 15 minutes before and 15, 30, 45, 60, 90, and 120 minutes after the injection for determinations of TSH response (Loosen et al., 1978).

In 51 female depressed inpatients, Linkowski, van Wettere, Kerkhofs, Brauman, and Mendlewicz (1983), found 4 subsequent suicides after a mean follow-up of 5 years. All four had shown an absence of TSH response (less than 1 microunit/ml) when first seen. One unexplained death had shown a blunted response (maximum change in TSH of 1.0 microunit/ml), and 3 natural deaths had all shown responses greater than the suicides. The pattern was interpreted to suggest that the TSH response to TRH might serve as a biological indicator of high suicide risk in depressed patients "if confirmed in prospective studies on larger groups of patients" (p. 404).

A subsequent report from the same investigators (Linkowski, van Wettere, Kerkhofs, Gregoire, Brauman & Mendlewicz, 1984) added 9 depressed female subjects and 42 normal female controls, and extended the follow-up to a mean of 8 years. Five of the seven suicides had very low TSH responses compared to the nonsuicide deaths and the controls. Subjects with a history of "violent" suicide attempts showed a significantly lower response than those with no history of suicidal behavior. The suggested use of this test as a marker of risk was limited to females, in view of an observed decrease in TSH response in normal males over 40.

Banki et al. (1984) found an opposite outcome with 141 female inpatient subjects, including 52 suicide attempts. The "violent" attempters showed a significantly higher mean TSH response than nonsuicidal subjects, and there was a marked overlap among the patient categories. Banki (1985) later refers to unpublished data indicating that the TSH response to TRH was more likely to be normal in "violent" suicide attempters. Another failure to support this approach was reported by Chabrol et al. (1983), who found a blunted TSH response in only 2 of 20 adolescent suicide attempters, who, however, were not clinically depressed.

With such mixed results to date, one can scarcely do more than note this test with interest, as any clinical application would have little data to support it. Until we have much more persuasive information to go on, the clinician can only watch and wait for new developments. One possible development that shows unusual promise, related to thyroid function, has been on the horizon for several years and is discussed below under "Psychoimmunology."

Urinary Norepinephrine-to-Epinephrine Ratio

Ostroff, Giller, Bonese, Ebersole, Harkness, and Mason (1982) took the urinary 17-OHCS idea a step further by exploring the hypothesis that a high urinary norepinephrine-to-epinephrine ratio is related to a tendency to turn anger outward, and a low ratio to directing anger inward (Funkenstein, King, & Drolette, 1954). The study was prompted by finding a low ratio in 2 suicides and 1 serious suicide attempter among their 22 male research subjects. Their rationale was that in the presence of high urinary cortisol levels, a second hormonal measure may enhance the significance of that finding. A low ratio would suggest risk of suicide, and a high ratio would suggest risk of assault. Findings consistent with this had been reported by Woodman (1979), who found a positive relationship between a consistently high ratio and assault-iveness in prison inmates. A subsequent effort to demonstrate a lower urinary norepinephrine-to-epinephrine ratio in patients with a history of suicide attempt (Ostroff, Giller, Harkness, & Mason, 1985) produced statistically significant differences in mean values, but the overlap was so great that its clinical usefulness is very questionable. It remains an intriguing idea, however, with such obvious psychodynamic implications that clinicians would be inclined to put special hope in this test's eventually warranting clinical use.

3-Methoxy-4-Hydroxyphenolglycol and Homovanillic Acid

Of the neurotransmitters available for study, serotonin and its metabolite 5-HIAA have dominated the field as regards depressive and suicidal states. For the sake of completeness, mention should be made of the two other neurotransmitters often studied in this context, norepinephrine and dopamine, and their major metabolites—respectively, 3-methoxy-4-hydroxyphenolglycol (MHPG) and homovanillic acid (HVA). With the exception of the urinary norepinephrine-to-epinephrine ratio discussed above, numerous efforts to define the relationship of these two compounds and their metabolites to suicidal thinking or behavior have thus far shown no role for them (Agren, 1983; Banki & Arato, 1983b; Banki et al., 1985; Roy et al., 1985; Traskman et al., 1981).

It is of theoretical interest that when a laboratory test for urinary MHPG was developed, the range of values found in depressed patients was essentially the same as in a normal population. This was interpreted by some to indicate three subtypes of depression, identified by low, intermediate, and high urinary MHPG, and efforts were undertaken to demonstrate differing responses to specific antidepressants in the three categories. This concept has not been related to suicidal behavior, but is reminiscent of Asberg's group's finding a bimodal distribution of CSF 5-HIAA in their patients and identifying the low-level group as at higher risk for suicide. Though MHPG levels have not yet proven useful, the creativity in the approach to a normal range of laboratory values seems noteworthy.

Tritiated Imipramine Binding

As an outgrowth of consistent findings of reduced serotonin metabolites in depression, a measure of this neurotransmitter's activity in the brain was developed that can be obtained from a simple blood specimen. Since the receptor sites of blood platelets and of brain tissue possess virtually identical binding characteristics, and since there is evidence that tritiated imipramine binding is associated with the neuronal uptake mechanism for serotonin, it was predictable that the platelets of depressed persons would show decreased binding sites for this compound. Extending this, Stanley, Virgilio, and Gershon (1982) demonstrated that the brain tissue of persons who had committed suicide showed reduced binding as compared with brains of persons who died of other causes. Prior efforts to measure serotonin levels in brain tissue of suicides had produced mixed results (Camps, & Eccleston, Shaw, 1967; Cochran, Robins, & Grote, 1976). The implied marker for suicide risk, then, would be a determination of tritiated imipramine binding in platelets as an indicator of the level of serotonin transmission activity in the brain. A lower level of activity would imply a higher suicide risk. The rationale only holds for those suicidal persons who have a primary major affective disorder. If a cutoff point could be established without excessive overlap with low-risk persons, the simplicity of such a blood test (as with the cortisol level) would be appealing. To the clinician, however, at present it remains just an interesting observation.

CSF Magnesium

Banki et al. (1985) added to the examination of CSF for markers of suicide risk by their finding that CSF magnesium levels were highly correlated with suicide attempts in 11 of their 56 patients. Details of the "suicidal" patients' diagnoses are lacking, but it is of interest that the correlation with suicide attempts was stronger for magnesium than for CSF 5-HIAA, which was the focus of attention in earlier studies. It has the appeal of a simple chemical test, but for the present, the absence of confirming data and the complexity of obtaining a sample render it only another interesting observation from a clinical viewpoint.

Electroencephalogram

Studies attempting to relate electroencephalogram (EEG) findings to suicidal behavior have not produced clinically usable results. Though suicidal ideation and attempts have been found to be associated with paroxysmal EEG dysrhythmia (Struve, 1979), the strength of these findings does not allow inferences as to suicide risk in individual cases.

Other Biological Aspects of Suicide

Though the biological measures discussed above have commanded most of the attention in recent years, a number of other biological issues deserve comment.

Genetics

Large bodies of evidence implicate a genetic factor in major psychotic and affective disorders, but no clear relation to suicide as such has been found. Studies of twin pairs have been inconclusive, and family and adoption studies have not yet satisfactorily separated suicide risk from risk for depression. Our present understanding of the possible role of an inheritable risk for suicide has been summarized by Rainer (1984) in the observation that "the interaction of psychological or biological precipitating factors for suicide with the genetic component of psychosis or personality disorder still needs further clarification" (p. 339). Genetic considerations do not play a role in contemporary clinical work with suicidal patients.

Plasma Drug Levels

Though only indirectly related to suicide, efforts to monitor the blood level of antidepressant medications have obvious implications for the clinician. Since the treatment of a suicidal state entails treatment of the underlying disorder, depressed and suicidal treatment-resistant patients constitute a very difficult clinical challenge, whether in the office or the hospital. The technology for measuring blood levels is now developed, but the therapeutic range is not firmly established. Nortriptyline was the first to be examined, apparently because it was one of the easiest to measure and was thought (mistakenly) to have no active metabolites. Its well-known "therapeutic window" of 50–150 ng/ml is now in some question, and there are mixed reports as to what the desired level of other antidepressant compounds should be (Hollister, 1985). Clinicians are more than ready to use such a potentially helpful biological measurement, and many already monitor nortriptyline and imipramine in spite of the limitations of the method, especially in inpatient settings. When there is firm evidence of therapeutic levels, this procedure will probably become standard practice in treatment-resistant cases and in monitoring compliance with medications, as well as in detecting and determining the severity of overdoses.

Electroconvulsive Therapy

Electroconvulsive therapy (ECT) requires mention because it retains a prominent role in the treatment of affective disorders, which in turn are closely associated with suicide. In spite of this centrality, its use has diminished in the past 20 years, primarily due to the wide availablity and vigorous marketing of antidepressant medications. The techniques of its use, however, have been progressively improved, and its neuroendocrine characteristics have been defined (Allen, Denney, Kendwall, Blachly, 1974; Elithorn, Bridges, & Hodge, 1968; Ylikorkola, Kauppila, Haapalahti, & Karppanen, 1976).

Clinical and methodological considerations prevent a controlled study of the potential of ECT for reducing suicide in depressed persons, though some efforts to do this have been made. Even in naturalistic studies, the low base rate of suicide and numerous extraneous variables pose serious obstacles.

Avery and Winokur (1978) reported a 1-year follow-up of 519 depressed inpatients, 257 of whom had received ECT. None of the subsequent 4 suicides were in the ECT group, and the rate of suicide attempts during the 6 months after treatment began was 0.85% in the ECT group compared to 7.0% in the "adequate antidepressant treatment" group. These investigators pointed out that during the 1960s, as the use of ECT declined and the treatment of depression with antidepressant medications increased, the incidence of suicide rose in hospitals in the

United States and Europe, and the reported rates of suicide attempts went up as well. The reciprocal trends of these two biological treatments were accompanied by changing admission policies and open wards, however, and these phenomena temper the interpretation of the data. Lonnqvist, Niskanen, Rinta-Manty, Achte, and Karha (1974) similarly reported that the suicide rate among psychiatric patients at the Helsinki University Hospital during the 1961–1971 period was more than double that of the prior decade.

The key to effectiveness in ECT is patient selection; the best results have occurred with primary endogenous depression. The current lull in the use of ECT is unfortunately creating a generation of practitioners with little training or experience in its use. Some notable exceptions (e.g., Frankel, 1984) preserve the hope that this uniquely valuable procedure will regain its role as a suicide prevention measure, and that research into its mechanism of action will provide clues to the basic nature of affective disorders.

Psychoimmunology

The immune system has long been suspect in the observed sequence of a physical disorder following a period of emotional stress. Recent work suggests that the opposite can also be true, such that an immunological disorder can produce a depressive state of suicidal intensity.

Gold, Pottash, and Extein (1982) report that early symptomless autoimmune thyroiditis (SAT) reveals no clear thyroid symptoms or laboratory abnormalities, but presents a picture of anergia, difficulty in concentrating, and depression. Apparently related to atrophic changes in the thyroid gland, the severe dysphoria observed in this condition often generates serious suicidal impulses. The patient's despair is worsened by the clinician's misinterpreting the symptoms as a major depressive disorder that does not respond to psychiatric treatment.

Gold's group points out that this condition is characterized by an exaggerated TSH response to TRH (in contrast to a blunted or absent response in depression), combined with a positive test for antithyroid microsomal antibodies. The TSH response is recommended as a screening test for patients who present with anergia or depression and do not respond to traditional treatment methods. Those with an exaggerated TSH response should have a comprehensive thyroid evaluation, using the presence of antithyroid antibodies for the thyroid microsome as a marker for SAT. This area of research thus puts the TSH response in a unique position as regards suicide potential, in that either a low or a high level indicates risk, though for different reasons.

One of the suicides reported by Beck-Friis *et al.* (1981) was a patient with thyroiditis who became depressed 2 weeks after treatment for this disorder was stopped, and Drummond, Lodrick, and Hallstrom (1984) reported four suicides of patients with thyroid abnormalities. These probably represent a number of different conditions, but from the clinician's viewpoint they support the rationale for examining the TSH response to TRH and antithyroid antibodies in patients who appear depressed but do not respond to antidepressant treatment. The recognition of SAT (and other thyroid disorders) is especially important because treatment, for example with thyroid replacement, can provide relief of symptoms.

Discussion

What does all this mean to the clinician trying to help a suicidal person? It is clear that the biological aspects of suicide have been a secondary research concern, growing out of the focus of the past two decades on the biology of depression. Only when patients in studies of depression committed suicide during or after the research program did attention turn to the implications of the biological data for suicidal behavior. This does not detract from the exciting possibilities of the findings. It is not surprising that persons hospitalized for a severe affective disturbance show self-destructive trends, and it would be a valuable supplement to the clinician's interview data to have a laboratory test to indicate which of these persons are at greatest risk for suicidal behavior.

Unfortunately, some research reports associate the biological observations only with primary major depressive disorders, while others only show significant findings when suicidal behavior is considered regardless of diagnosis. Still other studies require that "violent" suicides or suicide attempts be considered separately from "nonviolent" ones (overdose or single wrist cut). To the clinician this distinction has little meaning, especially in view of the sizeable proportion of suicidal deaths due to overdose, particularly in women. The fact that most antidepressant and antipsychotic medications are potentially lethal further clouds the usefulness of these categories. One could suggest that suicides and suicide attempts be considered entirely separately, due to the vastly different clinical implications of the two behaviors.

As additional biochemical studies appear, even more contradictions will arise due to selection bias or differing techniques (Stanley & Mann, 1984). Yet biological researchers are committed to pursue such studies, realizing that the problem of suicide is so serious that it deserves more biochemical attention (Braverman & Pfeiffer, 1985).

None of the 10 candidates for markers of suicide risk discussed above has a clear application for that purpose in clinical work at the present time. An opportunity exists in that the DST is widely used around the world in the diagnosis and monitoring of depressive states, primarily in hospital settings. Careful follow-up could add to the very limited published information available as to whether it can help determine the potential for suicide. Since the DST involves measurement of serum cortisol, follow-up data could also serve to test Krieger's (1974, 1975) very precise cutoff point for this hormone (20 µg/dl), beyond which he recommends special suicide precautions.

Though new reports are seen almost daily in this active area of study, all the potential biological markers of suicide risk must be considered to constitute areas of continuing research rather than established clinical tools until many more substantiating data are available. If time provides confirming data for these markers, we will have welcome additions to the risk factors already known to be associated with a suicidal outcome. Though suicide would still be unpredictable in a given case, we could have greater confidence in our estimate of risk with the addition of such objective information. Our assessment of changing risk could similarly be bolstered by changes in biological measures used as a monitoring device.

In the meantime, suicide prevention efforts would be well served by a judicious increase in the use of ECT in depression, and by a concerted effort to rule out underlying physical disorders in persons with treatment-resistant emotional disorders with a suicidal component. These are not areas that lend themselves easily to systematic investigation, but the neuroendocrine effects of ECT, for example, may well provide links to the newer endocrine observations in depressive and suicidal states.

The enthusiasm and optimism that researchers bring to their investigative work can sometimes elicit a like response in clinicians, generating a need to accept exciting research ideas as though they had established a new standard of clinical care. This misconception is often enhanced by energetic media coverage and by interested pharmaceutical companies or, as in the present case, by an unregulated laboratory industry. A timely caution in this regard was offered by Gelenberg, who urged a "healthy skepticism" regarding laboratory tests in psychiatry, pointing out, for example, that with the DST, "we have only hypotheses and very few answers," and referring to the TRH infusion test as "very interesting research" that might eventually aid in isolating a subgroup of depressed patients, but a "gimmick" when it comes to clinical use (quoted in "Using Laboratory Tests," 1982, p. 12).

At the same time, researchers' unflagging optimism must be recognized and responded to as the bridge to the future for all of us. Just as the

key to preventing suicide is to nurture and sustain hope even in the
absence of visible evidence of a better situation, we would do well to
maintain our own conviction that the proliferation of new biological
knowledge about suicidal states will ultimately contribute to our ability
to help persons in suicidal despair.

References

Agren, H. Life at risk: Markers of suicidality in depression. *Psychiatric Developments*,
    1983, *1*, 87–103.
Allen, J., Denney, D., Kendwall, J., Blachly, P. Corticortrophin release during ECT in
    man. *American Journal of Psychiatry*, 1974, *131*, 1225–1228.
Asberg, M., Traskman, L., & Thoren, P. 5-HIAA in the cerebrospinal fluid: A biochemical
    suicide predictor? *Archives of General Psychiatry*, 1976, *33*, 1193–1197.
Asberg, M., Hansson, R., Tomba, P., Aminoff, A., Martensson, B., Thorén, P., Träskman-
    Bendz, L., Eneroth, P., & Åström, G. Letter to the editor. *American Journal of
    Psychiatry*, 1981, *138*, 994–995.
Avery, D., & Winokur, G. Suicide, attempted suicide, and relapse rates in depression:
    Occurrence after ECT and antidepressant therapy. *Archives of General Psychiatry*,
    1978, *35*, 749–753.
Babigian, H. Personal communication at presentation *Suicide epidemiology and psychiatric
    care*, 18th Annual Meeting of the American Association of Suicidology, Toronto,
    Canada, April 18–21, 1985.
Banki, C. Biochemical markers for suicidal behavior. *American Journal of Psychiatry*,
    1985, *142*, 147–148.
Banki, C., & Arato, M. Amine metabolites and neuroendocrine responses related to
    depression and suicide. *Journal of Affective Disorders*, 1983, *5*, 223–232. (a)
Banki, C., & Arato, M. Amine metabolites, neuroendocrine findings, and personality
    dimensions as correlates of suicidal behavior. *Psychiatry Research*, 1983, *10*, 253–
    261. (b)
Banki, C., Arato, M., Papp, Z., & Kurcz, M. Biochemical markers in suicidal patients.
    Journal of Affective Disorders, 1984, *6*, 341–350.
Banki, C., Vojnik, M., Papp, Z., Balla, K. Z., & Arato, M. Cerebrospinal fluid magnesium
    and calcium related to amine metabolites, diagnosis, and suicide attempts. *Biological
    Psychiatry*, 1985, *20*, 163–171.
Beck-Friis, J., Aperia, B., Kjellman, B., Ljunggren, J., Petterson, U., Sara, V., Sjölin,
    Å., Unden, F., & Wetterberg, L. Suicidal behavior and the dexamethasone suppression
    test. *American Journal of Psychiatry*, 1981, *138*, 993–994.
Braverman, E., & Pfeiffer, C. Suicide and biochemistry. *Biological Psychiatry*, 1985, *20*,
    123–124.
Brown, G., Ebert, M., Goyer, P., Jimerson, D. C., Klein, W. J., Bunney, W. E., & Goodwin,
    F. K. Aggression, suicide, and serotonin: Relationships to CSF amine metabolites.
    American Journal of Psychiatry, 1982, *139*, 741–746.
Bunney, W. *The future of biologic psychiatry*. Paper presented at the San Diego Psychiatric
    Symposium, October 13, 1984.
Bunney, W., & Fawcett, J. Possibility of a biochemical test for suicide potential. *Archives
    of General Psychiatry*, 1965, *13*, 232–239.
Bunney, W., Fawcett, J., Davis, J., & Gifford, S. Further evaluation of urinary 17-
    hydroxycorticosteroids in suicidal patients. *Archives of General Psychiatry* 1969, *21*,
    138–150.
Carroll, B. Neurobiologic dimensions of depression and mania. In J. Angst (Ed.), *The
    origins of depression: Current concepts and approaches* (Dahlem Conference). New
    York: Springer, 1983.

Chabrol, H., Claverie, J., & Moron, P. DST, TRH test, and adolescent suicide attempts. *American Journal of Psychiatry*, 1983, *140*, 265.

Cochran, E., Robins, E., & Grote, S. Regional serotonin levels in brain: A comparison of depressive suicides and alcoholic suicides with controls. *Biological Psychiatry*, 1976, *11*, 283–294.

Coryell, W. Suicidal behavior and the DST: Lack of association. *American Journal of Psychiatry*, 1982, *139*, 1214.

Coryell, W., & Schlesser, M. Suicide and the DST in unipolar depression. *American Journal of Psychiatry*, 1981, *138*, 1120–1121.

Crumley, F. *The dexamethasone suppression test and adolescent suicide attempts.* Paper presented at the 16th Annual Meeting of the American Association of Suicidology, Dallas, Texas, 1983.

Drummond, L., Lodrick, M., & Hallstrom, C. Thyroid abnormalities and violent suicide. *British Journal of Psychiatry*, 1984, *44*, 213.

Elithorn, A., Bridges, P., & Hodge, J. Adrenocortical responsiveness during courses of electroconvulsive therapy. *British Journal of Psychiatry*, 1968, *114*, 575–580.

Fink, E., & Carpenter, W. Further examination of a biochemical test for suicide potential. *Diseases of the Nervous System*, 1976, *37*, 341–343.

Frankel, F. The use of electroconvulsive therapy in suicidal patients. *American Journal of Psychotherapy*, 1984, *38*, 384–391.

Funkenstein, D., King, S., & Drolette, M. The direction of anger during a laboratory stress-inducing situation. *Psychosomatic Medicine*, 1954, *16*, 404–413.

Gold, M., Pottash, A., & Extein, I. "Symptomless" autoimmune thyroiditis in depression. *Psychiatry Research*, 1982, *6*, 261–269.

Hollister, L. *Antidepressants and antipsychotics.* Paper presented at the conference on Frontiers in Psychiatric Therapy, Wichita, Kansas, March 15, 1985.

Kierkegaard, C., & Carroll, B. Disturbances of TSH and adrenocortical disturbances in endogenous depression. *Psychiatry Research*, 1980, *3*, 253–264.

Krieger, G. Biochemical predictors of suicide. *Diseases of the Nervous System*, 1970, *31*, 479–482.

Krieger, G. The plasma level of cortisol as a predictor of suicide. *Diseases of the Nervous System*, 1974, *35*, 237–240.

Krieger, G. Is there a biochemical predictor of suicide? *Suicide and Life-Threatening Behavior*, 1975, *5*, 228–231.

Kronfol, Z., Greden, J., Gardner, R., & Carroll, B. Suicidal behavior and the DST: Lack of association. *American Journal of Psychiatry*, 1982, *139*, 1214–1215.

Levy, B., & Hansen, E. Failure of the urinary test for suicide. *Archives of General Psychiatry*, 1969, *20*, 415–418.

Linkowski, P., van Wettere, J., Kerkhofs, M., Brauman, H., & Mendlewicz, J. Thyrotrophin response to thyreostimulin in affectively ill women: Relationship to suicidal behavior. *British Journal of Psychiatry*, 1983, *143*, 401–405.

Linkowski, P., van Wettere, J., Kerkhofs, M., Gregoire, F., Brauman, H. Violent suicidal behavior and the thyrotropin releasing hormone–thyroid stimulating hormone test: A clinical outcome study. *Neuropsychobiology*, 1984, *12*, 19–22.

Lonnqvist, J., Niskanen, P., Rinta-Manty, R., Achté, K., & Karha, E. Suicides in psychiatric hospitals in different therapeutic eras. *Psychiatrica Fennica*, 1974, 265–273.

Loosen, P., Prange, A., & Wilson, I. Influence of cortisol on TRH-induced TSH response in depression. *American Journal of Psychiatry*, 1978, *135*, 244–246.

Ninan, P., van Kammen, D., Scheinen, M., Linnoila, M., Bunney, W. E., & Goodwin, F. K. CSF 5-hydroxyindoleacetic acid levels in suicidal schizophrenic patients. *American Journal of Psychiatry*, 1984, *141*, 566–569.

Ostroff, R., Giller, E., Bonese, K., Ebersole, E., Harkness, L., & Mason, J. Neuroendocrine risk factors of suicidal behavior. *American Journal of Psychiatry*, 1982, *139*, 1323–1325.

Ostroff, R., Giller, E., Harkness, L., & Mason, J. The norepinephrine-to-epinephrine ratio in patients with a history of suicide attempts. *American Journal of Psychiatry*, 1985, *142*, 224–227.

Peselow, E., Goldring, N., Fieve, R., Wright, R. The dexamethasone suppression test in depressed outpatients and normal control subjects. *American Journal of Psychiatry*, 1983, *140*, 245–247.

Rainer, J. Genetic factors in depression and suicide. *American Journal of Psychotherapy*, 1984, *38*, 329–340.

Robbins, D., & Alessi, N. Suicide and the dexamethasone suppression test in adolescence. *Biological Psychiatry*, 1985, *20*, 107–110.

Roy, A., Ninan, P., Mazonson, A., Pickar, D., van Kammen, D., Linnoila, M., & Paul, S. CSF monoamine metabolites in chronic schizophrenic patients who attempt suicide. *Psychological Medicine*, 1985, *15*, 335–340.

Sachar, E., Asnis, G., Nathan, S., Halbreich, U., Tabrizi, A. & Halpern, F. Dextroamphetamine and cortisol in depression. *Archives of General Psychiatry*, 1980, *37*, 755–757.

Shaw, D., Camps, F., & Eccleston, E. 5-Hydroxytryptamine in the hindbrain of depressed suicides. *British Journal of Psychiatry*, 1967, *113*, 1407–1411.

Shneidman, E. *Definition of suicide*. New York: Wiley, 1985.

Stanley, M., & Mann, J. Suicide and serotonin receptors. *Lancet*, 1984, *i*, 349.

Stanley, M., Virgilio, J., & Gershon, S. Tritiated imipramine binding sites are decreased in the frontal cortex of suicides. *Science*, 1982, *216*, 1337–1339.

Struve, F. Clinical encephalography. In L. Hankoff, & B. Einsidler, (Eds.), *Suicide: Theory and clinical aspects*. Littleton, Mass: PSG, 1979.

Targum, S., Rosen, L., & Capodanno, A. The dexamethasone suppression test in suicidal patients with unipolar depression. *American Journal of Psychiatry*, 1983, *140*, 877–879.

Traskman, L., Asberg, M., Bertilsson, L., & Sjostrand, L. Monoamine metabolites in CSF and suicidal behavior. *Archives of General Psychiatry*, 1981, *38*, 631–636.

Traskman, L., Tybring, G., Asberg, M., Bertilsson, L., Lantto, O., & Schalling, G. Cortisol in the CSF of depressed and suicidal patients. *Archives of General Psychiatry*, 1980, *37*, 761–767.

Using laboratory tests in psychiatry: A good idea? *APA Psychiatric News*, October 1, 1982, p. 12.

van Praag, H. CSF 5-HIAA and suicide in non-depressed schizophrenics. *Lancet*, 1983, *ii*, 1256.

Van Wettere, J., Charles, G., & Wilmotte, J. Dexamethasone suppression test and suicide. *Acta Psychiatrica Belgica*, 1983, *83*, 569–578.

Woodman, D. Evidence of a permanent imbalance in catecholamine secretions in violent social deviants. *Journal of Psychosomatic Research*, 1979, *23*, 155–157.

Ylikorkola, O., Kauppila, A., Haapalahti, J., Karppanen, H. The effect of electric convulsion therapy on the circulating concentration of pituitary hormones, cortisol, and adenosine monophosphate. *Clinical Endocrinology*, 1976, *5*, 571–574.

CHAPTER 2

Affective Disorders and Aggression Disorders: Evidence for a Common Biological Mechanism

H. M. van Praag, MD, PhD
Department of Psychiatry, Albert Einstein College of Medicine/ Montefiore Medical Center

Relation of Mood Regulation to Central Serotonergic Systems

Ever since the introduction of the antidepressants in the late 1950s and the discovery that metabolism of central monoamines (MAs) is influenced by them, central MAs have been studied in depression. MAs serve as neurotransmitters in the central nervous system (CNS), and the most important representatives of this group are serotonin (5-hydroxytryptamine, or 5-HT) and the catecholamines, dopamine (DA) and noradrenaline (NA). What is the state of the art 25 years later? Are MAs related to depression or to certain features of depression, or are they not? In this chapter, I confine myself to 5-HT. A critical discussion of catecholamine research in depression can be found elsewhere (van Praag, 1982b).

I first formulate my answer, then present the argumentation. My answer is, cautiously, in the affirmative. Suggestive evidence indicates a relationship between 5-HT disturbances in the CNS and dysregulation of mood. Supportive evidence is derived from patients with a primary diagnosis of depression, as well as from patients suffering from certain somatic disorders who, in addition, show features of depression. Both groups of data are discussed consecutively.

However, signs of disturbed 5-HT metabolism have been found in aggression disorders as well, seemingly independent of depressive symptomatology. Rather than resort once more to a unimodal hypothesis—this time a 5-HT–aggression hypothesis—the hypothesis is launched that disturbances in central serotonergic functions form the common root for disturbances in regulation of mood *and* of aggression.

At this point, I underline that 5-HT research in suicidal behavior is clearly an offshoot of 5-HT research in depression. Until now, 5-HT research has formed the bulk of biological suicide research. It is true that some attention has been given to cortisol release, the dexamethasone suppression test, and the thyrotropin-releasing hormone–thyroid-stimulating hormone test; those data, however, are scanty and controversial, and do not present a coherent picture. Therefore, I refrain from discussing them and refer the interested reader to another paper (van Praag, 1986).

Data Derived from Patients with Depression as the Principal Diagnosis

It is not always clear in what types of depression the biological abnormalities have been found. My impression is that most findings pertain to the syndrome of vital or endogenous depression, which is rather similar to the DSM-III category of "major depressive disorder, melancholic type." If diagnostic categorization is unclear, I use the term "certain forms of depression."

CNS Studies

Cerebrospinal Fluid 5-Hydroxyindoles. In the late 1960s and early 1970s, three research groups independently and almost simultaneously introduced the probenecid technique in psychiatric research in order to study the metabolism of 5-HT in the CNS (van Praag, Korf, & Puite, 1970; Roos & Sjostrom, 1969; Tamarkin, Goodwin, & Axelrod, 1970). Probenecid blocks the efflux of 5-Hydroxyindoleacetic acid (5-HIAA) from the CNS, including the cerebrospinal fluid (CSF), to the bloodstream. 5-HIAA is the main degradation product of 5-HT. The resulting accumulation of 5-HIAA in CSF can be considered a crude yardstick of 5-HT degradation in the CNS. (For a description of the probenecid technique, see van Praag, 1977.) Several, though not all, authors have reported decreased probenecid-induced CSF 5-HIAA accumulation in a subgroup of patients suffering from the syndrome of vital (endogenous) depression (Figure 2-1). This observation has been regarded as indicative of diminished 5-HT metabolism in the CNS. The data on baseline CSF 5-HIAA in depression are more controversial (see Baldessarini, 1983; van Praag, 1978a, 1982b). The best baseline studies so far, however

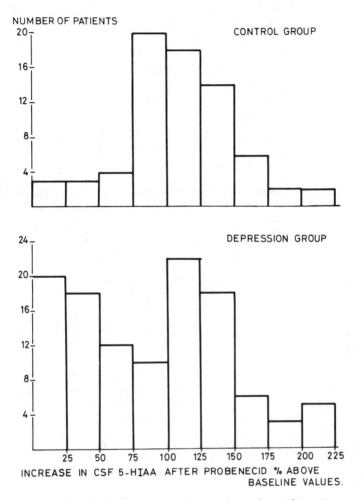

Figure 2-1.   Increase of CSF 5-HIAA concentration after probenecid in patients suffering from vital (endogenous) depression and in a nondepressed control group. The columns indicate the number of patients showing the increase in concentration given at the bottom of the column. (From van Praag, 1982a. Reprinted by permission.)

(in terms of group size, chemical methodology, and exclusion of factors interfering with CSF 5-HIAA concentration), repeatedly found decreased baseline values of CSF 5-HIAA in a subgroup of endogenously depressed patients (Asberg, Bertilsson, & Martensson, *et al.*, 1984; Traskman, Asberg, Bertilsson, & Thoren, 1984) (Figure 2-2).

Postmortem Studies.   Regional postmortem studies of CNS 5-hydroxy-indoles have been performed in suicide victims and depressed patients

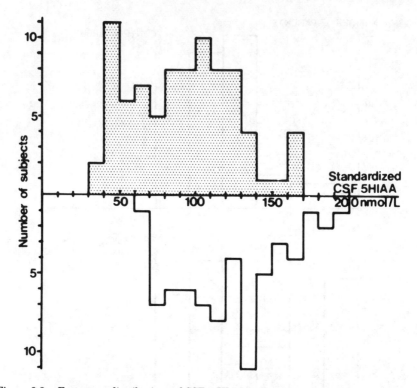

Figure 2-2.   Frequency distributions of CSF 5-HIAA in patients with melancholia (above center line) and healthy volunteer control subjects (below center line). Because of the dependence of metabolite concentrations on sex, age, and body height of the subjects, the levels were not directly comparable between the two groups of subjects (controls were younger and taller than the patients and more often male). All values were therefore been standardized to common age (45 years), body weight (170 cm), and unit sex (female) by means of a multiple-regression equation. (From Asberg, Bertilsson, & Martensson, 1984. Reprinted by permission.)

who died from natural causes (Birkmayer & Riederer, 1975; Farley, Deck, Hornykwicz, & Lloyd, 1974). Lowered concentrations of 5-HT and 5-HIAA have been found in certain raphe nuclei, these being the principal seat of cell bodies of serotonergic nerve fibers. The number of regional postmortem brain studies is too small for definitive conclusions.

Peripheral Data

Ratio of Tryptophan to Competing Amino Acids in Plasma.   Danish investigators have repeatedly reported a lowered plasma ratio of tryp-

tophan to the so-called competing amino acids in certain patients with
endogenous depression (Møller & Kirk, 1981; Møller, Kirk, & Fremming,
1976; Møller, Kirk, & Honore, 1980). This observation has now been
confirmed (Joseph, Brewerton, Reus, & Stebbins, 1984). The competing
amino acids are leucine, isoleucine, tyrosine, phenylalanine, and valine.
They compete with tryptophan for the same carrier system to cross the
blood–brain barrier (Figure 2-3). The ratio of tryptophan to competing
amino acids is the single most important factor determining transport
of tryptophan from plasma into the CNS (Wurtman, 1982). The availability of tryptophan in the CNS, in its turn, is an important determinant
of the synthesis rate of 5-HT. The decreased ratio can thus be expected
to lead to decreased CNS production of 5-HT. The relationship between
the decreased ratio and lowered CSF 5-HIAA has not yet been explored.

5-HT Uptake in Blood Platelets.   Several investigators have found 5-
HT uptake in blood platelets to be diminished in certain types of depression (see Rotman, 1983, for review). This finding is relevant since the
blood platelet is regarded as a reasonable model of a serotonergic nerve
ending.

The functional significance of this phenomenon is unknown. Several
explanations are conceivable. The serotonergic neuron could be primarily

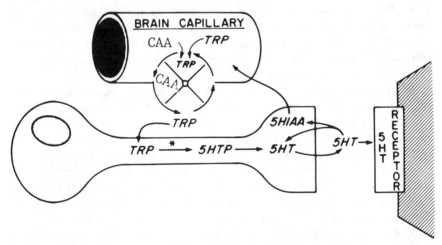

Figure 2-3.   The so-called neutral amino acids compete for the same transport mechanism
from plasma to CNS. These competing amino acids (CAA) are tryptophan, tyrosine,
valine, leucine, isoleucine, and phenylalanine. Since the carrier is satiable, the ratios
of tryptophan to CAA and tyrosine to CAA determine the influx of tryptophan and
tyrosine in the CNS. The CNS availability of those amino acids is an important regulator
of 5-HT and catecholamine synthesis, respectively. (From Fernstrom, 1982. Reprinted
by permission.)

hypoactive. The decreased 5-HT uptake, leading to increased 5-HT availability in the synapse, is a compensatory mechanism to restore function. Another explanation is that decreased 5-HT uptake is secondary to hypersensitivity of postsynaptic 5-HT receptors. Increased 5-HT availability would lead to desensitization of the receptors and possibly to normalization of function.

Direct Receptor Studies.   Some MA-related receptors are measurable in peripheral structures, in particular in white and red blood cells. In recent years, such peripheral receptor studies have been applied in biological depression and schizophrenia research. Very little is known, however, about the functional relationship between peripheral and corresponding central MA receptors. Are disturbances in central receptors reflected in the periphery, and, vice versa, is normality or abnormality of peripheral MA receptors indicative of their similar state in the CNS? Considerable animal work has to be done before the "marker value" of peripheral MA receptors for their central counterparts can be properly assessed. The following data should be reviewed with these restrictions in mind.

Imipramine recognition sites were discovered on blood platelets (Langer & Briley, 1981). These so-called imipramine receptors are probably modulators of the 5-HT uptake sites. The natural ligand of the imipramine receptor has not yet been identified, but promising progress has been made (Barbarccia, Gandolfi, Chaung, & Costa, 1983). High-affinity sites for imipramine, indistinguishable from the ones on platelets, have been found on CNS serotonergic nerve endings (Rehavi, Paul, Skolnick, & Goodwin, 1980).

At the present time the imipramine receptor is being intensively studied in humans. Preliminary data indicate that in depression their activity/density might be decreased (Briley, Langer, Raisman, Sechter, & Zarifian, 1980). Uncertainty exists as to whether this finding constitutes a trait or a state factor. A factor that is limiting progress in this area is the rather low interlaboratory reliability of the imipramine receptor assay. This is possibly related to the fact that both platelets and brain contain not only high-affinity binding sites for imipramine, but low-affinity binding sites as well. This state of affairs has only been recently reported (Ieni, Tobach, Zukin, Barr, & van Praag, 1985; Ieni, Zukin, & van Praag, 1984) and has not taken into account in previous studies.

Whether an association exists between imipramine receptor and 5-HT uptake in blood platelets is controversial (Wood, Suranyi-Cadotte, Nair, La Faille, & Schwartz, 1983). It is also unknown in which direction 5-HT uptake is influenced by activation of imipramine binding sites.

Henceforth, it is impossible even to speculate on the functional significance of the alleged decrease in imipramine binding sites in depression.

According to McBride, Mann, McEwen, and Biegon (1983), a 5-HT_2
receptor exists on blood platelets. Nothing is known on its indicator
value for the central counterpart. No studies on peripheral 5-HT_2 receptors in depression have as yet been published.

Indirect Receptor Studies.   Apart from direct measurement in the periphery, MA receptors—in this case, 5-HT receptors—can be studied
indirectly (i.e., via a so-called challenge test). A compound is administered
that increases functional activity in a particular MA-ergic system.
Subsequently a substance, usually a hormone, is measured whose release
is governed by that particular MA-ergic system. A blunted response
then indicates hyposensitivity, and an exaggerated response indicates
hypersensitivity, of that particular MA-ergic system (see Lemus & van
Praag, in press).

Two indirect 5-HT receptor tests have been described: release of the
pituitary hormone prolactin, and the release of the adrenal cortical
hormone cortisol in the response to compounds increasing 5-HT availability in the brain. Challengers that have been used are the 5-HT
precursors: tryptophan and 5-hydroxytryptophan (5-HTP) (Heninger,
Charney, & Sternberg, 1984; Kato, Nakai, Imura, Chihara, & Ohgo,
1974; Meltzer, Tricou, Robertson, & Lowry, 1983; Westenberg, van
Praag, de Jong, & Thyssen, 1982), and fenfluramine, an anorectic drug
increasing 5-HT release and decreasing 5-HT reuptake (Siever, Murphy,
Slater, de la Vega, & Lipper, 1984). Although there is considerable
evidence that increased 5-HT "tone" is a prolactin releasing factor, the
effect of 5-HT precursors on plasma prolactin in man has been controversial. Heninger *et al.* (1984), for example, found the prolactin response
to intravenous tryptophan blunted in depression (Figure 2-4); Westenberg
et al. (1982) found no consistent influence of 5-HT precursors on serum
prolactin (Table 2-1). Differences in dose could have been a factor (van
Praag, Lemus, & Kahn, in press). Perhaps even more important in this
respect is the fact that neither tryptophan nor 5-HTP is "5-HT-specific."
Both have measurable influences on the metabolism of CNS NA and
DA (see van Praag & Lemus, 1986). 5-HTP increases not only the
metabolism of 5-HT, but also that of DA and NA (van Praag, 1983b).
Large quantities of tryptophan will reduce the influx of tyrosine in the
CNS (Wurtman, 1982), and by doing so diminish the production rate
of catecholamines. The controversial data on prolactin response to 5-
HT precursors could be related to their dual effect on 5-HT and cate-
cholamine metabolism.

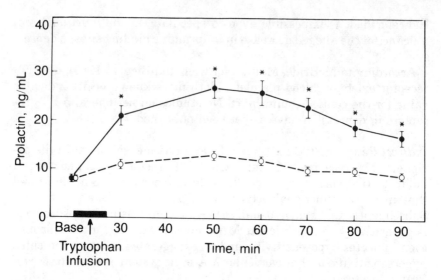

Figure 2-4. Average time course of mean (± *SEM*) prolactin response to tryptophan infusion for normal subjects (healthy controls) (solid line) (n = 19) and depressed patients (broken line) (n = 24). Asterisk indicates $p < .001$, Mann–Whitney U test, two-tailed. (From Heninger, Charney, & Sternberg, 1984. Reprinted by permission.)

The prolactin response to fenfluramine is described as being blunted in depression (Siever *et al.*, 1984) (Figure 2-5). These findings suggest that in those patients the 5-HT system is subresponsive. On the other hand, the cortisol response to 5-HTP seems to be increased (Meltzer, Umberkomaan-Wiita, Robertson, Tricou, Lowry, & Perline, 1984). This would indicate hyperresponsivity of the 5-HT system. Meltzer *et al.* hypothesize that the hyperresponsivity is a phenomenon secondary to an underlying 5-HT deficit (Figure 2-6).

The fact that the results of the indirect 5-HT receptors test are contradictory permits several interpretations: (1) The methodology is unreliable; (2) patients have been tested in different (biochemical) phases of a depressive episode; (3) in depression, different types of disordered 5-HT metabolism might occur. All three hypotheses deserve further exploration.

Pharmacological Strategies. In double-blind, controlled studies, we have repeatedly demonstrated that l-5-HTP is therapeutically active in patients with the syndrome of vital (endogenous) depression (van Praag, 1978b, 1983b; van Praag & Westenberg, 1983; van Praag, Korf, Dols, & Schut, 1972). It proved to be more active than placebo, and

29

equivalent to the tricyclic antidepressant clomipramine (Anafranil), whereas the combination of clomipramine and 5-HTP proved to be more efficacious than either compound alone. 5-HTP was always administered together with a peripheral decarboxylase inhibitor. Several groups, though not all, have confirmed our findings (see van Praag, 1981, for review). We found the low postprobenecid CSF 5-HIAA group of vital depression to be preferentially responsive to 5-HTP treatment. This study has not yet been repeated.

Several independent groups reported euphoric effects of 5-HTP in normal test subjects (Puhringe, Wirz-Justice, Graw, Lacoste, & Gastpar, 1976; Trimble, Chadwick, Reynolds, & Marsden, 1975). In myoclonus patients treated with 5-HTP, (hypo)mania has been reported to be a frequent side effect (Thal, Sharpless, Wolfson, & Katzman, 1980; van Woert, Rosenbaum, Howieson, & Bowers, 1977).

The data on l-tryptophan in depression are much more equivocal. The number of studies finding antidepressant effects almost equals the number of negative studies. However, it is fair to add that the largest and best-designed tryptophan study to date found l-tryptophan to be an effective antidepressant in depressive outpatients seen by general practitioners (Thomson, Rankin, Ashcroft, Yates, McQueen, & Cummings, 1982). Its efficacy was equivalent to that of amitriptyline (Tryptisol). In a double-blind comparative study of tryptophan and 5-HTP in depression, 5-HTP turned out to be significantly better than either tryptophan or placebo (van Praag, 1984). Tryptophan tended to be more efficacious than placebo, but not significantly so (Figure 2-7). This study was exclusively concerned with depressive inpatients, whose illness

TABLE 2-1. Baseline, Maximal Baseline, and Maximal Treatment Values of Prolactin (ng/ml) during 5-HTP and Tryptophan Loading in Depressive Patients and Controls

Treatment and dose	Groups	Baseline		Maximal baseline		Maximal treatment	
		Mean	SD	Mean	SD	Mean	SD
Tryptophan	Patients ($n = 9$)	8.5^a	4.2	9.7	5.3	10.4^a	4.9
(5 g)	Controls ($n = 5$)	4.0	1.3	4.5	1.6	5.2	1.2
5-HTP	Patients ($n = 9$)	8.9	5.3	10.5	5.2	10.3	5.5
(200 mg)	Controls ($n = 5$)	5.0	1.1	5.9	1.3	5.2	0.5

Note. From Westenberg, van Praag, de Jong, & Thyssen (1982). Reprinted by permission. For baseline and maximal baseline values, plasma samples were collected at -40, -20, and 0 minutes before administration of the amino acids. For baseline values, plasma concentrations at these times were averaged. Thereafter, samples were collected at 20-minute intervals between $+20$ and $+180$ minutes. [a]Statistically significant compared to controls (Mann–Whitney U test, $p < .05$).

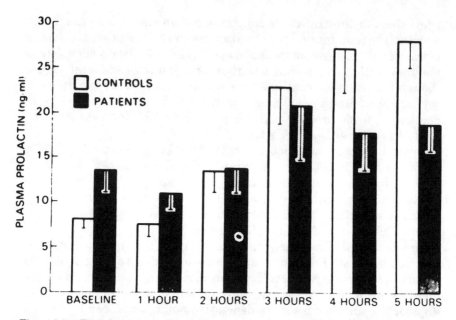

Figure 2-5.   Time course of the elevation in plasma prolactin following 60 mg fenfluramine in sex- and age-matched patients suffering from depression (n = 9) and controls (n = 9). Means ± *SEM*'s are indicated. (From Siever, Murphy, Slater, de la Vega, & Lipper, 1984. Reprinted by permission.)

was considerably more severe than the patients involved in the above-mentioned tryptophan study of Thomson *et al.* (1982).

The reason for the discrepant findings with the two 5-HT precursors may be found in their disparate effects on central catecholamines. As stated under "Indirect Receptor Studies" (above), 5-HTP increases the metabolism both of 5-HT and of DA and NA. This has been observed in animals and humans (van Praag, 1983b). In animals, large doses of tryptophan decrease central catecholamine metabolism by decreasing the transport of tyrosine into the CNS, via diminishing the ratio of tyrosine to competing amino acids (Wurtman, 1982). Whether the same occurs in humans is uncertain (van Praag & Lemus, 1986). According to the MA hypothesis of depression, decreasing the catecholamine availability in the brain constitutes a depressogenic principle. This could counteract the therapeutic potential of increased 5-HT availability.

There has been one study published in which an inhibitor of 5-HT synthesis was used, namely, para-chlorophenylalanine (PCPA) (Shopsin, Gershon, Goldstein, Friedman, & Wilk, 1974). It was reported that the antidepressant response of tricyclic antidepressants was blocked by PCPA.

Recently, a number of selective inhibitors of 5-HT uptake have been developed. Examples are zimelidine, indalpine, fluoxetine, and fluvoamine. All of them possess antidepressant properties. This finding also speaks in favor of involvement of central serotonergic functions in mood regulation.

Data Derived from Patients with Somatic Disorders and a Concomitant Depression

Parkinson's Disease

Depression is diagnosed in approximately 50% of patients with Parkinson's disease (Mayeux, Stern, Rosen, & Leventhal, 1981; Mindham, 1970). Correlation between the severity of the Parkinson syndrome and the severity of depression is lacking. Moreover, depression not infrequently antedates Parkinson's disease. Thus, the depressive syndrome is not likely to be solely a psychological reaction to a disabling disease.

Hornykiewicz (1981) demonstrated Parkinson's disease to be, at least in part, a DA-deficiency syndrome. In addition, he found CNS 5-HT to be lowered in this disease. In accordance with postmortem findings, the postprobenecid CSF concentrations of homovanillic acid (HVA)—the main degradation product of DA—and of 5-HIAA were found to be lowered in Parkinson's disease (Lakke, Korf, van Praag, & Schut, 1972).

Recently Mayeux, Stern, Cote, and Williams (1984) both confirmed our findings and found a significant correlation in Parkinson patients

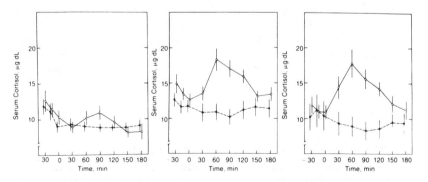

Figure 2-6. Effect of placebo (filled circles) or 5-HTP (open circles), 200 mg orally, in normal controls (left), depressed patients (center), and manic patients (right), on serum cortisol. Each point represents mean ± SEM. (From Meltzer, Umberkomaan-Wiita, Robertson, Tricou, Lowry, & Perline, 1984. Reprinted by permission.)

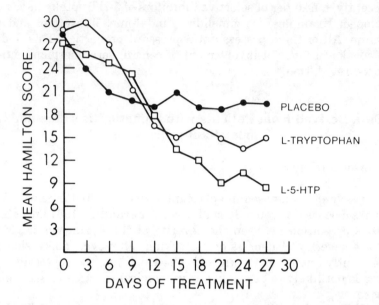

Figure 2-7.   Comparative, controlled study of l-5-HTP (200 mg/day) in combination with carbidopa (150 mg/day), l-tryptophan (5 g/day), and placebo in patients suffering from the syndrome of vital (endogenous) depression. 5-HTP was significantly superior to tryptophan and placebo. Tryptophan treatment was not significantly different from placebo treatment. (From van Praag, 1984. Reprinted by permission.)

between low CSF 5-HIAA and the occurrence of major depressive disorder (Figure 2-8). This is suggestive evidence that depression in Parkinson patients relates to involvement of serotonergic systems. The concentration of HVA and 3-methoxy-4-hydroxyphenylglycol (MHPG)—the main degradation product of NA in the CNS—did not relate to depression.

Coeliac Disease

Coeliac disease is a malabsorption syndrome characterized by gluten intolerance. Hallert and Sedvall (1983) demonstrated an increased depression morbidity in this intestinal disorder. Using the same reasoning as mentioned above in connection with Parkinson's disease, this finding should not be exclusively considered as a psychological reaction to chronic somatic suffering.

In patients with this disorder, Hallert and Sedvall (1983) found CSF 5-HIAA to be lowered (Figure 2-9). The concentrations of HVA and MHPG were also decreased.

At this time, it is unclear to what extent decreased CSF 5-HIAA and mood lowering interrelate. The fact that depression in coeliac patients responded to pyridoxine speaks in favor of such a relationship. Pyridoxine, which comes from dietary sources, is a cofactor required for 5-HT and catecholamine synthesis, and is poorly absorbed in coeliac disease.

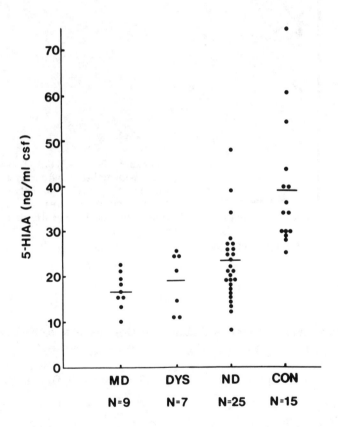

Figure 2-8.   CSF content of 5-HIAA in Parkinson patients according to their psychiatric diagnosis. MD refers to major depression, DYS to dysthymic disorder, ND to no psychiatric disorder, and CON to the age-matched controls. The horizontal lines reflect means for each group. (From Mayeux, Stern, Cote, & Williams, 1984. Reprinted by permission.)

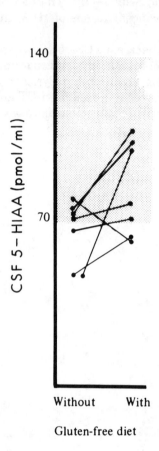

Figure 2-9. 5-HIAA in CSF of seven adult coeliac patients before and during treatment with a gluten-free diet. Normal range: 70–140 pmol/ml (shaded area). (From Hallert & Sedvall, 1983. Reprinted by permission.)

Are the 5-HT Disorders Related to Depression, to Suicide, or to Disturbed Regulation of Aggression?

Syndromal or Symptomatological Specificity of 5-HT Disorders

Assuming now that central 5-HT metabolism can be disturbed in depression, the question arises to what extent those disturbances are specific for depression. Systematic specificity studies have been conducted for only one 5-HT-related variable, CSF 5-HIAA.

Biological research in psychiatry so far has a definite nosological/ syndromal orientation. The ultimate goal is to find *the* biological causes of, for example, schizophrenia, depression, or the like. Previously we have questioned this approach and pleaded another one (van Praag, Korf, Lakke, & Schut, 1975). We then summarized the evidence that biological variables in behavioral disorders seem to correlate better with particular psychological dysfunctions than with a particular syndrome or nosological entity as a whole. Particular psychological dysfunctions are seldom syndromally or nosologically specific, but tend to occur in many behavioral disorders. Biological dysfunctions are specifically related, we hypothesized, to particular psychological dysfunctions; they are syndromally and nosologically nonspecific. The best basis for biological psychiatry is, we suggested, a "functional psychopathology"—that is, a psychopathology in which psychological dysfunctions rather than syndromes or nosological entities are the units of classification. To this end, syndromes have to be "dissected" into their component psychological dysfunctions, such as disturbances in motor activity, perception, information processing, and so on. In fact, this consideration constitutes an application of Claude Bernard's principles to psychiatry. Collaboration between psychiatrists and experimental clinical psychologists is a prerequisite for this venture to be successful.

5-HT Disorders and Suicidal Acts

Recent data regarding CSF 5-HIAA seem to support the relevance of the "functional strategy." In 1976 Asberg, Traskman, and Thoren reported that low CSF 5-HIAA occurred in particular in those depressed patients who had attempted suicide (Figure 2-10). The correlation was stronger in those who had used violent means than in those who had used nonviolent methods (Figure 2-11). Drug overdose by ingestion and superficial wrist cuts were classified as nonviolent; all other methods were classified as violent. The chance of rescue was not taken into account in determining the lethality of the attempt. According to Asberg's group (Traskman, Asberg, Bertilsson, & Sjostrand, 1981), CSF 5-HIAA contains prognostic information, in that low 5-HIAA levels predict increased subsequent suicide risk. Another group found that low CSF 5-HIAA entails increased relapse risk in patients with unipolar and bipolar depression (van Praag & de Haan, 1979).

The relation between low CSF 5-HIAA and suicidal behavior has been confirmed in several studies of dissimilar design (Table 2-2). In some studies, CSF 5-HIAA was measured in depressed patients after

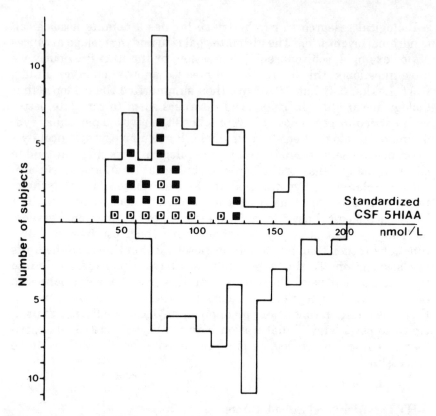

Figure 2-10.   Standardized concentrations of CSF 5-HIAA (see Figure 2-2) in patients
who had attempted suicide (above center line) and healthy volunteer control subjects
(below center line). The squares indicate suicide attempts by a violent method (any
method other than a drug overdose, taken by mouth, or a superficial wrist cut). D
indicates a subject who subsequently died from suicide, in all cases but one within 1
year after the lumbar puncture. (From Asberg, Bertilsson, & Martensson, 1984. Reprinted
by permission.)

admission for suicide attempt (Banki & Arato, 1983; Banki, Molnar,
& Vojnik, 1981; Oreland, Widberg, Asberg, Traskman, Sjostrand, Thoren,
Bertilsson, & Tybring, 1981; van Praag, 1982a). Others correlated CSF
5-HIAA with lifetime history of suicide attempts (Agren, 1980; Montgomery & Montgomery, 1982), or with suicidal ideation at the time of
admission (Agren, 1980). Banki and Arato (1983) confirmed that the
correlation between low CSF 5-HIAA and suicidal acts resulted mostly
from violent suicide attempters. I (van Praag, 1982a), on the other
hand, found the correlation to apply equally to violent and nonviolent
attempters (see Table 2-2). On the risk–rescue scale developed by Weis-

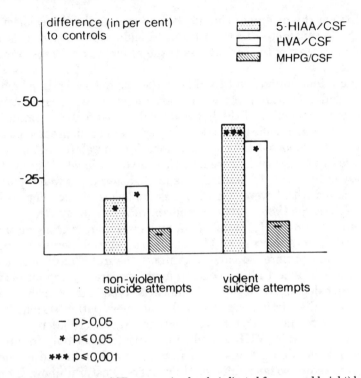

Figure 2-11. Differences in CSF monoamine levels (adjusted for age and height) between controls and violent and nonviolent suicide "attempters." (From Traskman, Asberg, Bertilsson, & Sjostrand, 1981. Reprinted by permission.)

man and Worden (1972), the low 5-HIAA patients tended to cluster in the patient mode with high risk–rescue scores, but the correlation reached no statistical significance (van Praag, Plutchik, & Conte, in press). The risk–rescue scale determines separately the deadliness of the method used in the attempt and the chance of being rescued. The combined assessment results in a score indicating the seriousness (or

TABLE 2-2. Incidence of Suicide Attempts in 203 Patients Hospitalized with Depressions of Varying Symptomatology, Related to Central 5-HT Disorders

	Total	Admitted after suicide attempts	Number of violent suicide attempts
Low CSF 5-HIAA level	51	24	4
Normal CSF 5-HIAA level	152	30	3

Note. From van Praag (1982a). Reprinted by permission.

lethality) of the attempt. The higher one scores, the more serious the attempt is considered to have been. Suicide method per se is not a reliable indicator of the seriousness of the attempt (van Praag, Plutchik, & Conte, in press).

Agren (1980) found low CSF 5-HIAA levels to be correlated not only with suicidal ideation, but with overt anger as well. He considered these data supportive of the hypothesis that low 5-HIAA patients are prone to violent suicides. His test group consisted of depressed patients.

One study reported that suicidal ideation correlates not only with decreased but also with increased CSF 5-HIAA levels (Agren, 1983). Interestingly, low CSF 5-HIAA in suicide attempters was reported to be correlated with lowered CSF magnesium levels (Banki, Vojnik, Papp, Balla, & Arato, 1985). Little is known, however, about the influence of magnesium on 5-HT metabolism and serotonergic transmission.

According to Asberg et al. (1976), the correlation between low CSF 5-HIAA and attempted suicide exists in both "neurotic" and "endogenous" depressions. The best-fitting DSM-III diagnoses are "dysthymic disorder" and "major depressive disorder, melancholic type," respectively. In other studies this distinction was not made, but most patients seem to have suffered from major depressive disorder. Agren (1983) reported the correlation between 5-HIAA and suicidality to occur only in unipolar, not in bipolar, depressions. It is noteworthy that in one of the two negative studies so far published (Roy-Byrne, Post, Rubinow, Linnoila, Savard, & Davis, 1983), the majority of patients (70%) suffered from bipolar depression. Violent suicides were too few to be analyzed separately. In the second negative study (Vestegaard, Sørenson, Hoppe, Rafaelson, Yates, & Nicolaou, 1978), it is not stated whether the data pertain to recent suicide attempt or lifetime history of suicide. Violent and nonviolent attempts were not analyzed separately. We were unable to confirm Agren's (1980) finding of low CSF 5-HIAA in suicidal ideation (van Praag, in press; van Praag, Lemus, & Kahn, in press). The phenomenon was only found in subjects with recent or past suicide attempts.

I (van Praag, 1982a) measured postprobenecid CSF 5-HIAA; all others measured baseline levels.

Apart from CSF 5-HIAA, the only other 5-HT-related variables that have been studied in suicide are imipramine binding sites and 5-HT$_2$ receptors in postmortem brain tissues. The data, however, are confusing. Imipramine binding has been reported as increased (Meyerson, Wennogle, Abel, Coupet, Lippa, Rau, & Beer, 1982), decreased (Perry, Marshall, Blessed, Tomlinson, & Perry, 1983; Stanley, Virgilio, & Gershon, 1982), and normal (Crow, 1985); 5-HT$_2$ receptors have been reported as increased (Stanley & Mann, 1983) and normal (Crow, 1985).

In conclusion, most studies, but not all, have found a correlation between suicidal behavior and low CSF 5-HIAA. The evidence that in particular the violence of the attempt is implicated is equivocal. The finding that low CSF 5-HIAA predicts increased suicide risk awaits confirmation.

CSF 5-HIAA in So-Called Nondepressed Suicide Attempters

A few years after their original publication (Asberg et al., 1976), the group of Asberg (Traskman et al., 1981) replicated the finding of low CSF 5-HIAA in depressed suicide attempters, but added an important observation—namely, that the same correlation had been found, albeit to a lesser degree, in what they called nondepressed and nonpsychotic suicide attempters (Figure 2-12). The latter group consisted of patients

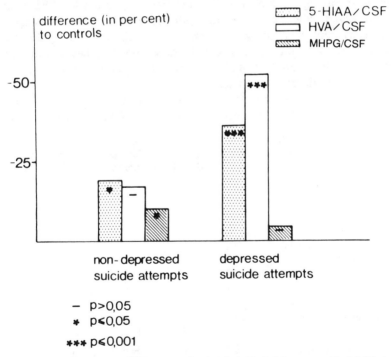

Figure 2-12. Differences in CSF monoamine levels (adjusted for age and height) between controls and depressed and nondepressed suicide attempters. (From Traskman et al., 1981. Reprinted by permission.)

with personality disorder and anxiety disorder. This finding has been confirmed in suicide attempters diagnosed with minor depressive illness, anxiety state, borderline personality, and substance abuse (Banki & Arato, 1983; Brown, Ebert, Goyer, Jimerson, Klein, Bunney, & Goodwin, 1982; Brown, Goodwin, Ballenger, Goyer, & Major, 1979; Oreland *et al.*, 1981). None of these studies analyzed violent and nonviolent attempts separately.

From these observations, it was tentatively concluded that the central 5-HT disorder as represented by lowered CSF 5-HIAA is related to disturbed aggression regulation, rather than being an indicator of certain forms of affective disorder. This conclusion, however, seems premature, for the following reasons:

1. A vast majority of nonpsychotic patients admitted to a psychiatric ward because of attempted suicide were found to have suffered from a considerable degree of depression in the 2 months prior to the attempt (van Praag, 1982a). After the suicide attempt, a significant drop of depression ratings was observed (van Praag & Plutchik, 1985) (Table 2-3); no such drop was observed after admission to the ward for depressed patients without prior suicide attempts. The diagnosis of a nondepressed suicide attempter should therefore be based on data pertaining to the presuicidal condition. In the above-mentioned studies, however, it was based on postsuicidal observations.

2. Suicide attempts with violent means are more likely to occur in major depressive disorder, melancholic type, than in other forms of

TABLE 2-3. Depression Scores 1 Week Prior to Suicide Attempt and After Admission for 25 Suicide Attempters

Score	Before		After		
	$\bar{x}$	SD	$\bar{x}$	SD	t
Global Scores					
Independent physician	2.4	1.2	1.9	1.0	2.22*
Treating physician	2.4	1.1	1.7	.9	2.63*
Patient	2.7	1.5	1.3	1.1	3.99***
Important others	2.0	1.4	1.3	.8	2.38*
Hamilton Rating Scale					
Independent physician	18.6	6.6	15.6	5.2	2.17*
Treating physician	18.0	6.4	15.8	5.7	1.33
Zung Depression Scale	58.4	12.6	50.8	10.1	3.33**

Note. From van Praag & Plutchik (1985). Reprinted by permission.
* $p < .05$.
** $p < .01$.
*** $p < .001$.

TABLE 2-4. Syndromal Depression Diagnosis in 31 Depressed Patients Who Had
Made Violent Suicide Attempts and in 31 Depressed Patients Who Had Made
Nonviolent Suicide Attempts

		Diagnosis	
	n	Vital depression	Other depression types
Violent suicide attempt	31	26	5
Nonviolent suicide attempt	31	13	18

Note. From van Praag & Plutchik (1984). Reprinted by permission. Vital (endogenous) depressions
were found significantly more frequently in violent suicide attempters (χ^2 = 11.68, p < .001).

depression (van Praag & Plutchik, 1984) (Table 2-4). From the available
data, it is impossible to conclude whether lowered CSF 5-HIAA levels
are related to violent autoaggression as such or to that particular
depression type in which the likelihood of violent autoaggression is
increased.

Other data, however, support the assumption that a relation between
lowered CSF 5-HIAA and dyscontrol of (auto) aggression indeed exists.
In the following section, these data are discussed.

Low CSF 5-HIAA and Disorders in Aggression Regulation

Low CSF 5-HIAA has been found in schizophrenic patients without
major affective symptoms, who had attempted suicide because "voices"
had ordered them to do so (van Praag, 1983a). Those who scored high
on the risk–rescue scale had the lowest 5-HIAA levels (Figure 2-13).
Ninan, van Kammen, Scheinin, Linnoila, Bunney, and Goodwin (1984),
studying schizophrenic patients, found a correlation between suicidal
ideation and lowered CSF 5-HIAA. We (van Praag, in press; van Praag,
Lemus, & Kahn, in press) nor Roy, Ninan, Mazonson, Piekar, van
Kammen, Linnoila, and Paul (1985) found a relationship between low
CSF 5-HIAA and life time history of suicide attempts in chronic schizophrenics.

A second piece of evidence indicating linkage of low CSF 5-HIAA
and aggression was derived from a study in which two groups of psy-
chopathologically similar patients with major depression, melancholic
type, were compared on several aggression measures (van Praag, in
press). One group was characterized by normal CSF 5-HIAA, the other
by low postprobenecid CSF 5-HIAA. The latter group distinguished
itself from the former in two ways: (1) higher rate of suicide attempts;

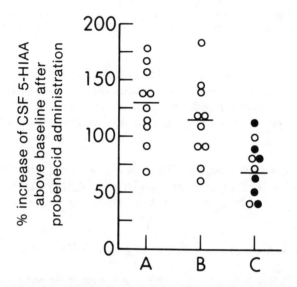

A = Non-psychiatric control group

B = Schizophrenic without suicidal history

C = Schizophrenic with suicidal history

O = Non-violent suicide

● = Violent suicide

Figure 2-13.   Postprobenecid CSF 5-HIAA in nondepressed schizophrenic patients with and without suicidal histories and in nonpsychiatrically disturbed controls. Mean CSF 5-HIAA in group c was lower than in the other two groups ($p < .05$, Fisher's exact test). (From van Praag, 1983a. Reprinted by permission.)

(2) higher hostility scores on a variety of measures (Table 2-5). Brown *et al.* (1982), in the same vein, reported a trivariate relation among history of aggression, history of suicide, and low CSF 5-HIAA in patients with personality disorders. Those studies confirm the purely psychopathological study of Weissman, Fox, and Klerman (1973), in which the single most important factor distinguishing between patients admitted for depression and patients admitted for suicide attempts turned out to be a higher degree of hostility in the suicidal patients.

Supportive evidence for a relation between 5-HT and aggression is also provided by studies conducted in nondepressed patients with aggressive behavior against others. These studies have been carried out in patients with several types of personality disorder (Bioulac, Benezich, Renaud, Noel, & Roche, 1980; Brown et al., 1979, 1982) and in prison inmates convicted for violent crimes (Lidberg, Asberg, & Sundquist-Stensman, 1984; Lidberg, Tuck, Asberg, Scalia-Tomba, & Bertilsson, 1985; Linnoila, Virkkunen, Scheinin, Nuutila, Rimon, & Goodwin, 1983). The ways in which aggression ratings were derived differed widely: aggression scores on a personality inventory, lifetime history of aggressive acts, and measurement of CSF MA metabolites directly after a violent crime (Table 2-6). Yet all studies reported a negative correlation between CSF 5-HIAA and outward-directed aggression. Two studies found evidence that it is not aggressive behavior as such, but rather lack of impulse control, that constitutes the behavioral correlate of deficient 5-HT metabolism (Lidberg et al., 1985; Linnoila et al., 1983).

One should not overrate the findings relating 5-HT and outward-directed aggression. In men, the biology of aggression is hard to study. This behavioral state is pre-eminently influenced by environmental (social) factors for which it is difficult to control and by preceding of alcohol and drugs; in addition, disturbances in aggression regulation are generally short-lasting, in contrast to pathological disturbances in mood regulation. Nevertheless, it would be inappropriate to ignore the fact that no negative reports have been published so far, and the fact that in animal literature a host of data is found indicating the importance of serotonergic systems for the regulation of (certain forms of) aggression (Valzelli, 1981, 1984).

A possible case in point of some kind of relationship between 5-HT and aggression is, finally, formed by the Lesch–Nyhan syndrome. This

TABLE 2-5. Characteristics of Low 5-HIAA
Depressives as Compared to Normal 5-HIAA
Depressives

---

1. More suicide attempts**
2. Greater number of contacts with police*
3. Increased arguments with:
     Relatives*
     Spouses**
     Colleagues*
     Friends*
4. More hostility at interview*
5. Impaired employment history (arguments)*

Note. From van Praag (in press). Reprinted by permission.
* $p < .05$.
** $p < .01$.

TABLE 2-6. Studies in Which CSF 5-HIAA and Aggression Were Negatively Correlated

Study	Number and sex of subjects	Diagnosis	Measurements of aggression	Assay of CSF 5-HIAA	Postprobenecid or baseline 5-HIAA	Other MA metabolites in CSF
Brown, Goodwin, Ballenger, Goyer, & Major (1979)	26 males	Personality disorder	Checklist for lifetime history of aggressive acts	Fluorometric	Baseline	HVA unchanged; MHPG increased
Brown, Ebert, Goyer, Jimerson, Klein, Bunney, & Goodwin (1982)	12 males	Borderline personality	Checklist for lifetime history of aggressive acts; Buss–Durkee Inventory; MMPI	Mass fragmentography	Baseline	HVA unchanged; MHPG unchanged
Bioulac, Benezich, Renaud, Noel, & Roche (1980)	6 males	XYY personality disorder	Lifetime history of aggressive behavior	Fluorometric	Postprobenecid	HVA unchanged; MHPG not measured
Linnoila, Virkkunen, Scheinin, Nuutila, Rimon, & Goodwin (1983)[a]	36 males	Severe personality disorders	21 had killed and 15 had made attempts to kill; all were alcohol abusers	Liquid chromatography	Baseline	HVA unchanged; MHPG unchanged
Lindberg, Asberg, & Sundquist-Stensman (1984)	2 males, 1 female	Depression: 2; acute psychotic episode: 1	All had killed one of their children and attempted suicide subsequently	Not stated	Baseline	Not mentioned
Lidberg, Tuck, Asberg, Scalia-Tomba, & Bertilsson	16 males	Alcoholism: 10; schizophrenia: 1; no further diagnoses mentioned	All had committed criminal homicide	Mass fragmentography	Baseline	HVA unchanged; MHPG unchanged

[a]This study examined low CSF 5-HIAA in impulsive violent offenders as opposed to those who had premeditated their acts.

syndrome is an inborn error of purine metabolism characterized by, among other things, growth retardation and severe self-mutilation. Some authors found CSF 5-HIAA to be lowered (Castels, Chakrabarti, Windsberg, Hurwic, Perel, & Nyhan, 1979) and self-mutilative behavior to be ameliorated by administration of the 5-HT precursor 5-HTP (Mizuno & Yugari, 1975). No studies of 5-HT metabolism in other forms of self-mutilation have been published, but they seem, in the light of the above-mentioned research, to be indicated.

In summary, a correlation between low CSF 5-HIAA and aggressive behavior, both outward-directed and directed to oneself, seems fairly likely.

The Linkage between Depression and Aggression: A Biological Hypothesis

Most evidence today suggests a correlation between disturbed aggression regulation or disturbed impulse control and low CSF 5-HIAA, an indicator of decreased 5-HT metabolism in the CNS. These findings do not, per se, contradict a relation between low CSF 5-HIAA and mood disorder. It is conceivable that disturbances in serotonergic functions could give rise to both mood and aggression dysregulation. Several observations speak in favor of this assumption. First, low CSF 5-HIAA has been found in depressed patients without suicidal history (Asberg et al., 1976; van Praag, 1982a). Second, CSF 5-HIAA values have been found to be lowest in depressed patients who had made violent suicide attempts (Traskman et al., 1981). Finally, pharmacological manipulation of central 5-HT induces mood changes. 5-HTP has a mood-elevating effect (van Praag & Westenberg, 1983); tryptophan depletion, on the other hand, causes a rapid lowering of mood (Young, Smith, Pihl, & Ervin, 1985). A common factor in the central regulation of mood and aggression would provide a biological explanation for the clinical observation that dysregulation of mood and dysregulation of aggression frequently go hand in hand (Conte & Plutchik, 1974; Freud, 1917/1957; Gershon, Cromer, & Klerman, 1968; Plutchik, van Praag, & Conte, Weissman et al., 1973).

Summary and Conclusion

Ever since the discovery that the classical antidepressants—tricyclics and MA oxidase inhibitors—exert an influence on central 5-HT, this neurotransmitter has been studied in depression, particularly in those forms responsive to this type of treatment. This chapter reviews the evidence in favor of a relationship between depression and central 5-HT dysfunctions. Most of the findings have been derived from patients with depression as the principal diagnosis. Some data have originated from patients suffering from a somatic illness and from depression as well. Both peripheral and central data are discussed.

Although no single 5-HT-related finding in depression has so far been unequivocally established, the available evidence, in balance, justifies the tentative conclusion that disturbances in 5-HT metabolism can occur in depression.

Lowered CSF 5-HIAA, the major indicator of disturbed central 5-HT metabolism in depression, has also been reported in aggression disorders, both in patients who had committed suicidal acts and in those with outward-directed aggression. The finding can not be explained by a concomitant state of depression.

Rather than to discard the classical 5-HT–depression hypothesis, in favor of a 5-HT–aggression hypothesis, the hypothesis is launched that disturbances in serotonergic regulation can give rise to both mood *and* aggression disorders. This would provide a biological explanation for the clinical observation that those disorders frequently go hand in hand.

References

Agren, H. Symptom patterns in unipolar and bipolar depression correlating with mono-amine metabolites in the cerebrospinal fluid. *Psychiatry Research*, 1980, *3*, 225–236.

Agren, H. Life at risk: Markers of suicidality in depression. *Psychiatric Developments*, 1983, *1*, 87–104.

Asberg, M., Bertilsson, L., & Martensson, B. CSF monoamine metabolites, depression, and suicide. In E. Usdin, M. Asberg, L. Bertilsson, & F. Sjoqvist (Eds.), *Frontiers in biochemical and pharmacological research in depression*. New York: Raven Press, 1984.

Asberg, M., Bertilsson, L., Martensson, B., Scalia-Tomba, G.-P., Thoren, P., & Traskman, L. CSF monoamine metabolites in melancholia. *Acta Psychiatrica Scandinavica*, 1984, *69*, 201–219.

Asberg, M., Traskman, L., & Thoren, P. 5-HIAA in the cerebrospinal fluid: A biochemical suicide predictor? *Archives of General Psychiatry*, 1976, *33*, 1193–1197.

Asberg, M. Traskman, L. & Thoren, P. Serotonin depression: A biochemical subgroup within the affective disorders? *Science*, 1976, *131*, 478–480.

Baldessarini, R. J. *Biomedical aspects of depression*. New York: Academic Press, 1983.

Banki, C. M., & Arato, M. Amine metabolites and neuroendocrine responses related to depression and suicide. *Journal of Affective Disorders*, 1983, *5*, 223–232.

Banki, C. M., Molnar, G., & Vojnik, M. Cerebrospinal fluid amine metabolites, tryptophan and clinical parameters in depression: Psychopathological symptoms. *Journal of Affective Disorders*, 1981, *3*, 91–99.

Banki, C. M., Vojnik, M., Papp, Z., Balla, K. Z., & Arato, M. Cerebrospinal fluid magnesium and calcium related to amine metabolites, diagnosis, and suicide attempts. *Biological Psychiatry*, 1985, *20*, 163–171.

Barbarccia, M. L., Gandolfi, O., Chaung, D., & Costa, E. Modulation of neuronal serotonin uptake by a putative endogenous ligand of imipramine recognition sites. *Proceedings of the National Academy of Sciences USA*, 1983, *80*, 5134–5138.

Bioulac, B., Benezich, M., Renaud, B., Noel, B., & Roche, D. Serotonergic dysfunctions in the 47, XYY syndrome. *Biological Psychiatry*, 1980, *15*, 917–923.

Birkmayer, W., & Riederer, P. Biochemical post-mortem findings in depressed patients. *Journal of Neural Transmission*, 1975, *37*, 95–109.

Briley, M. S., Langer, S. Z., Raisman, R., Sechter, D., & Zarifian, E. Tritiated imipramine binding sites are decreased in platelets of untreated depressed patients. *Science*, 1980, *209*, 303–305.

Brown, G. L., Ebert, M. E., Goyer, P. F., Jimerson, D. C., Klein, W. J., Bunney, W. E., & Goodwin, F. K. Aggression, suicide and serotonin: Relationships to CSF amine metabolites. *American Journal of Psychiatry*, 1982, *139*, 741–746.

Brown, G. L., Goodwin, F. K., Ballenger, J. C., Goyer, P. F., & Major, L. F. Aggression in humans correlates with cerebrospinal fluid metabolites. *Psychiatry Research*, 1979, *1*, 131–139.

Castells, S., Chakrabarti, C., Windsberg, B. G., Hurwic, M., Perel, J. M., & Nyhan, W. L. Effects of l-5-hydroxytryptophan on monoamine and amino acids turnover in the Lesch–Nyhan syndrome. *Journal of Autism and Developmental Disorders*, 1979, *9*, 95.

Conte, H. R., & Plutchik, R. Personality and background characteristics of suicidal mental patients. *Journal of Psychiatric Research*, 1974, *10*, 181.

Crow, T. *Monoamine neurons and reward: Can they be related to clinical syndrome?* Paper presented at the 14th Annual Meeting of the Society of Biological Psychiatry, Dallas, May 15–19, 1985.

Fernstrom, J. D. Acute effects of tryptophan and single meals on serotonin synthesis in the rat brain. In B. T. Ho, J. C. Schoolar, & E. Usdin (Eds.), *Serotonin in biological psychiatry*. New York: Raven Press, 1982.

Freud, S. Mourning and melancholia. In J. Strachey (Ed.), *Standard edition of the complete psychological works of Sigmund Freud* (Vol. 14). London: Hogarth Press, 1957. (Originally published, 1917.)

Gershon, E. S., Cromer, M., & Klerman G. L. Hostility and depression. *Psychiatry*, 1968, *31*, 224.

Hallert, C., & Sedvall, G. Improvement in central monoamine metabolism in adult coeliac patients starting a gluten-free diet. *Psychological Medicine*, 1983, *13*, 267–271.

Heninger, G. R., Charney, D. S., & Sternberg, D. E. Serotonergic function in depression. *Archives of General Psychiatry*, 1984, *41*, 398–402.

Hornykiewicz, O. Biochemical determinants of Parkinson's disease. In H. M. van Praag, M. H. Lader, O. J. Rafaelsen, & E. J. Sachar (Eds.), *Handbook of biological psychiatry, Part IV*. New York: Marcel Dekker, 1981.

Ieni, J. R., Tobach, E., Zukin, S., Barr, G., & van Praag, H. M. Multiple [3H]imipramine binding sites in brains of male and female fawn-hooded and Long–Evans rats. *European Journal of Pharmacology* 1985, *112*, 261–265.

Ieni, J. R., Zukin, S. R., & van Praag, H. M. Complex interactions of 3H-imipramine with platelet and brain binding sites: implication for clinical research. *Clinical Neuropharmacology*, 1984, *7*, 128–129.

Joseph, M. S., Brewerton, T. D., Reus, V. I., & Stebbins, G. T. Plasma l-tryptophan/ neutral amino acid ratio and dexamethasone suppression in depression. *Psychiatry Research*, 1984, *11*, 185–192.

Kato, Y., Nakai, Y., Imura, H., Chihara, K., & Ohgo, S. Effect of 5-hydroxytryptophan (5-HTP) on plasma prolactin in man. *Journal of Clinical Endocrinology and Metabolism*, 1974, *38*, 695–697.

Lakke, J. P. W. F., Korf, J., van Praag, H. M., & Schut T. Predictive value of the probenecid test for the effect of l-dopa therapy in Parkinson's disease. *Nature: New Biology*, 1972, *236*, 208–209.

Langer, S. Z., & Briley, M. High affinity 3H-imipramine binding: A new biological tool for studies in depression. *Trends in Neuroscience*, 1981, *4*, 28.

Lemus, C., & van Praag, H. M. Monoamine precursors: Effects on neuroendocrine parameters. In C. Nemeroff & P. Loosen (Eds.), *Handbook of psychoneuroendocrinology*. New York: Guilford Press, in press.

Lidberg, L., Asberg, M., & Sundquist-Stensman, U. B. 5-Hydroxyindoleacetic acid levels in attempted suicides who have killed their children. *Lancet*, 1984, *ii*, 928.

Lidberg, L., Tuck, J. R., Asberg, M., Scalia-Tomba, G. P., & Bertilsson, L. Homicide, suicide and CSF 5-HIAA. *Acta Psychiatrica Scandinavica*, 1985, *71*, 230–236.

Linnoila, M., Virkkunen, M., Scheinin, M., Nuutila, A., Rimon, R., & Goodwin, F. K. Low cerebrospinal fluid 5-hydroxyindoleacetic acid concentration differentiates impulsive from non-impulsive violent behavior. *Life Sciences*, 1983, *33*, 2609–2614.

Lloyd, K. J., Farley, I. J., Deck, J. H. N., & Hornykiewicz, O. Serotonin and 5-hydroxyindoleacetic acid in discrete areas of the brainstem of suicide victims and control patients. *Advances in Biochemical Psychopharmacology*, 1974, *11*, 387–397.

Mayeux, R., Stern, Y., Cote., L., & Williams, J. B. W. Altered serotonin metabolism in depressed patients with Parkinson's disease. *Neurology*, 1984, *34*, 642–646.

Mayeux, R., Stern, Y., Rosen, J., & Leventhal, J. Depression, intellectual impairment and Parkinson's disease. *Neurology*, 1981, *31*, 645–650.

McBride, P. A., Mann, J. J., McEwen, B., & Biegon, A. Characterization of serotonin binding sites on human platelets. *Life Sciences*, 1983, *33*, 2033.

Meltzer, H. Y., Tricou, B. J., Robertson, A., & Lowry, M. Hormone response to 5-HTP. *Psychiatry Research*, 1983, *10*, 151.

Meltzer, H. Y., Umberkomaan-Wiita, B., Robertson, A., Tricou, B. J., Lowry, M., & Perline, R. Response of serum cortisol to 5-HTP in depression. *Archives of General Psychiatry*, 1984, *41*, 366–374.

Meyerson, L. R., Wennogle, L. P., Abel, M. S., Coupet, J., Lippa, A. S., Rau, C. E., & Beer, B. Human brain receptor alterations in suicide victims. *Pharmacology, Biochemistry and Behavior*, 1982, *17*, 159–163.

Mindham, R. H. S. Psychiatric syndromes in parkinsonism. *Journal of Neurology, Neurosurgery and Psychiatry*, 1970, *30*, 188–191.

Mizuno, T., & Yugari, Y. Prophylactic effect of l-5-hydroxytryptophan on self-mutilation in the Lesch–Nyhan syndrome. *Neuropediatrie*, 1975, *6*, 13.

Møller, S. E., & Kirk, L. Decreased tryptophan availability in endogenous depression caused by disturbed plasma leucine clearance. *Progress in Neuropsychopharmacology and Biological Psychiatry*, 1981, *5*, 277–279.

Møller, S. E., Kirk, L., & Fremming, K. H. Plasma amino acids as an index for subgroup in manic depressive psychosis: Correlation to effect of tryptophan. *Psychopharmacology*, 1976, *49*, 205–213.

Møller, S. E., Kirk, L., & Honore, P. Relationship between plasma ratio of tryptophan to competing amino acids and the response to l-tryptophan treatment in endogenously depressed patients. *Journal of Affective Disorders*, 1980, *3*, 47–50.

Montgomery, S. A., & Montgomery, D. Pharmacological prevention of suicidal behavior. *Journal of Affective Disorders*, 1982, *4*, 291.

Ninan, P. T., van Kammen, D. P., Scheinin, M., Linnoila, M., Bunney, W. E., & Goodwin, F. K. CSF 5-hydroxyindoleacetic acids levels in suicidal schizophrenic patients. *American Journal of Psychiatry*, 1984, *141*, 566–569.

Oreland, L., Widberg, A., Asberg, M., Traskman, L., Sjostrand, L., Thoren, P., Bertilsson, L., & Tybring, G. Platelet MAO activity and monoamine metabolites in cerebrospinal fluid in depressed and suicidal patients and in healthy controls. *Psychiatry Research*, 1981, *4*, 21–29.

Perry, E. K., Marshall, E. F., Blessed, G., Tomlinson, B. E., & Perry, R. H. Decreased imipramine binding in the brains of patients with depressive illness. *British Journal of Psychiatry*, 1983, *142*, 188–192.

Plutchik, R., van Praag, H. M., & Conte, H. R. *Variables related to suicide, violence, depressions and impulsivity*. Paper presented at the IV World Congress of Biological Psychiatry, Philadelphia, September 1985.

Puhringe, W., Wirz-Justice, A., Graw, P., Lacoste, V., & Gastpar, M. Intravenous l-5-hydroxytryptophan in normal subjects: An interdisciplinary precursor loading study. I. Implication of reproducible mood elevation. *Pharmakopsychiatrie*, 1976, *9*, 260–268.

Rehavi, M., Paul, S. M., Skolnick, P., & Goodwin, F. Demonstration of specific high affinity binding sites for 3H-imipramine in human brain. *Life Sciences*, 1980, *26*, 2273–2279.

Roos, B. E., & Sjostrom, R. 5-Hydroxyindoleacetic acid and homovanillic acid levels in the cerebrospinal fluid after probenecid application in patients with manic–depressive psychosis. *Journal of Clinical Pharmacology*, 1969, *1*, 153–155.

Rotman, A. Blood platelets in psychopharmacological research. *Progress in Neuropsychopharmacology and Biological Psychiatry*, 1983, *7*, 135–151.

Roy, A., Ninan, P. H., Mazonson, A., Pickar, D., van Kammen, D. P., Linnoila, M., & Paul, S. M. CSF monoamine metabolites in chronic schizophrenic patients who attempted suicide. *Psychological Medicine*, 1985, *15*, 335–340.

Roy-Byrne, P., Post, R. M., Rubinow, D. R., Linnoila, M., Savard, R., & Davis, D. CSF 5-HIAA and personal and family history of suicide in affectively ill patients: A negative study. *Psychiatry Research*, 1983, *10*, 263–274.

Shopsin, B., Gershon, S., Goldstein, S., Friedman, M., & Wilk, S. Use of synthesis inhibition in defining a role for biogenic amines during imipramine treatment in depressed patients. *Psychopharmacological Bulletin*, 1974, *10*, 52.

Siever, L. J., Murphy, D. L., Slater, S., de la Vega, E., & Lipper, S. Plasma prolactin changes following fenfluramine in depressed patients compared to controls: An evaluation of central serotonergic responsivity in depression. *Life Sciences*, 1984, *34*, 1029–1039.

Stanley, M., & Mann, J. J. Increased serotonin-2 binding sites in frontal cortex of suicide victims. *Lancet*, 1983, *i*, 214–216.

Stanely, M., Virgilio, J., & Gershon, S. Tritiated imipramine binding sites are decreased in the frontal cortex of suicides. *Science*, 1982, *216*, 1337–1339.

Tamarkin, N. R., Goodwin, F. K., & Axelrod, J. Rapid elevation of biogenic amine metabolites in human CSF following probenecid. *Life Sciences*, 1970, *9*, 1397–1408.

Thal, L. J., Sharpless, N. S., Wolfson, L., & Katzman, R. Treatment of myoclonus with l-5-hydroxytryptophan and carbidopa. Clinical, electrophysiological and biochemical observation. *Annals of Neurology*, 1980, *7*, 570–576.

Thomson, J., Rankin, H., Ashcroft, G. W., Yates, C. M., McQueen, J. K., & Cummings S. W. The treatment of depression in general practice: A comparison of l-tryptophan, amitriptyline, and a combination of l-tryptophan and amitriptyline with placebo. *Psychological Medicine*, 1982, *12*, 741–751.

Traskman, L., Asberg, M., Bertilsson, L., & Sjostrand, L. Monoamine metabolites in CSF and suicidal behavior. *Archives of General Psychiatry*, 1981, *38*, 631–636.

Traskman, L., Asberg, M., Bertilsson, L., & Thoren, P. CSF monoamine metabolites of depressed patients during illness and after recovery. *Acta Psychiatrica Scandinavica*, 1984, *69*, 333–342.

Trimble, M., Chadwick, D., Reynolds, E., & Marsden, C. D. l-5-Hydroxytryptophan and mood. *Lancet*, 1975, *i*, 583.

Valzelli, L. *Psychobiology of aggression and violence*. New York: Raven Press, 1981.

Valzelli, L. Reflections on experimental and human pathology of aggression. *Progress in Neuropsychopharmacology and Biological Psychiatry*, 1984, *8*, 311–325.

van Praag, H. M. *Depression and schizophrenia: A contribution on their chemical pathologies*. New York: Spectrum, 1977.

van Praag, H. M. Amine hypotheses of affective disorders. In L. L. Iversen, S. D. Iversen, & S. H. Snyder (Eds.), *Handbook of psychopharmacology (Vol. 13, Biology of mood and anti-anxiety drugs)*. New York: Plenum Press, 1978. (a)

van Praag, H. M. *Psychotropic drugs: A guide for the practitioner*. NewYork: Brunner/Mazel, 1978. (b)

van Praag, H. M. Management of depression with serotonin precursors. *Biological Psychiatry*, 1981, *16*, 291-310.

van Praag, H. M. Depression, suicide and the metabolism of serotonin in the brain. *Journal of Affective Disorders*, 1982, *4*, 275-290. (a)

van Praag, H. M. Neurotransmitters and CNS disease: Depression. *Lancet*, 1982, *ii*, 1259-1264. (b)

van Praag, H. M. CSF 5-HIAA and suicide in non-depressed schizophrenics. *Lancet*,

1983, *ii*, 977-978. (a)

van Praag, H. M. In search of the action mechanism of antidepressants. 5-HTP/tyrosine mixtures in depression. *Neuropharmacology*, 1983, *22*, 433-440. (b)

van Praag, H. M. Studies in the mechanism of action of serotonin precursors in depression. *Psychopharmacological Bulletin*, 1984, *20*, 599–602.

van Praag, H. M. Brain serotonin and human (auto) aggression. In J. D. Barchas & W. E. Bunney (Eds.), *Perspectives in psychopharmacology*. New York: Alan R. Liss, in press.

van Praag, H. M. Biological suicide research: Outcome and limitations. *Biological Suicide*, 1986*a*.

van Praag, H. M. (Auto) Aggression and CSF 5-HIAA in Depression and schizophrenia. *Psychopharmacology Bulletin* (in press).

van Praag, H. M., & de Haan, S. Central serotonin metabolism and frequency of depression. *Psychiatry Research*, 1979, *1*, 219–224.

van Praag, H. M., Korf, J., Dols, L. C. W., & Schut, T. A pilot study of the predictive value of the probenecid test in application of 5-hydroxytryptophan as antidepressant. *Psychopharmacology* 1972, *25*, 14–21.

van Praag, H. M., Korf, J., Lakke, J. P. W. F., & Schut, T. Dopamine metabolism in depressions, psychoses and Parkinson's disease: The problem of the specificity of biological variables in behavior disorders. *Psychological Medicine*, 1975, *5*, 138–146.

van Praag, H. M., Korf, J., & Puite, J. 5-Hydroxyindoleacetic acid levels in the cerebrospinal fluid of depressive patients treated with probenecid. *Nature*, 1970, *225*, 1259–1260.

van Praag, H. M., & Lemus, C. Monoamine precursors in the treatment of psychiatric disorders. In J. J. Wurtman & R. J. Wurtman (Eds.), *Nutrition and the brain* (Vol. 7). New York: Raven Press, 1986.

van Praag, H. M., Lemus, C., & Kahn, R. Hormonal probes of central serotonoergic activity. Do they really exists? *Biological Psychiatry*, (in press).

van Praag, H. M., & Plutchik, R. An emperical study on the "cathartic effect" of attempted suicide. *Psychiatry Research*, 1985, *16*, 123–130.

van Praag, H. M., Plutchik, R., & Conte, H. The serotonin-hypothesis of (auto) aggression. Critical appraisal of the evidence. *Annals of the N.Y.Academy of Sciences*, (in press).

van Praag, H. M., & Plutchik, R. Depression-type and depression-severity in relation to risk of violent suicide attempt. *Psychiatry Research*, 1984, *12*, 333–338.

van Praag, H. M., & Westenberg, H. G. M. The treatment of depressions with l-5-hydroxytryptophan. In J. Mendlewicz & H. M. van Praag (Eds.), *Management of depression with monoamine precursors*. Basel: S. Karger, 1983.

van Woert, M. H., Rosenbaum, D., Howieson, J., & Bowers, M. B. Long term therapy of myoclonus and other neurological disorders with l-5-hydroxytryptophan and carbidopa. *New England Journal of Medicine*, 1977, *296*, 70–75.

Vestegaard, P., Sørensen, T., Hoppe, E., Rafaelson, O. J., Yates, C. M., & Nicolaou, N. Biogenic amine metabolites in cerebrospinal fluid of patients with affective disorders. *Acta Psychiatrica Scandinavica*, 1978, *58*, 88–96.

Weisman A. D., & Worden, J. W. Risk/rescue rating in suicide assessment. *Archives of General Psychiatry*, 1972, *26*, 553–560.

Weissman, M., Fox, K., & Klerman, J. L. Hostility and depression associated with suicide attempts. *American Journal of Psychiatry*, 1973, *130*, 450.

Westenberg, H. G. M., van Praag, H. M., de Jong, J. T. V. M., & Thyssen, J. H. H. Post-synaptic serotonergic activity in depressive patients: Evaluation of the neuroendocrine strategy. *Psychiatry Research*, 1982, *7*, 361–371.

Wood, P. L., Suranyi-Cadotte, B. E., Nair, N. P. V., LaFaille, F., & Schwartz, G. Lack of association between [3H]imipramine binding sites and uptake of serotonin in control, depressed and schizophrenic patients. *Neuropharmacology*, 1983, *22*, 1211–1214.

Wurtman, R. J. Nutrients that modify brain function. *Scientific American*, 1982, *42*, 246.

Young, S. N., Smith, S. E., Pihl, R. O., & Ervin, F. R. Tryptophan depletion causes a rapid lowering of mood in normal males. *Psychopharmacology Bulletin*, 1985, *87*, 173–177.

CHAPTER 3

Clinical Electroencephalography and the Study of Suicide Behavior

Frederick A. Struve, PhD

Department of Psychiatry and Behavioral Science, Eastern Virginia Medical School; Virginia Consortium for Professional Psychology

It is certain that many will be initially perplexed to find clinical electroencephalography (EEG) included as a topic area in a volume on suicide. Primarily this is because in the minds of health professionals and laypersons alike, clinical EEG is closely bound by strong fundamental ties to the fields of epilepsy and classical clinical neurology. For many, its relevance to the mystery and tragedy of self-destruction seems obscure.

Historically, both electroencephalographers and suicidologists have uniformly ignored the possibility that EEG–suicide relationships may exist or that EEG study may contribute to the understanding of at least some aspects of self-destructive behavior. Although behavioral symptoms and psychiatric disorders have to some extent received limited attention in major reference works on EEG, discussion of suicide behavior is completely absent from such volumes (Cohn, 1949; Craib & Perry, 1975; Gibbs & Gibbs, 1952, 1964; Glaser, 1963; Hill & Parr, 1963; Kiloh, McComas, & Osselton, 1972; Kiloh & Osselton, 1966; Klass & Daly, 1979; Kooi, 1971; Schwab, 1951; Strauss, Ostow, & Greenstein, 1952; Wilson, 1965a). Conversely, with only one exception known to me (Hankoff & Einsidler, 1979), substantive discussion of EEG has not previously been included in the numerous volumes devoted to the study of suicide. This is not surprising. For vast periods of time, the formal study of suicide has excluded biological considerations of any kind. In our efforts to understand self-destruction, the march from moral and

This work was supported by Grant No. MH20662 from the National Institute of Mental Health, United States Public Health Service.

51

philosophical conceptualizations to sociological and then psychological or psychodynamic formulations has been prolonged and gradual. Within this context, studies of "organic" or biological variables of potential relevance to suicide—most of which stem from neurochemistry, neuroendocrinology, and psychopharmacology—have only emerged and begun to increase within the past three decades. The first serious attempts to include ratings of suicide behavior in broad surveys of EEG–behavior relationships within psychiatric populations did not occur until 1964 (Small & Small) and 1965 (Tucker, Detre, Harrow, & Glaser), and it was not until 1972 (Struve, Klein, & Saraf) that investigations specifically designed to focus explicitly on EEG–suicide relationships appeared.

That EEG may be used as a tool in the study of suicide becomes less perplexing when one considers the historical roots of EEG as a clinical science. It did not spring forth from the field of neurology, but instead had its origin in psychiatry. Following a period of 40 years during which studies demonstrating electrical activity recorded from the brains of animals were largely rejected by leading neurological authorities, Hans Berger, a German psychiatrist, began in 1929 to publish his classic series of studies of the human EEG (Berger, 1929). Dr. Berger was deeply committed to biological psychiatry, and he had conducted numerous biological and cerebrophysiological studies of emotion, cognition, and behavior. His successful development of EEG grew out of such concerns and represented the development of a powerful tool with which he hoped to understand more fully the physiology of consciousness and the pathophysiology of aberrant behavior. Within this perspective, EEG studies of behavior, including suicide, are but logical extensions of the philosophy and work begun over 50 years ago by EEG's founder.

Synopsis and Overview

The potential usefulness of clinical EEG in understanding the wide spectrum of suicide behaviors can be viewed from several directions. In one approach, EEG can be considered as one of several valuable screening techniques used to uncover previously unrecognized covert physical diseases in some psychiatric patients. In this instance, one is not seeking a direct linkage between EEG abnormality and self-destructive impulses. Instead, EEG abnormality, when encountered, may result in subsequent detection of unsuspected biological illnesses that may produce serious psychiatric disturbances—some types of which (i.e., depression) have the potential to introduce risk for suicide. Presumably, correction of the underlying physical disease will lessen the psychiatric symptoms, with a consequent reduction of self-destructive potential.

Another approach, which is more directly concerned with the potential for cerebral dysrhythmias to increase suicide tendencies, involves study of the prevalence of suicide behaviors among patients with known seizure disorders. Regardless of EEG findings (the interictal EEG may be normal in some seizure patients), the existence of a well-documented seizure disorder implies episodic disruption of cerebral electrical activity, which in turn either may or may not modify suicide risk. Unfortunately, studies of suicide among epileptics suffer from numerous conceptual confounds, some of which are reviewed later. Because of this, empirical relationships between cerebral dysrhythmia and suicide—if they exist at all—must be sought among individuals free of overt convulsive phenomena, and such investigative attempts have been confined largely to psychiatric populations.

Studies of EEG–suicide relationships among psychiatric patients can be divided into two basic types. In the first of these, the focus is not directly on suicide; rather, ratings of some aspect of suicide behavior are simply included among a broad array of symptomatic, diagnostic, and demographic variables to be cross-tabulated with EEG findings. In the second approach, studies are explicitly designed for the exclusive purpose of examining potential EEG–suicide relationships. Finally, EEG studies of suicide behaviors can be conceptualized as falling within the broader context of episodic dysconstrol syndromes, where a variety of episodic dyscontrol acts are presumed to be mediated by ictal discharges in the limbic system and elsewhere in the cortical and subcortical brain.

Limitations of Noninvasive Scalp EEG

In all discussion to follow, the limitations of scalp EEG recording must be kept in mind. Such limitations place very real constraints upon the sensitivity of EEG to electrical dysregulation within the brain, and it is important that they be recognized. The limiting constraints inherent in EEG technology have received extensive treatment elsewhere (Struve, 1985a), and will only be given in summary fashion here.

Because of several factors, abnormal electrical discharges may occur within the brain, yet may not be detected by external scalp EEG recordings. In essence we have a situation where "false-negative" EEGs can occur, and this has both clinical and research implications. A primary factor that limits detection of electrical signals is the structural housing of the brain itself. Surrounded and encased by skull, only about one-third of the outer convexity of the cortex is accessible to external scalp recording (Gibbs & Gibbs, 1964; Glaser, 1963). A large amount of mesial, inferior, and deep-buried cortical tissue is far removed from exploring electrodes on the scalp, as are subcortical and cerebellar structures. Intertwined with this constraint is the fact that the skin, skull, dura, and brain tissue itself impose substantial impedance to the propagation of electrical potentials. Thus electrical signals may occur within the brain, yet may not be recorded because either they are too weak to reach scalp leads or they originate at locations too remote for detection to be possible. It has long been established that electrical events recorded from depth electrodes inserted within the brain or from electrodes applied directly to the exposed cortex may at times be absent from scalp EEG tracings (Abraham & Ajmone-Marsan, 1958; Cooper, Winter, Crow, et al., 1965; Heath, 1975; Heath & Mickle, 1960; Spencer, Williamson, Spencer, et al., 1982; Walter & Crow, 1964).

A number of EEG abnormalities are fairly continual during the recording (e.g., generalized slowing), and they are not likely to remain undetected. However, many important findings are "paroxysmal" in nature. That is, they only appear in the EEG tracing briefly and episodically (Gibbs & Gibbs, 1952, 1964; Kiloh et al., 1972; Klass & Daly, 1979; Kooi, 1971). A paroxysmal dysrhythmia (e.g., focal spiking) may appear only once or twice during a prolonged EEG recording, or it may appear as frequently as every few seconds. Furthermore, some paroxysmal discharges may appear only during a sleep tracing or perhaps only during that brief transition between waking and sleeping. It is possible that electrical discharges may exist but occur only at such widely spaced intervals that they remain undetected. Should this happen, the problem of "false-negative" EEG results emerges again.

Because of these constraints and limitations, as well as others discussed elsewhere (Struve, 1985a), a normal waking, sleeping, and activated EEG can only suggest "presumptive evidence" that a scalp-recordable cerebral dysrhythmia does not exist; it cannot be construed as positive evidence of absence of such activity.

Covert Physical Disease

The Linkage of Physical Disease with Psychiatric Disturbance

Many years ago, we published a case study (Fader & Struve, 1972) of a 23-year-old woman who made two suicide attempts—one of which was exceptionally serious and nearly fatal—because of intense dysphoria associated with undetected physiological dysfunction. She functioned at a high level of social and occupational competence without psychiatric complaint or history up until she underwent a thyroidectomy for thyroid carcinoma. After her surgery she was placed on appropriate replacement thyroid, and her physical recovery appeared to proceed smoothly. However, she gradually became increasingly despondent and irritable and experienced feelings of worthlessness. She became psychotically depressed and for 15 consecutive months received both inpatient and outpatient psychiatric care, involving trials with antidepressant and antipsychotic medications as well as psychotherapy—none of which was of any help to her at all. During this entire period, the continuing medical opinion was that no physical dysfunction existed. In our laboratory, the screening EEG showed abnormality that was compatible with endocrinological dysfunction (hypothyroidism); because of this, and despite contrary consultant medical opinion, we *increased* her thyroid replacement schedule by 1 grain per day. Over a period of 2 weeks, the increase in replacement thyroid resulted in a normalization of her EEG and a complete remission of her depression, with a return to an optimistic attitude and normal socialization. When the extra 1 grain of thyroid was later changed to placebo without the patient's knowledge, she again became clinically depressed and her EEG again became abnormal. Reinstatement of active thyroid again resulted in normalization of both her EEG and her behavior. Prolonged follow-up indicated that she had returned to work in a demanding job and had married. There was no recurrence of depression or suicidal behavior. Her symptomatic depression and attendant profound suicidal behavior were apparently "caused" by a relative hypothyroid state, which for a very long time remained medically undetected.

In such a case as the one described above, we are reminded that unrecognized physical dysfunction can produce profound psychiatric disturbance, which in some cases may be associated with clearly life-threatening self-destructive acts. One is tempted to view such cases as exceptional, but in fact they might not be as rare as one might suppose. This is because *all* behavioral or psychiatric symptoms *without exception* are "nonspecific," in that they can arise from a variety of both functional psychosocial and/or physical disease causes. That a wide variety of organic dysfunctions and biological illnesses can effectively "masquerade" as functional psychiatric disturbance is known and documented in the literature, yet all too frequently this possibility is neglected by mental health practitioners of all disciplines. In Table 3-1, existing prevalence studies of physical disease in psychiatric inpatient and outpatient populations are summarized. Prevalence of biological illness is seen to range from 9% to 80%, with a weighted average of 35.6% for the combined sample (all studies) of 6,238 patients. In this table it is also seen that

TABLE 3-1. Prevalence of Physical Illness and Unsuspected (Covert) Illness in Psychiatric Patients

Study	Sample size	Population type	Patients with physical disease	Percentage of all patients with psychiatric symptoms caused or increased by physical disease	Percentage of all patients with "unsuspected" disease
Phillips (1937)	164	Inpatient	112 (68%)	42%	Not given
Marshall (1949)	175	Inpatient	77 (44%)	21%	2%
Herridge (1960)	209	Inpatient	103 (49%)	26%	Not given
D. W. Davies (1965)	36	Outpatient	21 (58%)	42%	Not given
Maguire & Granville-Grossman (1968)	200	Inpatient	67 (34%)	Not given	17%
Romano (1970)	92	Inpatient	49 (53%)	Not given	3%
Burke (1972)	200	Inpatient	86 (43%)	Not given	Not given
Koranyi (1972)	100	Outpatient	≃50 (≃50%)	10%	≃33%
Hall, Popkin, Devaul, Faillace, & Stickney (1978)	658	Outpatient	63 (9%)	9%	7%
Burke (1978)	133	Day hospital	67 (50%)	Not given	29%
Koranyi (1979)	2,090	Outpatient	902 (43%)	30%	20%
Hall, Gardner, Stickney, LeCann, & Popkin (1980)	100	Inpatient	80 (80%)	46%	80%
Karasu et al. (1980) Study 1	612	Inpatient	95 (16%)	Not given	Not given
Karasu et al. (1980) Study 2	200	Outpatient	104 (52%)	Not given	Not given
Muecke & Krueger (1981)	910	Outpatient	185 (20%)	0%	20%
Hoffman (1982)	215	Inpatient	123 (57%)	13%	19%
Barnes et al. (1983)	144	Outpatient	38 (26%)	Not given	13%

Note. Total n = 6,238. Weighted average percentage for each patient category: physical disease, 35.6%; psychiatric symptoms caused or increased by physical disease, 20%; "unsuspected" disease, 19%.

overall 20% of psychiatric patients (range 0% to 46%) may have their psychiatric symptoms either directly caused by or exacerbated by biological illness. Furthermore, averaged over all studies in Table 3-1, 19% of psychiatric patients (range 2% to 80%) may have previously unrecognized and undetected physiological dysfunction or disease. The published data that are available force the conclusion that biological disease, which often may be covert, represents a significant factor in the genesis of some psychiatric disturbance, and thus in some depression with suicide risk as well.

Recent reviews of the area of undetected disease and psychopathology (Gross, 1981–1982; Hall, Beresford, Gardner, & Popkin, 1982; Hoffman & Koran, 1984; Koranyi, 1980) indicate clearly that virtually every organ system (i.e., pulmonary, gastrointestinal, endocrinological, cardiovascular, etc.) is capable of developing disease that can be reflected initially by behavioral or psychiatric symptom presentations. Behavioral symptoms or even syndromes that can be etiologically related to underlying and often undetected organic factors are referred to as "secondary" symptoms, and the recently increased interest in this area has spawned important and significant reviews of "secondary mania" (Krauthammer & Klerman, 1978), organic or "secondary" anxiety disorders (Dietch, 1981), and, pertinent to our concern with suicide, organic depressive disorders (Dietch & Zetin, 1983). Furthermore, with respect to the thrust of this present publication, it is important to note that the above-mentioned reviews (plus large amounts of related literature) suggest that the most frequently encountered behavioral symptom originating from undetected organic cause is depression, which may range from mild to extreme in intensity. The available literature also suggests that of all biological illnesses, those involving endocrinological disease are most frequently seen to masquerade as psychiatric disturbance. In many endocrinological imbalances, disturbances of mood, especially depression, are likely to occur.

EEG and Detection of Covert Disease

It is important to consider covert disease in the assessment of emotional disturbance. Clinical EEG represents one technique that is useful in this respect, although it is seriously underutilized as a screening assessment procedure. Mental health professionals correctly assume that EEG is useful in identifying psychiatric patients who may have seizure disorders or structural brain lesions; however, they are generally not aware that this view of EEG's utility is exceptionally retrictive and narrow. EEG is sensitive to alterations in the electrical activity of the brain that are related to a truly wide variety of factors. Among other things, EEG is sensitive to cerebral electrical dysregulation caused by underlying diffuse and focal cerebral disturbances, encephalitic processes, vascular lesions, endocrinological and metabolic disorders, nutritional disorders, exposures to toxic substances, pharmacotoxicity, and idiopathic and iatrogenic seizures of various kinds (Gibbs & Gibbs, 1964; Kooi, 1971; Kiloh et al., 1972; Klass & Daly, 1979; Rémond & Glaser, 1977; Rémond & Radermecker, 1977; Wilson, 1965b). The value of this wide spectrum of sensitivity to screening patients with emotional or psychiatric complaints has been stressed elsewhere (Itil, 1982; Lutz, 1982; Struve, 1985).

In Table 3-1, it can be seen that the overall prevalence of physical disease as well as the prevalence of "covert" or previous undetected physical disease among psychiatric patients is high—perhaps higher than conventional clinical wisdom has recognized to date. Similarly, empirical reports of routine EEG testing of psychiatric patients (R. K. Davies, Neil, & Himmelhock, 1975; Gibbs & Novick, 1977; Struve & Pike, 1974; Tucker et al., 1965) point to high yields of EEG abnormalities ranging from 20% to 50%. Furthermore, since 1976 we have conducted a series of empirical studies (Struve, 1984) of the value of routine EEG screening for psychiatric patients; these studies demonstrate that nearly two-thirds (66.3%) of all recorded EEG abnormalities may occur in patients for which no pre-EEG suspicion of physical illness existed. Of patients with the most serious EEG abnormalities, more than half (54.6%) were not suspected of having any organic dysfunction prior to the screening EEG. Although with some patients no organic cause for the EEG finding could be demonstrated, with many a wide variety of previously unrecognized physical dysfunctions and disease states were uncovered following further medical scrutiny. In a recent study of 103 consecutive patients' EEGs containing generalized and/or focal slowing (Struve, 1985c), it was found that 82.6% of patients who received additional medical study had demonstrable organic dysfunction or disease, and that 8% of these cases had covert thyroid dysfunction underlying their psychiatric mood disturbances and affective symptoms.

An abnormal EEG does not readily denote specific etiology (Struve, 1985a). Frequently, additional medical tests are necessary to determine the medical cause, if any, of the EEG irregularity. When such a search is successful, the patient often can be greatly helped. Certainly near-tragedies similar to the case presented at the beginning of this section can be avoided more often.

Suicide and Seizure Disorders

That cerebral dysrhythmias may themselves directly contribute to some aspects of suicidal behavior is an intriguing notion. In examining this possibility, it is appropriate to give some consideration to the prevalence of suicide among persons with known seizure disorders. The reason for this is that convulsive phenomena are mediated by dysregulation of electrical activity within the brain; even when interictal EEGs are normal (and they may be in some epileptics), a firm clinical diagnosis of convulsive disorder implies an underlying disruption of cerebral electrical activity, even if not externally measured. Stated somewhat differently, a study of suicide behavior among known epileptics nicely circumvents the problem of "false-negative" EEGs discussed earlier. If a seizure disorder exists, it must be based on a cerebral dysrhythmia. Many research strategies are, of course, twin-edged swords that cut both ways. Certainly the positive value of examining suicide within the context of seizures is counterbalanced by equally important conceptual confounds that operate to cloud and obscure the data relationships observed. Elevated suicide prevalence among seizure patients, if found, does not unequivocally support the existence of associations between cerebral dysrhythmia and suicide. Seizure patients often face a life adjustment made exceptionally difficult by social stigmatization, vocational and insurance obstacles, medication side effects, and numerous other factors, and they may also have pre-existing or secondarily acquired brain damage superimposed upon their seizure disorder. Often depressive affect and suicidal symptoms may relate to these factors as plausibly as to EEG irregularities.

One of the more interesting case studies of suicide in seizure patients was published over 30 years ago by Weil (1954). He studied six patients with temporal lobe seizures and concurrent depressive episodes, the latter of which also cleared up with anticonvulsant medication. In two of these cases followed over a considerable time period, the depressive episodes were found to covary with increased or decreased severity of the EEG dysrhythmia. In fact with one of the six cases, suicide ideation only occurred during periods when the EEG spike discharges intensified. The covariation of depressive affect and suicide thoughts with the presence and absence of recorded EEG dysrhythmia suggests some contribution of the underlying cerebral dysrhythmia to behavioral symptoms, at least in these cases. Larger studies (Barande, 1958; Delay, Deniker, & Barande, 1957) suggest that in some populations of seizure patients the prevalence of suicide attempt behavior may be as high as one-third—approaching similar data for general psychiatric populations. One can also compare the rates of completed suicides among epileptics with similar rates for the general population. When this is done, some workers (Henriksen, Juul-Jensen, & Lund, 1970; Krohn, 1963; Prudhomme, 1941; Taylor & Falconer, 1968) have found that successful suicides among some epileptic populations exceed actuarial rates from the general population. In a large, well-designed study, Gunn (1973) contrasted epileptic prisoners with nonepileptic prisoners carefully matched for age, sex, institution, length of time served, and length of sentence. Using clinical interviews he found a significantly higher frequency of suicide ideation ($p < .005$) and affective symptoms ($p < .025$) among the prisoners with convulsive seizure disorders. However, Gunn was careful to note that "prisoners" with seizures may not be truly representative of epileptics in general.

Data suggesting an elevated prevalence of both suicide ideation and suicide attempts among persons with seizure disorders are compatible with the hypothesis that underlying cerebral dysrhythmias may somehow operate directly to elevate suicide risk. However, the material reviewed does not permit acceptance of this idea, and the conceptual difficulties mentioned above have not received adequate control. The data from seizure populations do, however, encourage further study in this area, and they heighten the importance of more direct EEG–suicide investigations in nonepileptic patient groups.

EEG and Suicide among Psychiatric Patients

Examination of potential EEG–suicide relationships among psychiatric patients free of seizures avoids the interpretive problems posed by the numerous seizure-related effects on life adjustment faced by the epileptic. However, relevant studies within psychiatry are few in number, and of these, some only approach EEG–suicide relationships in a minor or tangential manner. In Table 3-2, a summary of psychiatric population studies with a bearing on cerebral dysrhythmia and self-destructive behavior is provided. As noted in the synopsis and overview, the studies listed in Table 3-2 and discussed in this section can be divided into either general survey approaches that do not focus closely on suicide, or more detailed studies designed quite explicitly to study possible EEG–suicide phenomena.

General Survey Approaches

In Table 3-2, nine of the studies listed have not focused explicitly on suicide, but rather have employed broad survey approaches in which patients with a given EEG finding are contrasted with controls on a wide array of demographic, diagnostic, and symptomatic variables. In these studies, the primary quest has involved a search for possible clinical correlates of the particular EEG pattern in question; of course, self-destructive behavior would only constitute one potential correlate out of a great many. Furthermore, since these studies by and large have been concerned with different EEG phenomena, they cannot be compared directly with one another. Finally, although all of the studies contain some data relevant to the EEG–suicide issue, the assessments of suicide that have been conducted are quite limited in scope and usually involve simple ratings of only one or two suicide behavior items. These general survey studies (Types A and B in Table 3-2) should be viewed as providing a preliminary or cursory first look into the possibility that cerebral dysrhythmias may influence suicidal behavior.

Four of the nine general survey studies (Small, 1968; Small, Sharply, & Small, 1968; Small & Small, 1964; Tucker *et al.*, 1965) reported negative findings, in that no significant EEG–suicide associations were found. For the most part, these negative studies involved minor EEG dysrhythmias of possible interest to psychiatry (Struve, 1985a), but of the sort considered controversial by some electroencephalographers and most neurologists (Kiloh *et al.*, 1972; Klass & Daly, 1979). In two well-controlled investigations, Small and associates (Small, 1968; Small *et al.*, 1968) demonstrated that suicide behavior and specifically suicide attempts were unrelated to the presence or absence of either the 6/sec spike-and-wave EEG pattern or the psychomotor variant pattern (rhythmic midtemporal discharges). In fact, patients with EEGs containing the 6/sec spike-and-wave EEG dysrhythmia were more likely *not* to have made suicide attempts than were normal EEG psychiatric patients. One of the survey studies with positive findings—that of Greenberg and Pollack (1966), who used clinical judgments—reported a significant ($p < .025$) tendency for patients with the 14 and 6/sec positive-spike EEG pattern, a subcortical dysrhythmia, to be judged higher in suicide-risk than in matched normal EEG patients. However, the Greenberg and Pollack study was small and contained only nine patients with the 14 and 6/sec positive-spike finding. Larger-sample investigative studies by Small, already mentioned (Small *et al.*, 1968; Small & Small, 1964) report an absence of significant associations between the 14 and 6/sec positive-spike pattern and suicide; this is supported by our own work (Struve, Saraf, Arko, Klein, & Becka, 1977), in which a large-sample intensive study found the 14 and 6/sec positive-spike subcortical dysrhythmia to be evenly distributed across control and symptom groups, and hence unrelated to suicide.

A general survey study with especially strong methodology was conducted by Tucker *et al.* (1965). In their study of 95 psychiatric inpatients with EEGs classified as showing either diffuse, paroxysmal, or focal abnormality, as well as 45 patients with normal EEGs, they were careful to collect EEG and clinical symptom measures independently and to report interrater reliability figures for important variables. Although the study involved a wide variety of potential clinical correlates to the EEG findings, they included measures of "suicide ideation" as

TABLE 3-2. Summary of EEG–Suicide Associations Reported within Psychiatric Populations

Reference	Type	Description	Basic findings
Small & Small (1964)	A	25 patients with 14 and 6/sec positive spikes matched for age and sex with 25 normal EEG patients. Groups contrasted on numerous variables. Suicide not main emphasis of study.	Negative findings: Groups not significantly different for current suicide attempts or past history of attempts.
Tucker, Detre, Harrow, & Glaser (1965)	A	95 patients with abnormal EEGs contrasted with 45 normal EEG controls on numerous variables. Suicide not main emphasis of study.	Negative findings: No significant between group differences for either depression or suicide ideation.
Greenberg & Pollack (1966)	A	9 patients with 14 and 6/sec positive spikes contrasted with 10 normal EEG patients on numerous variables. Suicide not main emphasis of study.	14 and 6/sec positive spikes related ($p < .025$) to clinical judgment of increased suicide risk.
Flood & Seager (1968)	B	Chart review of 73 completed suicides, 73 nonsuicide random controls, and 70 nonsuicide matched control patients. Comparison on numerous variables. Only half of each group had EEG data.	Negative findings: No significant difference between suicide and control groups on incidence of EEG abnormality.
Small (1968)	A	50 patients with 6/sec spike and wave, matched for age, sex, education with normal EEG controls and "other abnormal" EEG comparison group. Groups contrasted on numerous variables. Suicide not main emphasis of study.	Negative findings: Patients with 6/sec spike and wave had *fewer* suicide attempts ($p < .02$) than normal-EEG controls.
Small, Sharpley, & Small (1968)	A	Patients with either 14 and 6/sec positive spikes, 6/sec spike and wave, or psychomotor variant contrasted with age-, sex-, and education-matched normal-EEG controls on numerous variables. Suicide not main emphasis of study.	Negative findings: Ratings of suicide behavior unrelated to all three abnormal EEG categories.

Study	Type	Design	Findings
Small (1970)	A	45 patients with Small Sharp Spikes contrasted with age, sex, and education-matched normal EEG patient controls on numerous variables. Suicide not main emphasis of study.	Psychotic affective reactions related to Small Sharp Spikes ($p < .01$). History of suicide attempts three times more frequent in Small Sharp Spike EEG group.
Small (1971)	A	60 patients with photoconvulsive EEG responses contrasted with age, sex, and education-matched normal-EEG patient controls on numerous variables. Suicide not main emphasis of study.	Incidence of suicide attempts significantly related ($p < .01$) to photoconvulsive EEG response.
Struve, Klein, & Saraf (1972)	C	Chart review of 219 patients resulted in assignment to following groups: (1) suicide ideation only, (2) suicide attempts, (3) mixed suicide–assaultive, (4) controls.	Paroxysmal EEGs related to suicide ideation alone ($p < .02$), suicide attempts ($p < .009$), and mixed suicide–assaultive symptoms ($p = .05$).
R. K. Davies, Neil, & Himmelhock (1975)	A	50 patients with normal EEGs, 33 patients with paroxysmal EEG abnormality, and 31 patients with nonparoxysmal EEG abnormality. Numerous between-group comparisons. Suicide not main emphasis of study.	A 2×3 contingency with "impulsively suicidal behavior" contrasted across three EEG groups approached significance ($p < .10$). Reanalysis by present author collapsed normal and nonparoxysmal EEG groups together and found item "impulsively suicidal" related ($p = .03$) to paroxysmal EEGs.
Struve, Saraf, Arko, Klein, & Becka (1977)	C	698 patients rated on 11 suicide variables and three temper dyscontrol variables. Analyses involved 115 patients with suicide ideation only, 187 patients with suicide attempts, 189 mixed suicide–assaultive patients, and 168 controls.	For both males and females, paroxysmal EEG related to suicide ideation alone, suicide attempts, and mixed suicide–assaultive symptoms at high levels of statistical significance. EEG – suicide relationships did not hold for adolescents. The 14 and 6/sec positive-spike pattern unrelated to suicide.

Note. Description of study types:

A: Measures of suicide were found within a large array of variables in a larger study. The study was *not* explicitly designed to focus on EEG–suicide relationships.

B: Study did focus on suicide; however, EEG was only one of a large number of variables examined. Study was not explicitly designed to focus on EEG–suicide relationships.

C: Study was explicitly designed to focus on EEG–suicide relationships.

(Table continues on p. 64.)

TABLE 3-2. (*Continued*)

Reference	Type	Description	Basic findings
Gibbs & Novick (1977)	A	Report of EEG findings in a sample of 1,000 consecutive psychiatric inpatients aged 20 and above. Suicide not main emphasis of study.	Of 27 patients judged to be "suicidal," 66.7% had abnormal EEGs.
Volow, Zung, & Green (1979)	C	216 patients aged 18 to 84 given the Zung Index of Potential Suicide and EEG testing.	Mixed findings: Abnormal EEG related ($p < .001$) to suicide threat behavior. Abnormal EEG not significantly related to suicide attempts. Paroxysmal EEG abnormality not significantly related to suicide measures.
Struve (1983)	C	Subanalysis of 281 patients with suicide symptoms drawn from 1977 study. Patients dichotomized into paroxysmal EEG versus nonparoxysmal EEG. Also, EEGs of 26 completed suicides contrasted with various matched control groups.	Paroxysmal EEG patients had suicide ideation more reactive to stress, more intense, and more frequent. Suicide attempters with normal EEGs had significantly more medical attempt hazard and thorough plan formulation. Attempters with paroxysmal EEG more reactive to stress. No relationship between EEG and completed suicide.
Struve (1985)	C	Pilot study of the potential interaction between oral contraceptive use and paroxysmal EEGs in increasing suicide attempt prevalence. 160 female patients studied.	For women with paroxysmal EEGs, oral contraceptive use was significantly related to suicide attempts. For women with normal EEGs, pill use had no effect on suicide attempt rate.

well as clinical depression, and neither of these items was found to be related to EEG abnormality. This and other negative survey studies already mentioned are consistent with the negative EEG–suicide findings of Flood and Seager (1968), who used a different investigative approach. They started by collecting, retrospectively, a large sample of 73 completed suicides, and examined their hospital charts in comparison with charts from two carefully selected nonsuicidal contol groups matched for age, sex, admission time, hospital location, and diagnosis. About half of the suicide and control groups had had EEG studies completed during their hospitalizations, and the reports were contained in the charts. Flood and Seager found that reports of EEG abnormality were similar in incidence across the suicide group and both control groups, suggesting a lack of salient EEG–suicide relationships. It must be stressed that Flood and Seager studied completed suicides only. They did not examine sublethal suicide behavior, such as ideation, threats, and unsuccessful attempts (both serious and gestures), and data germane to EEG associations with these later behaviors were not presented.

In addition to the Greenberg and Pollack study already mentioned, other general survey studies listed in Table 3-2 have been more encouraging regarding the possibility that cerebral dysrhythmias may play some role in either the genesis or modulation of self-destructive thought and action. Gibbs and Novick (1977) conducted a large-scale EEG examination series of 1,000 consecutively admitted psychiatric patients. In addition to routine use of sleep EEG activation, they employed exclusive monopolar recording, which, as stated by Lutz (1982), is a technique that will maximize the detection of various paroxysmal dysrhythmias that are quite capable of being "canceled out" or made invisible with certain bipolar recording montages. Of the 1,000 patients, 27 were judged to be suicidal by treating staff, and 66.7% of these suicidal patients had abnormal EEGs. Although this was a high prevalence of EEG abnormality, the suicidal patients did not have overt convulsive seizures. Qualitative aspects of suicidal behavior characteristic of these patients with EEG abnormality were not noted. It would seem that many more patients in the sample of 1,000 should have had some degree of present or past suicide ideation or behavior; however, a detailed assessment of suicide symptoms throughout the population apparently was not done.

R. K. Davies *et al.* (1975) conducted an interesting study that classified EEGs in a manner similar to our own later studies. These authors studied 64 patients with abnormal EEGs, of which about half were "paroxysmal abnormalities" (i.e., they occurred suddenly and episodically during a tracing) and about half were "nonparoxysmal" EEG patterns. All were contrasted with 50 normal EEG patients on many measures.

Their published analysis indicated only a statistical trend ($p < .10$) linking ratings of "impulsively suicidal behavior" to EEG abnormality. However, their EEG classification allowed reanalysis of their published data in a way that matched our own methods of EEG analyses (Struve *et al.*, 1972, 1977). We reanalyzed their findings by contrasting their paroxysmal EEG patients against normal and nonparoxysmal EEGs lumped together; when this was done, we found that "impulsively suicidal behavior" was significantly related to presence of paroxysmal EEG dysrhythmia ($p = .03$).

Although Small and her associates provided many of the negative EEG–suicide findings listed in Table 3-2, they were also among the first investigators to report positive associations of interest. In one study (Small, 1970), the Small Sharp Spike EEG pattern (so named because of its low amplitude—hence "small"—sharp biphasic wave form) was found to have a significant association ($p < .01$) with depressive affective reactions, and chart review analyses indicated that suicide attempts were three times more frequent among patients with the Small Sharp Spike EEG dysrhythmia than among controls. In a classic paper published later (Small, Small, Millstein, & Moore, 1975) they presented evidence that the Small Sharp Spike EEG signal could be a marker for manic–depressive disease, thus suggesting that this particular EEG dysrhythmia might have special importance for affective dys-regulation and hence for suicide potential. For over 10 years we have also been impressed with the apparently strong association between Small Sharp Spikes and depression, although we have never systematically catalogued and published these observations. Almost all patients with Small Sharp Spikes seen in our previous laboratory had referral consults indicating either (1) depressive diagnosis, (2) treatment with antidepressant medication, or (3) recent electroconvulsive therapy (ECT) for psychotic depression. Furthermore, it is interesting that of 16 Small Sharp Spike patients in our suicide–EEG study sample (Struve *et al.*, 1977), *all* displayed strong suicide ideation. In a different study, Small (1971) reported that patients with positive photoconvulsive EEG responses (dysrhythmic EEG responses to intense stroboscopic flash at various frequencies) had sig-nificantly more suicide attempts than those unresponsive to photic flash. The use of photic stimulation is not an uncommon activation procedure in many EEG laboratories, and this observation could easily receive follow-up study.

Specific EEG–Suicide Studies

Prior to 1972, we had noted that the admission EEGs of a very small number of psychiatric patients who had successfully completed suicide were abnormal. This serendipitous observation prompted our curiosity about potential EEG–suicide relationships and led to efforts to formalize specific studies of EEG correlates of self-destructive behavior.

In our first study (Struve *et al.*, 1972), we employed retrospective clinical chart reviews rather than direct patient interviews. The clinical records of 219 consecutively admitted psychiatric patients aged 15 to 25 were reviewed by two specially trained research psychologists who had no knowledge of EEG findings and who also had no knowledge that they were even participating in a study of EEG–suicide relationships. Under an experimental "guise" of rating "criminal and precriminal tendencies," the research psychologists rated the clinical charts on a wide variety of "criminal" items, among which we had buried our critical study items of presence of (1) suicide ideation, (2) suicide attempts, (3) assaultive and/or destructive ideation, (4) assaultive and/or destructive acts, and (5) temper dyscontrol. Assessments of assaultive/destructive behavior and temper dyscontrol were made for very specific reasons. Since it has long been recognized that associations between cerebral dysrhythmia and outward-directed aggression or violence may exist (Andrulonis, Donnelly, Glueck, *et al.*, 1980; Bach-y-Rita, Lion, *et al.*, 1971; R. K. Davies *et al.*, 1975; Elliott, 1981; Maletzky, 1973; Mark & Ervin, 1970; Monroe, 1970; Struve and Struve, 1985), attempts at demonstrating pure suicide–EEG relationships must first involve exclusion of outwardly aggressive patients. If this is not done, then to the extent that inward- and outward-directed aggression are correlated, any EEG–suicide associations that are found could be partially or totally accounted for by expected correlations between EEG and temper dyscontrol. Of the 219 patients reviewed in this study, 91 were omitted because of mixed symptom pictures (i.e., assaultive and suicidal behavior combined), incomplete study data, or incomplete or absent EEG results. During this time period every admitted patient was given a routine screening EEG. The final sample contained 44 control patients free of any rated suicidal or assaultive symptoms, 32 patients with pure suicide ideation only, 21 patients who had made suicide attempts, and 31 patients with assaultive/destructive behavior but no present or past suicide symptoms.

In Table 3-3, the results of this early study (Struve *et al.*, 1972) are summarized. The differences between symptom and control groups were analyzed for males and females separately. As can be seen, both males and females with suicide ideation had more than twice the incidence of paroxysmal EEG dysrhythmias as did corresponding control patients who were free of rated suicide and assaultive behavior. Furthermore, the elevation of paroxysmal EEG incidence among those expressing suicide ideation alone (i.e., without attempts) as contrasted with controls was statistically significant. As mentioned above in the discussion of

TABLE 3-3.   Paroxysmal EEGs in Male and Female Symptom and Control Groups

Study groups	n	% with paroxysmal EEGs	Comparison with controls (Fisher's exact test)
Males			
Control group	24	29.2	—
Suicide ideation only	16	68.8	$p = .016$
Suicide ideation and attempts	6	100.0	$p = .003$
Assaultive–destructive (no suicide)	18	66.7	$p = .017$
Females			
Control group	20	15.0	—
Suicide ideation only	16	37.5	$p = .004$
Suicide ideation and attempts	15	60.0	$p = .008$
Assaultive–destructive (no suicide)	13	53.8	$p = .024$

Note. Adapted from Struve, Klein, & Saraf (1972). Reprinted by permission.

seizure disorders, Weil (1954) was the first to document occurrence of suicidal "thinking" related to EEG recordings of spike discharges in temporal lobe epileptics. Our data extend such observations and suggest that cerebral dysrhythmia in psychiatric patients free of convulsive symptoms may influence the occurrence of "suicidal thinking," even in the absence of overt suicide attempt behavior. The data in Table 3-3 also indicate statistically significant positive associations between paroxysmal EEG dysrhythmia and suicide attempt behavior, with the reported incidence of paroxysmal EEGs being from three (males) to four (females) times higher among attempters than nonsuicidal controls. The significant association between EEG findings and assaultive/destructive behavior would be expected from the prevailing literature, and it underscores the importance of controlling for outward-directed aggressive behavior in seeking organic correlates to suicide symptomatology.

Studies that rely on retrospective chart reviews involve a potential bias from underreporting of symptomatology. That is, the clinical records reviewed may mention suicide behavior, if it is a salient issue of clinical concern, but may fail to document "ideation" that is considered transient or no longer active. Treating clinical staff members may display considerable variation in what they select for documentation in the formal record and in how they describe or stress the symptomatology included. We cannot know if and to what extent underreporting bias occurred, and therefore cannot know whether or not it would have altered the study findings as reported.

Our next investigation (Struve *et al.*, 1977) attempted to address several shortcomings of our earlier 1972 study. This was a large-scale investigation and involved initial screening of 1,199 consecutively admitted psychiatric inpatients between the ages of 14 and 49. Most importantly, after a complete clinical chart review, each subject was individually interviewed by a research psychiatrist and a research psychologist using a scale especially designed to rate seven different aspects of both current and/or past suicide ideation, three aspects of current and/or past suicide attempt behavior, and three aspects of assaultiveness or temper dyscontrol. (The specific variables assessed are discussed later.) The interviewers also judged the adequacy of the interview data, and cases in which the interview content was deemed unreliable (i.e., due to subject uncooperativeness, subject confusion, florid psychoses, etc.) were omitted from further analyses. All interview assessments were secured without knowledge of the EEG results, and adequate interrater reliabilities for all rated aspects of suicide or assaultive behavior were presented. Similarly, all EEGs were secured and interpreted without knowledge of the patient's diagnosis or suicide behavior rating results. A sample of 511 EEGs was interpreted independently by a second electroencephalographer, with high inter-interpreter agreement (93%) and significant levels of interpretive reliability ($p < .001$) reported. As in all of our studies, EEGs were dichotomized into those with paroxysmal abnormalities versus all normal EEGs, and tracings with nonparoxysmal findings (i.e., slowing) combined. Without access to EEG information, subjects with complete data ($n = 696$) were classified into the following study groups:

1. Control group ($n = 168$): No significant ratings of suicide, assaultive, or temper symptoms.
2. Suicide ideation only ($n = 115$): *Current* suicide ideation of minimal to marked degree. Subjects had never made a suicide attempt or gesture. No evidence of assaultive or temper dyscontrol behavior.
3. Suicide attempts ($n = 187$): Subjects had made one or more suicide attempts or gestures. They had no significant assaultive or temper dyscontrol symptoms.
4. Mixed suicide–assaultive ($n = 189$): Subjects displayed suicide ideation and/or attempts, and also displayed significant assaultive or temper dyscontrol behavior.
5. Pure assaultive–destructive ($n = 37$): Absence of any suicidal behavior. This group was not studied further.

As a result of this investigation, a large number of data analyses were performed for various purposes; they cannot all be described in detail here, but they are contained in the original report (Struve *et al.*,

1977). The basic findings from the initial overall data analyses are shown in Table 3-4, where it can be seen that patients with either (1) suicide ideation alone, (2) suicide ideation as well as attempts, or (3) mixed suicide–assaultive behavior had significantly elevated rates of paroxysmal EEG abnormality, as contrasted with controls free of both suicide and assaultive symtomatology. As before, there was a statistically significant positive association between EEG dysrhythmia and suicide ideation existing without the presence of overt attempt behavior.

Additional age-stratified analyses performed at that time (Struve *et al.*, 1977) indicated that although EEG–suicide associations were in the predicted direction for adolescents, the magnitude of the relationships did not reach statistical significance. Primarily, this was because the overall prevalence of paroxysmal EEG dysrhythmia was higher among adolescents than among adults, with the consequence that the incidence of EEG dysrhythmia in the adolescent control group was sufficiently high to wash out differences between the symptom group and controls. Significant associations were, however, maintained for adults. Furthermore, it was found that one EEG pattern, the 14 and 6/sec positive-spike signal, was evenly distributed across control and symptom groups stratified by age as well as divided by sex, and as such was unrelated to suicide behavior. Table 3-5 shows the results of a corrected analysis that took these two findings into account. As can be seen, there was a sharp drop in paroxysmal EEG incidence rates for all study groups when (1) the analysis was confined to subjects age 19 or older and (2) the 14 and 6/sec positive-spike pattern was classified as normal. Nonetheless, the analyses continued to show statistically significant positive associations between EEG dysrhythmia and suicide ideation alone, suicide attempts, and mixtures of suicide and assaultive symptoms, and this was true for both males and females considered separately. Numerical analyses (not shown here) in which, for each item of the suicide interview scale, rating scale distributions for paroxysmal EEG (excluding 14 and 6/sec positive spikes) and nonparoxysmal EEG subjects

TABLE 3-4. Incidence of Paroxysmal EEGs in Control and Symptom Groups: All Subjects

Study groups	n	% with paroxysmal EEGs	Comparison with controls
Control group	168	25.6	—
Suicide ideation	115	40.0	$\chi^2 = 6.571, df = 1, p = .005$
Suicide attempts	187	44.4	$\chi^2 = 13.646, df = 1, p < .0005$
Mixed suicide–assaultive	189	44.4	$\chi^2 = 13.788, df = 1, p < .0005$

Note. Adapted from Struve, Saraf, Arko, Klein, & Becka (1977). Reprinted by permission.

TABLE 3-5.   Paroxysmal EEGs (Omitting 14 and 6/sec Positive Spikes) in Adult Male and Female Symptom and Control Groups

Study groups	n	% with paroxysmal EEGs	Comparison with controls
Males age 19 and above			
Control group	69	4.3	—
Suicide ideation only	43	14.0	$\chi^2 = 3.308, df = 1, p = .034$
Suicide ideation and attempts	46	17.4	$\chi^2 = 5.428, df = 1, p = .01$
Mixed suicide– assaultive	78	10.3	$\chi^2 = 1.846, df = 1, p = .09$
Females age 19 and above			
Control group	61	9.8	—
Suicide ideation only	42	30.9	$\chi^2 = 7.373, df = 1, p = .004$
Suicide ideation and attempts	99	23.2	$\chi^2 = 4.564, df = 1, p = .02$
Mixed suicide– assaultive	49	24.5	$\chi^2 = 4.263, df = 1, p = .02$

Note. Adapted from Struve *et al.* (1977). Reprinted by permission.

were contrasted (*t* tests) revealed numerous significant differences, with paroxysmal EEG subjects having higher or "more severe" mean item ratings. Such findings were viewed (Struve *et al.*, 1977) as confirming the contingency results presented by use of a different methodological analysis.

The finding that the 14 and 6/sec positive-spike EEG pattern was unrelated to our suicide measures needs additional comment, since this EEG signal contributed heavily to the EEG findings reported in our earlier study (Struve *et al.*, 1972). It is possible that, had this EEG pattern been omitted in our earlier study, significant EEG–suicide associations might not have emerged. When our earlier sample data (Struve *et al.*, 1972) were reanalyzed after omitting the 14 and 6/sec signal, the positive association between paroxysmal EEG dysrhythmia and suicide behavioral remained ($\chi^2 = 6.296, df = 1, p < .007$).

In 1979, Volow, Zung, and Green (1979) attempted, for the most part unsuccessfully, to replicate our findings. Their attempt was sophisticated, in that it focused explicitly on EEG–suicide relationships, used an EEG interpretive method blind to suicide ratings or diagnosis, and employed a formalized assessment of suicide potential. Their study differed substantially from our investigations (Struve *et al.*, 1972, 1977) in a number of ways that are reviewed below. In the Volow *et al.* study, 216 consecutive patients admitted to an inpatient psychiatry service were given the self-rating form of the Index of Potential Suicide (IPS) (Zung, 1974) as well as clinical EEG studies. In Table 3-6, some of the salient data findings from their publication (Volow *et al.*, 1979) have been abstracted. Essentially, they were unable to demonstrate significant relationships between EEG abnormality and suicide behavior as contrasted with the behavior of nonsuicidal comparison patients. This was true when they examined all EEG abnormalities combined, as well as when they focused on paroxysmal EEG dysrhythmias separately, as we had done. Their findings did not support an association between EEG findings and suicide attempts, nor did they produce any significant relationships between EEG patterns and outward-directed aggressive behavior. As indicated in Table 3-6, they did report a significant positive relationship between total EEG abnormality and suicide threat behavior, and they stressed that this relationship was retained even after EEG–age relationships were partialed out. This may be similar to our positive associations between EEG and suicide ideation (without attempts). Whether this relationship between suicide threateners and EEG abnormality would hold for paroxysmal EEG dysrhythmias treated separately (as in our studies) is not clear.

There are a number of methodological differences between the study of Volow *et al.* and our own investigations. Age differences between the studies were substantial. While patients in the Volow study had a median age of 45 and an upper age limit of 84, our own studies involved young patients with a *maximum* age of 25 in our 1972 sample and an upper age limit of 49 in our 1977 study. Over half of our psychiatric sample was female, whereas the Volow population was 99% male in composition. Furthermore, in our studies EEGs had to contain long monopolar drowsiness and sleep recordings to be acceptable. Volow and associates failed to obtain sleep tracings in 18% of their sample,

TABLE 3-6. Selected EEG–Suicide Findings from Volow, Zung, and Green (1979)

	A Nonsuicidal patients ($n = 122$)	B Suicidal patients ($n = 94$)	C Suicide threatener subgroup ($n = 35$)
All abnormal EEGs	8 (6.6%)	14 (14.9%)	11 (31.4%)
Paroxysmal EEGs only	3 (2.5%)	5 (5.3%)	Not given

Note. Volow *et al.*'s findings were abstracted by me. I calculated between-groups differences as follows: A × B, no significant difference; A × C, $\chi^2 = 15.816$, $df = 1$, $p < .005$.

and they also noted that "in view of the nonadolescent age composition, no special attempt was made to extend sleep or use special runs" (1979). Sleep is critically important in the activation of a wide variety of paroxysmal EEG findings (Struve, 1985a); furthermore, several of the paroxysmal EEG dysrhythmias that we reported would be less commonly seen in patients of advanced age. Of interest is the fact that both studies reported very different overall prevalence rates for paroxysmal EEG findings—3.7% in the study by Volow *et al.*, versus between 37.8% and 50.1% in our study populations. Clearly, the EEG profiles of the studies were vastly different. In addition, 20.8% of the patients in the Volow *et al.* sample were diagnosed as having organic disorders or as alcoholic, whereas among our inpatient psychiatric population such diagnoses were very rare.

Perhaps underlying EEG–suicide relationships are of insufficient strength to transcend such wide methodological differences, whereas stronger, more robust phenomena would be visible over more diverse conditions. This is an empirical issue for which there is no present answer. It is certain that there is little direct methodological comparability between the study done by Volow *et al.* and the ones conducted by ourselves. It is equally clear that EEG–suicide associations are not of sufficiently overriding salience to be discernible under all conditions.

For some time we have been investigating the general hypothesis that patients with EEG dysrhythmia will have an elevated vulnerability for medication side effects, as contrasted with normal EEG patients exposed to the same pharmacological agents. Such studies are not relevant to suicide and are not reviewed in this space. However, as part of that concern, we noted (Struve, Saraf, Arko, Klein, & Becka, 1976) that female patients with paroxysmal EEG dysrhythmias had a substantially elevated incidence of both somatic and psychiatric side effects from oral contraceptives, as compared with women with normal EEGs who were also taking the "pill." Since these same women had participated in both our study of EEGs and oral contraceptives (Struve *et al.*, 1976) and our second EEG–suicide study (Struve *et al.*, 1977), we were able to analyze the joint study data to determine whether oral contraceptives and dysrhythmic EEGs operated interactively to increase suicide risk. A pilot study addressing this issue has recently been published (Struve, 1985b), and the primary findings are reproduced in Table 3-7. Among females with normal EEGs, the presence or absence of oral contraceptive use had no discernible effect on the incidence of suicide attempts. However, with the addition of paroxysmal EEGs alone, the suicide attempt rate can be seen to have increased by 9%, and the combination of paroxysmal EEG patterns with oral contraceptive use yielded an additional 28% increase in suicide attempt rates, resulting

TABLE 3-7.   Suicide Attempt Incidence in Female Psychiatric Patients as a Function
of EEG Category and Oral Contraceptive Use

	All ages				Age 19 and above			
	Paroxysmal EEG		Normal EEG		Paroxysmal EEG		Normal EEG	
	Pill	No pill	Pill	No pill	Pill	No pill	Pill	No pill
Suicide attempt	15	15	27	35	14	4	24	19
No attempt	2	10	26	30	2	5	22	20

Note. Adapted from Struve (1985b); used by permission. Significance of relationship between pill use and suicide attempt rate (Fisher's exact test): all ages, paroxysmal EEG, $p = .048$; all ages, normal EEG, n.s.; age 19 and above, paroxysmal EEG, $p = .034$; age 19 and above, normal EEG, n.s.

in a high 88% attempt incidence. Among females with normal EEGs, there was no statistically significant relationship between "pill" use and suicide attempt rate. However, among those female patients with paroxysmal EEGs, "pill" use was significantly associated with increased suicide attempt rate for all women studied ($p = .048$), as well as for those age 19 or older considered separately ($p = .034$). Broad generalizations from this pilot study would be hazardous. However, the reduced neurophysiological control of some patients with cerebral dysrhythmia may allow low-intensity and/or low-frequency psychiatric side effects of the "pill" (e.g., depression) to become more manifest. Possibly a hypothesized "pill"-related dysphoria is less well tolerated or is experienced subjectively as more severe in patients with altered cerebral function, thus making suicide attempts more likely. These relationships—especially as manifested in those females with psychiatric disability—deserve additional careful scrutiny.

Qualitative Considerations and Completed Suicides

The studies reviewed and presented so far have only addressed the issue of the relationship of EEG findings to the *presence* or *absence* of suicide behavior per se. With the exception of R. K. Davies *et al.* (1975), who suggested that paroxysmal EEG patients may be "impulsively" suicidal, the qualitative characteristics of suicidal behavior as a function of EEG dysrhythmia have received insufficient study. In order to determine whether or not qualitative differences in suicide expression exist between suicidal populations with and without cerebral dysrhythmias, one must focus narrowly on only those subjects who display suicide symptoms. Suicidally asymptomatic control patients are not germane to this issue and can be omitted.

The suicide interview rating scale used in our second study (Struve *et al.*, 1977) was designed to assess qualitative aspects of suicide behavior as well as simple presence or absence of the phenomena. All subjects were rated on the following variables, using an 8-point scale for each item: present illness *and* past history of (1) frequency of suicide ideation, (2) intensity of suicide ideation, (3) duration of ideation, (4) degree of "reactivity" of ideation to psychosocial variables, (5) ability to control (dismiss) suicide thoughts, (6) subjects' concern over suicide ideation, and (7) degree of formulation (i.e., specificity) of suicide plans. If actual suicide attempts had been made, similar ratings were made for current illness *and* past history of (1) number of suicide attempts, (2) seriousness (i.e., medical hazard) of suicide attempts, and (3) degree of "reactivity" of attempts to psychosocial variables. Additional ratings for assaultive/destructive behavior and temper dyscontrol were also made, but they are not relevant to our present concern. In a recent study (Struve, 1983), we reanalyzed the suicide interview rating scale data for a sample of 281 patients (all ages) with suicide symptomatology. These suicidal patients were dichotomized into those with paroxysmal EEG patterns ($n = 70$) and those with normal or nonparoxysmal EEGs ($n = 211$). For each of the suicide symptom items, rating scores (8-point scale) of the paroxysmal versus nonparoxysmal EEG patients were contrasted using a one-way analysis of variance. This analytical procedure was performed twice. The first analysis involved all 281 suicidal patients; the second analysis was confined to those suicidal patients ($n = 172$) who had actually made one or more suicide attempts.

The results of these statistical procedures (Struve, 1983) are summarized in Table 3-8. In essence, paroxysmal EEG suicidal patients tended to display suicide ideation that was more "reactive" to specific identified psychosocial precipitants (i.e., loss of job, romance rejection, school failure, etc.) than that of normal-EEG suicidal patients, who instead had ideation emerging from a chronic long-term matrix of failure, disappointment, or depressive affect devoid of a clearly delineated precipitant. Those with paroxysmal EEGs also tended to have ideation that was more frequent and more intense than the suicide ideation reported by patients with normal EEGs. Among suicide attempters, those with paroxysmal EEGs again tended to experience suicide ideation that was more frequent, more intense, and more highly reactive to precipitating events, as contrasted with normal-EEG patients.

Conversely, there was a trend ($p = .08$) for patients with normal or nonparoxysmal EEGs to have a more highly developed and well-thought-out suicide plan than paroxysmal EEG patients. When only the data from suicide attempters were examined, the relationship between non-paroxysmal EEG and degree of suicide plan formulation was significant

TABLE 3-8. Qualitative Aspects of Suicide: Paroxysmal EEG versus Nonparoxysmal EEG

Group and scale item	Direction	F	df	p
Patients with suicide ideation (paroxysmal, $n = 70$; nonparoxysmal, $n = 211$)				
1. Degree of plan formulation (present illness)	Nonparoxysmal > paroxysmal	3.14	1, 276	.08
2. Reactivity of ideation (present illness)	Paroxysmal > nonparoxysmal	6.35	1, 278	.01
3. Frequency of ideation (past history)	Paroxysmal > nonparoxysmal	3.77	1, 277	.05
4. Intensity of ideation (past history)	Paroxysmal > nonparoxysmal	4.62	1, 279	.03
Patients with suicide attempts (paroxysmal, $n = 42$; nonparoxysmal, $n = 130$)				
1. Degree of plan formulation (present illness)	Nonparoxysmal > paroxysmal	4.25	1, 167	.04
2. Medical seriousness of attempt (present illness)	Nonparoxysmal > paroxysmal	3.45	1, 170	.06
3. Past history of ideation	Nonparoxysmal > paroxysmal	4.22	1, 170	.04
4. Frequency of ideation (past history)	Paroxysmal > nonparoxysmal	5.38	1, 169	.02
5. Intensity of ideation (past history)	Paroxysmal > nonparoxysmal	7.00	1, 170	.009
6. Reactivity of ideation (past history)	Paroxysmal > nonparoxysmal	3.59	1, 170	.06

Note. Adapted from Struve (1983). Reprinted by permission.

(p = .04). Congruent with this finding was the additional observation that nonparoxysmal and normal EEG patients tended to make suicide attempts that were of greater medical seriousness than the attempts made by paroxysmal EEG patients. In addition, nonparoxysmal EEG suicidal patients displayed suicide ideation that was less identified with obvious precipitants, less frequent, and less intense than that reported by patients with paroxysmal cerebral dysrhythmia.

Over a number of years, we were able to collect a series of patients who (1) had successfully completed suicide and (2) had pre-existing EEGs secured at our laboratory. These were not patients who had been enrolled in our formal EEG–suicide studies. From a total sample of 32 completed suicides, 26 were found to have had adequate EEG studies containing recordings made during waking, drowsiness, and sleep. All EEGs had been secured and interpreted without knowledge of the patients' suicide potential. These 26 patients were contrasted with three retrospectively selected control groups in terms of incidence of EEG abnormality. A first control group (n = 131) was selected from the carefully screened nonsuicidal control group used in our large-scale EEG–suicide study (Struve et al., 1977), and from this population patients were selected to match the same age and sex distribution of the suicide cases. A second control group (n = 245) was obtained from our general EEG laboratory files using the following method: Upon entering the laboratory files with an index case, we proceeded alphabetically through the files selecting the next 10 cases meeting the criteria of same sex, age of index case ± 1 year, date of index case EEG ± 1 year, and adequate EEG test. In forming the third control group, the clinical hospital records of all 245 patients in the second group just described were inspected carefully, and all patients who had made one or more suicide attempts in their entire psychiatric history were omitted. This third control group contained 137 patients. The EEG was abnormal in 34.6% of the 26 patients who had succeeded in taking their lives. However, contingency analyses (Struve, 1983) indicated that this was not significantly different from the abnormal EEG incidence in either the first control group (33.6%), the second control group (40.0%), or the third control group (42.3%). Examination of "paroxysmal" EEG abnormality across completed-suicide and control groups also failed to produce significant differences.

Episodic Behavior Disorders and Episodic Acts of Dyscontrol

A relationship between EEG abnormality and suicide behavior does appear to exist; however, the nature of this association is complex, and its theoretical significance remains unclear. Although Volow *et al.* (1979) were unable to concur, the available data suggest that only those kinds of EEG abnormalities that are "paroxysmal" are potentially related to suicidal behaviors (R. K. Davies *et al.*, 1975; Small, 1970, 1971; Struve *et al.*, 1972, 1977; Weil, 1954). Nonparoxysmal EEG abnormalities (e.g., focal slowing, generalized slowing, amplitude asymmetries, and the like) may not relate strongly to suicide, although this issue deserves additional study. In a broad sense, paroxysmal EEG dysrhythmia has been related to both suicide ideation occurring alone (Struve *et al.*, 1972, 1977; Weil, 1954), as well as to actual suicide attempt behavior (Small, 1970, 1971; Struve *et al.*, 1972, 1977). At this juncture, it is imperative to point out that although the incidence of paroxysmal EEG findings is significantly elevated among suicidal as contrasted with nonsuicidal patients, the *absolute incidence* of paroxysmal dysrhythmia is not high, and the majority of suicidal patients display normal EEGs (see Tables 3-4 and 3-5). However, when one focuses only on those psychiatric patients with paroxysmal EEGs, 87.9% of such patients display at least some type of suicidal symptomatology (Struve *et al.*, 1977). Thus, the presence of suicidal behavior does not permit the inference that a paroxysmal EEG will be found. However, the existence of a paroxysmal EEG creates a strong presumption that at least some suicidal symptoms will occur as part of the clinical picture. This suggests that adult psychiatric patients with paroxysmal EEG findings may be at high risk for suicidal behavior, but that such patients comprise a relatively small proportion of all suicidal psychiatric patients.

There are qualitative differences in expressivity of suicidal behavior between patients with and those without paroxysmal EEG dysrhythmia. Our reanalysis of the data presented by R. K. Davies *et al.* (1975) suggests that paroxysmal EEGs are associated with suicidal behavior that is "impulsive." Their data are thus consistent with our findings (Struve, 1983) that suicidal behavior associated with paroxysmal EEGs is sudden, impulsive, and highly reactive to immediate precipitating events, and that it involves suicide plans that are poorly defined and not well formulated. Conversely, patients without paroxysmal EEG findings tend to engage in ideation that develops insidiously and which is not reactive to immediate events. Furthermore, their suicide ideation involves plans that are less fragmented and more carefully worked out, and when actual attempts occur they are of greater medical hazard than the typical attempts made by paroxysmal EEG patients. This suggests the possibility that different variables may operate in the genesis of suicidal behavior between these EEG groupings.

Monroe has developed the concept of "episodic behavioral disorders" (Monroe, 1959, 1970, 1979, 1982a, 1982b; Monroe & Mickle, 1967) to reflect the influence of presumed limbic system electrical dysregulation or other cerebral dysrhythmia on altered behavior. The pathological behavior is episodic, and behavioral disruption is usually sudden in onset, with durations of behavioral disturbance lasting from hours to days and even several weeks. During periods of episodic dyscontrol behavior, emotional instability, sudden alterations in mood, and impulsive acting out (which may involve both outward aggression and suicide symptoms) are commonly encountered. Others have also suggested that episodic behavioral dyscontrol involving sudden aggressive behaviors may be related to cerebral dysrhythmia (Andrulonis et al., 1980; Bach-y-Rita et al., 1971; Neil et al., 1978; R. K. Davies et al., 1975; Elliott, 1981, 1982; Jonas, 1965; Maletzky, 1973; Mark & Ervin, 1970). The poorly planned and highly reactive suicidal behavior of paroxysmal EEG patients may fit within this overall concept of behavioral dyscontrol, and thus may represent yet another manifestation of the short-sighted and impulsive actions characterizing such patients. As such, cerebral dysrhythmia may impair emotional and behavioral control during periods of high situational stress, thus making suicidal symptoms as well as other ineffective reactions more likely. Cerebral dysrhythmia may operate as an ill-defined neurophysiological handicap that interacts with psychiatric disability, making optimal control during stress less likely. Conversely, suicidal behavior in patients without paroxysmal EEGs may be more heavily influenced by other variables, such as psychodynamic considerations or the pathophysiology and clinical course of major depressive disease.

Epilogue

This chapter has shown that EEGs can be used to help screen for the presence of covert disease that may produce psychiatric depressive symptomatology, as well as to denote cerebral dysrhythmias that may directly influence suicidal behavior. It must be stressed that although significant EEG–suicide associations may exist, the strength of the statistical relationships found cannot permit individual case prediction to be attempted. At this time, the clinical EEG cannot effectively predict suicide attempt risk, nor can it reasonably guide treatment intervention. We may hope that continuing EEG study of self-destructive behavior ultimately will allow a more complete understanding of how disordered cerebral electrophysiological events may influence the type and quality of suicide behavior observed. As increased understanding of the biological aspects of suicide emerges from various disciplines, we may hope that increased effectiveness of clinical intervention and prevention will be seen.

References

Abraham, A., & Ajmone-Marsan, C. Patterns of cortical discharges and their relation to routine scalp electroencephalography. *Electroencephalography and Clinical Neurophysiology*, 1958, *10*, 447–461.

Andrulonis, P. A., Donnelly, J., Glueck, B. C., Stroebel, C. F., & Szarek, B. L. Preliminary data on ethosuximide and the episodic dyscontrol syndrome. *American Journal of Psychiatry*, 1980, *147*, 1455–1456.

Bach-y-Rita, G., Lion, Jr., Climent, C. E., & Ervin, F. R. A study of 130 violent patients. *American Journal of Psychiatry*, 1971, *127*, 1473–1478.

Barande, R. Contribution à Petude de l'état dangereux chez les épileptiques. *International Society of Criminology Bulletin* (Paris), 1958, *00*, 38–75.

Barnes, R. F., *et al.* Medical illness in chronic psychiatric outpatients. *General Hospital Psychiatry*, 1983, *5*, 191–195.

Berger, H. Uber das Elektrenkephalogramm des Menschen: I Mitteilung. *Archivs für Psychiatrie*, 1929, *87*, 527–570.

Burke, A. W. Physical illness in psychiatric patients in Jamaica. *British Journal of Psychiatry*, 1972, *121*, 321–322.

Burke, A. W. Physical disorder among day hospital patients. *British Journal of Psychiatry*, 1978, *133*, 22–27.

Cohn, R. *Clinical electroencephalography*. New York: McGraw-Hill, 1949.

Cooper, R., Winter, A. L., Crow, J. H., & Walter, W. G. Comparison of subcortical, cortical, and scalp activity using chronically indwelling electrodes in man. *Electroencephalography and Clinical Neurophysiology*, 1965, *18*, 217–228.

Craib, A. R., & Perry, M. *The EEG handbook* (2nd ed.).: Beckman Instruments, 1975.

Davies, D. W. Physical illness in psychiatric outpatients. *British Journal of Psychiatry*, 1965, *111*, 27–33.

Davies, R. K., Neil, J. F., & Himmelhock, J. M. Cerebral dysrhythmias in schizophrenics receiving phenothiazines—clinical correlates. *Clinical Electroencephalography*, 1975, *5*, 103–115.

Delay, J., Deniker, P., & Barande, R. Le suicide des épileptiques. *Encephale.*, 1957, *46*, 401–436.

Dietch, J. T. Diagnosis of organic anxiety disorders. *Psychosomatics*, 1981, *22*, 661–669.

Dietch, J. T., & Zetin, M. Diagnosis of organic depressive disorders. *Psychosomatics*, 1983, *24*, 971–979.

Elliott, F. A. Episodic dyscontrol—neurological findings. In C. Perris, G. Struwe, & B. Jansson (Eds.), *Developments in psychiatry* (Vol. 5, Biological psychiatry 1981). Amsterdam: Elsevier, 1981.

Elliott, F. A. Neurological findings in adult minimal brain dysfunction and the dyscontrol syndrome. *Journal of Nervous and Mental Disease*, 1982, *170*, 680–687.

Fader, B. W., & Struve, F. A. The possible valve of the electroencephalogram in detecting subclinical hypothyroidism associated with agitated depression: A case study. *Clinical Electroencephalography*, 1972, *3*, 94–101.

Flood, R. A., & Seager, C. P. A retrospective examination of psychiatric case records of patients who subsequently committed suicide. *British Journal of Psychiatry*, 1968, *114*, 443–450.

Gibbs, F. A., & Gibbs, E. L. *Atlas of electroencephalography* (Vol. 2, Epilepsy). Reading, Mass.: Addison-Wesley, 1952.

Gibbs, F. A., & Gibbs, E. L. *Atlas of electroencephalography* (Vol. 3, *Neurological and psychiatric disorders*). Reading, Mass.: Addison-Wesley, 1964.

Gibbs, F. A., & Novick, R. G. Electroencephalographic findings among adult patients in a private psychiatric hospital. *Clinical Electroencephalography*, 1977, *8*, 79–88.

Glaser, G. H. (Ed.). *EEG and behavior*. New York: Basic Books, 1963.

Greenberg, I. M., & Pollack, M. Clinical correlates of 14 & 6/sec. positive spiking in schizophrenic patients. *Electroencephalography and Clinical Neurophysiology*, 1966, *20*, 197–200.

Gross, D. A. Medical origins of psychiatric emergencies: The systems approach. *International Journal of Psychiatry in Medicine*, 1981–1982, *11*, 1–23.

Gunn, J. Affective and suicidal symptoms in epileptic prisoners. *Psychological Medicine*, 1973, *3*, 108–114.

Hall, R. C. W., Beresford, T. P., Gardner, E. R., & Popkin, M. K. The medical care of psychiatric patients. *Hospital and Community Psychiatry*, 1982, *33*, 25–34.

Hall, R. C. W., Gardner, E. R., Stickney, S. K., LeCann, A. F., & Popkin, M. K. Physical illness manifesting as psychiatric disease: II. Analysis of a state hospital inpatient population. *Archives of General Psychiatry*, 1980, *37*, 989–995.

Hall, R. C. W., Popkin, M. K., Devaul, R. A., Faillace, L. A., & Stickney, S. K. Physical illness presenting as psychiatric disease. *Archives of General Psychiatry*, 1978, *35*, 1315–1320.

Hankoff, L. D., & Einsidler, B. (Eds.). *Suicide: Theory and clinical aspects.* Littleton, Mass.: PSG, 1979.

Heath, R. G. Brain function and behavior. *Journal of Nervous and Mental Disease*, 1975, *160*, 159–175.

Heath, R. G., & Mickle, W. A. Evaluation of 7 years experience with depth electrode studies in human patients. In E. Hamey & D. O'Doherty (Eds.), *Electrical studies on the unanesthestized brain.* New York: Paul B. Hoeber, 1960.

Henriksen, B., Juul-Jensen, P., & Lund, M. The mortality of epileptics. In R. Brakenridge (Ed.) *Life assurance medicine: Proceedings of the 10th International Congress of Life Assurance Medicine.* London: Pitman, 1970.

Herridge, C. F. Physical disorders in psychiatric illness: A study of 209 consecutive admissions. *Lancet*, 1960, *2*, 949–951.

Hill, D., & Parr, G. *Electroencephalography.* New York: Macmillan, 1963.

Hoffman, R. S. Diagnostic errors in the evaluation of behavioral disorders. *Journal of the American Medical Association*, 1982, *248*, 964–967.

Hoffman, R. S., & Koran, L. M. Detecting physical illness in patients with mental disorders. *Psychosomatics*, 1984, *25*, 654–660.

Itil, T. M. The use of electroencephalography in the practice of psychiatry. *Psychosomatics*, 1982, *23*, 799–813.

Jonas, A. *Ictal and subictal neurosis: Diagnosis and treatment.* Springfield, Ill.: Charles C Thomas, 1965.

Karasu, T. B., *et al.* The medical care of patients with psychiatric illness. *Hospital and Community Psychiatry*, 1980, *31*, 463–472.

Kiloh, L. G., McComas, A. J., & Osselton, J. W. *Clinical electroencephalography* (3rd ed.). London: Butterworths, 1972.

Kiloh, L. G., & Osselton, J. W. *Clinical electroencephalography.* London: Butterworths, 1966.

Klass, D. W., & Daly, D. D. *Current practice of clinical electroencephalography.* New York: Raven Press, 1979.

Kooi, K. A. *Fundamentals of electroencephalography.* New York: Harper & Row, 1971.

Koranyi, E. K. Physical health and illness in a psychiatric outpatient department population. *Canadian Psychiatric Association Journal*, 1972, *17*(Suppl.), 109–116.

Koranyi, E. K. Morbidity and rate of undiagnosed physical illness in a psychiatric clinic population. *Archives of General Psychiatry*, 1979, *36*, 414–419.

Koranyi, E. K. Somatic illness in psychiatric patients. *Psychosomatics*, 1980, *21*, 887–891.

Krauthammer, C., & Klerman, G. L. Secondary mania: Manic syndromes associated with antecedent physical illness or drugs. *Archives of General Psychiatry*, 1978, *35*, 1333–1339.

Krohn, W. Causes of death among epileptics. *Epilepsia*, 1963, *4*, 315–322.

Lutz, E. G. Electroencephalography in psychiatry. *Frontiers of Psychiatry*, 1982, *12*, 13–14.

Maguire, G. P., & Granville-Grossman, K. L. Physical illness in psychiatric patients. *British Medical Journal*, 1968, *115*, 1365–1369.

Maletzky, B. M. The episodic dyscontrol syndrome. *Diseases of the Nervous System*, 1973,

34, 178–185.

Mark, V. H., & Ervin, F. R. *Violence and the brain.* New York: Harper & Row, 1970.

Marshall, H. E. S. Incidence of physical disorders among psychiatric inpatients: A study of 175 cases. *British Medical Journal,* 1949, *2*, 468–470.

Monroe, R. R. Episodic behavior disorders—Schizophrenia or epilepsy. *Archives of General Psychiatry,* 1959, *1*, 101–110.

Monroe, R. R. *Episodic behavior disorders: A psychodynamic and neurophysiological analysis.* Cambridge, Mass.: Harvard University Press, 1970.

Monroe, R. R. Epileptoid mechanism in episodic dyscontrol of aggressive criminals. In L. Bellak (Ed.), *Psychiatric aspects of minimal brain dysfunction in adults* New York: Grune & Stratton, 1979.

Monroe, R. R. DSM III style diagnoses of the episodic disorders. *Journal of Nervous and Mental Disease,* 1982, *170*, 664–669. (a)

Monroe, R. R. Limbic ictus and atypical psychoses. *Journal of Nervous and Mental Disease,* 1982, *170*, 711–716. (b)

Monroe, R. R., & Mickle, W. A. Alpha chloralose activated electroencephalograms in psychiatric patients. *Journal of Nervous and Mental Disease,* 1967, *144*, 59–68.

Muecke, L. N., & Krueger, D. W. Physical findings in a psychiatric outpatient clinic. *American Journal of Psychiatry,* 1981, *138*, 1241–1242.

Neil, J. F., Merikangas, J. R., Davies, R. K., & Himmelhoch, J. M. Validity and clinical utility of neuroleptic facilitated electroencephalography in psychotic patients. *Clinical Electroencephalography,* 1978, *9*, 38–48.

Phillips, R. J. Physical disorder in 164 consecutive admissions to a mental hospital: The incidence and signficance. *British Medical Journal,* 1937, *2*, 363–366.

Prudhomme, C. Epilepsy and suicide. *Journal of Nervous and Mental Disease,* 1941, *94*, 722–731.

Rémond, A., & Glaser, G. H. *Handbook of electroencephalography and clinical neurophysiology* (Vol. 15C, *Metabolic, endocrine, and toxic diseases*). Amsterdam: Elsevier, 1977.

Rémond, A., & Radermecker, F. J. *Handbook of electroencephalography and clinical neurophysiology* (Vol. 15A, *Infections and inflammatory reactions, allergy and allergic reactions, degenerative diseases*). Amsterdam: Elsevier, 1977.

Romano, J. The elimination of the internship—An act of regression. *American Journal of Psychiatry,* 1970, *126*, 1565–1576.

Schwab, R. S. *Electroencephalography in clinical practice.* Philadelphia: W. B. Saunders, 1951.

Small, J. G. The six per second spike and wave: A psychiatric population study. *Electroencephalography and Clinical Neurophysiology,* 1968, *24*, 561–568.

Small, J. G. Small sharp spikes in a psychiatric population. *Archives of General Psychiatry,* 1970, *22*, 275–284.

Small, J. G. Photoconvulsive and photomyoclonic responses in psychiatric patients. *Clinical Electroencephalography,* 1971, *2*, 77–88.

Small, J. G., Sharpley, P., & Small, I. F. Positive spikes, spike–wave phantoms, and psychomotor variants. *Archives of General Psychiatry,* 1968, *18*, 232–238.

Small, J. G., & Small, J. F. Fourteen and six per second positive spikes in psychiatry. *Archives of General Psychiatry,* 1964, *11*, 645–650.

Small, J. G., Small, J. F., Millstein, V., & Moore, D. F. Familial associations with EEG variants in manic–depressive disease. *Archives of General Psychiatry,* 1975, *32*, 43–48.

Spencer, S. S., Spencer, D. D., Williamson, P. D., *et al.* The localizing value of depth electroencephalography in 32 patients with refractory epilepsy. *Annals of Neurology,* 1982, *12*, 248–253.

Strauss, H., Ostow, M., & Greenstein, L. *Diagnostic electroencephalography,* New York: Grune & Stratton, 1952.

Struve, F. A. Electroencephalographic relationships to suicide behavior—Qualitative considerations and a report on a series of completed suicides. *Clinical Electroencephalography,* 1983, *14*, 20–26.

Struve, F. A. Selective referral versus routine screening in clinical EEG assessment of psychiatric inpatients. *Psychiatric Medicine*, 1984, *1*, 317–343.

Struve, F. A. Clinical electroencephalography as an assessment method in psychiatric practice. In R. Hall & T. Beresford (Eds.), *Handbook of psychiatric diagnostic procedures* (Vol. 2). New York: Spectrum, 1985. (a)

Struve, F. A. Possible potentiation of suicide risk in patients with EEG dysrhythmias taking oral contraceptives: A speculative empirical note. *Clinical Electroencephalography*, 1985, *16*, 88–90. (b)

Struve, F. A. *Somatopsychic implications of generalized and/or focal slowing in psychiatric screening EEGs*. Paper presented at the 14th Annual Scientific Meeting of the Society of Biological Psychiatry, Dallas, May 15–19, 1985. (c)

Struve, F. A., Klein, D. F., & Saraf, K. R. Electroencephalographic correlates of suicide ideation and attempts. *Archives of General Psychiatry*, 1972, *27*, 363–365.

Struve, F. A., & Pike, L. E. Routine admission electroencephalograms of adolescent and adult psychiatric patients awake and asleep. *Clinical Electroencephalography*, 1974, *5*, 67–72.

Struve, F. A., Saraf, K. R., Arko, R. S., Klein, D. F., & Becka, D. R. Electroencephalographic correlates of oral contraceptive use in psychiatric patients. *Archives of General Psychiatry*, 1976, *33*, 741–745.

Struve, F. A., Saraf, K. R., Arko, R. S., Klein, D. F., & Becka, D. R. Relationship between paroxysmal electroencephalographic dysrhythmia and suicide ideation and attempts in psychiatric patients. In C. Shagass, S. Gershon, & A. Friedhoff (Eds.), *Psychopathology and brain dysfunction* New York: Raven Press, 1977.

Struve, F. A., & Struve, E. J. *Scalp derived EEG dysrhythmia and episodic dyscontrol in hospitalized psychiatric patients*. Paper presented at the 14th Annual Scientific Meeting of the Society of Biological Psychiatry, Dallas, May 15–19, 1985.

Taylor, D. C., & Falconer, M. A. Clinical, socioeconomic, and psychological changes after temporal lobectomy for epilepsy. *British Journal of Psychiatry*, 1968, *114*, 1247–1261.

Tucker, G. J., Detre, T., Harrow, M., & Glaser, G. H. Behavior and symptoms of psychiatric patients and the electroencephalogram. *Archives of General Psychiatry*, 1965, *12*, 278–286.

Volow, M. R., Zung, W. W. K., & Green, R. L. Electroencephalographic abnormalities in suicidal patients. *Journal of Clinical Psychiatry*, 1979, *40*, 213–216.

Walter, W. G., & Crow, H. J. Depth recording from the human brain. *Electroencephalography and Clinical Neurophysiology*, 1964, *16*, 68–72.

Weil, A. A. Depressive reactions in temporal lobe uncinate seizures. *Electroencephalography and Clinical Neurophysiology*, 1954, *6*, 701.

Wilson, W. P. (Ed.). *Applications of electroencephalography in psychiatry*. Durham, N.C.: Duke University Press, 1965. (a)

Wilson, W. P. The electroencephalogram in endocrine disorders. In W. P. Wilson (Ed.), *Applications of electroencephalography in psychiatry*. Durham, N.C.: Duke University Press, 1965. (b)

Zung, W. W. K. Index of Potential Suicide (IPS): A rating scale for suicide prevention. In A. Beck, H. Resnik, & D. Lettier (Eds.), *The prediction of suicide*. New York: Charles Press, 1974.

CHAPTER 4

A Mathematical Model of Evolutionary Pressures Regulating Self-Preservation and Self-Destruction

Denys de Catanzaro, PhD
Department of Psychology, McMaster University

The typical focus of suicide research is upon some subset of cases in contemporary human culture. This article focuses more broadly upon the antithesis of suicide, self-preservation, as it pervades the general patterns of behavior of all organisms—not only in current generations, but over the totality of biological evolution. From the perspective of modern evolutionary theory, it is evident that self-preservation has definable limitations that can be modeled mathematically. It can be demonstrated that the observed ecologies of suicide and other deviations from self-preservation generally correspond to the circumstances predicted by these theoretical limitations. This correspondence, in conjunction with various lines of empirical evidence, supports a tentative conclusion that humans' heritable motivational constitution is such that the degree of self-preservation varies with personal circumstances.

One commonly hears the phrase "self-preservation instincts" with reference to both human and animal behavior, and such a characterization is probably accurate in many instances. All behaving organisms normally seek food, water, and shelter, and avoid harsh elements, predation, and other perceptible threats to survival. These patterns usually constitute the better part of organisms' behavioral repertoires, and they clearly function to keep the individual alive. A perusal of any modern text in physiological psychology (e.g., Carlson, 1981) shows that there are stereotyped, heritable, physiological substrates of avoidance of pain and danger, of hunger and thirst, and of more complicated components of self-preservation, such as emotional behavior.

Self-preservation is so ubiquitous that many researchers and laypeople appear to have assumed that deviations from it must reflect grossly abnormal or pathological conditions. However, the reasoning below suggests that natural selection does not invariably favor tendencies toward self-preservation, and may indeed favor outright self-destructiveness under limited, definable conditions. I suppose that this may lend renewed credence to the notion of a "death instinct."

Natural selection is often characterized as "survival of the fittest." This phrase has unfortunately been excessively prominent in popular conceptions of evolution and should be discarded. It employs the concept of "fitness" in a manner that is not consistent with modern scientific definitions. Moreover, it mistakenly leaves the impression that survival is the governing force in biological evolution. Reproduction, not survival, is that governing force. This follows by logical necessity. An organism that reproduces passes on its heritable traits to subsequent generations, whereas one that does not reproduce passes on none of its heritable traits. The genetics of each new generation are constituted by that subset of the previous generation that has reproduced. Accordingly, a better characterization of natural selection is found in the phrase "differential reproduction," if we must have any such phrase.

Survival is nonetheless critical, within limits, in the determination of the differential reproduction that constitutes evolution, Survival to the age of reproductive maturity is clearly a necessary condition for reproduction. However, a long-lived individual who never reproduces does not pass on any heritable traits to future generations, whereas a short-lived individual who is extremely fecund makes a significant genetic contribution to the next generation. Thus, longevity per se is not necessarily selected for by natural selection. It is only selected for, or passed on over generations, insofar as it facilitates reproduction. Genetically mediated traits subserving longevity and self-preservation can logically be expected to have survived numerous generations of natural selection only to the extent that they have helped organisms to reproduce.

Members of many species die subsequent to one major reproductive effort (such species are "semelparous"; see Wilson, 1975). A well-known example is that of spawning salmon, and there are numerous instances among plants and insects. In humans and certain other species, life may continue in a postreproductive state, as, for example, in postmenopausal women. We must consider that nurturance and other kin-solicitous behavior, in species where these occur, may have an impact upon the value of self-preservation in the context of natural selection. Offspring and other biological relatives share an individual's genes. If that individual has any impact upon the potential for reproduction of these relatives, his or her survival and self-preservation indirectly influence the propagation of his or her genes as they exist in relatives. Unmarried aunts or aging grandmothers may indirectly be of value to the replication of their genes to the extent that they aid in raising nieces and nephews and grandchildren. Members of sterile castes of social insects reproduce indirectly by facilitating the reproduction of the colony queen, who is typically a mother or sister (see Wilson, 1971). The general nature of this logic follows from "inclusive fitness" theory, which considers that individuals' reproductive success (which defines their true *fitness* in a biological sense) should include not only their progeny but those of their kin weighted by their genetic relatedness (see W. D. Hamilton, 1964).

Presentation of the Model

I would like to propose that the contingency of self-preservation upon reproductive relevance can be summarized through the following formula, which defines ψ_i as the optimal degree of self-preservation expressed by individual i:

$$\psi_i = \rho_i + \sum_k b_k \rho_k r_k$$

where ρ_i = the remaining reproductive potential of i;
ρ_k = the remaining reproductive potential of each kinship member k;
b_k = a coefficient of benefit or cost to the reproduction of each k provided by the continued existence of i;
r_k = the coefficient of genetic relatedness of each k to i.

This represents a summation of i's future likelihood of reproduction and that of all of i's kin weighted by i's impact on their reproduction and the degree to which they share genes with i. Let me now explain each of the terms in detail to show how they are measured and why self-preservation ought to be a function of ψ.

The variable ρ can be defined as the likely number of offspring that an individual will produce in his or her remaining natural lifetime, *not* inclusive of those already realized. The mean value of ρ for any age cohort can be defined empirically from the actuarial statistics for any particular human culture. It can similarly be applied for any other species where such actuarial data can be obtained. This mean can be equated to Fisher's (1958) "reproductive value" or W. D. Hamilton's (1966) modification of this, which can be entitled "expected reproduction beyond age a." The latter function, which is simpler, is represented by w_a, such that

$$w_a = \int_a^{\infty} \lambda^{-x} 1_x f_x \, dx$$

where λ^{-x} = the Malthusian parameter, which simply adjusts the statistic for possible shifts in total population size over time, and which for many purposes can simply be ignored;

1_x = the fraction of individuals of an age cohort living at age x;

fx = the age-specific fertility rate.

This quantity is integrated from each age a to ∞, or more realistically to the highest age at which any offspring are produced. A typical function of reproductive value is given in Figure 4-1.

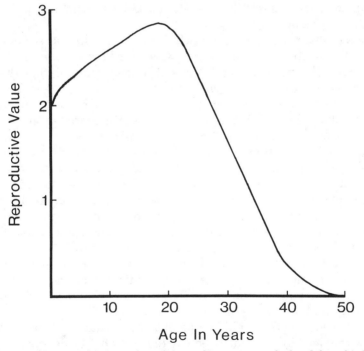

Figure 4-1. The reproductive value of Australian women calculated from birth and death rates current in 1911. This employs Fisher's formula, which differs slightly from that of W. D. Hamilton but yields a very similar curve. (From Fisher, 1958, p. 28. Reproduced with permission of Dover Publications, Inc.)

While age is clearly an important predictor of probable fertility, w_a or reproductive value can only represent the mean ρ at each age and will for many purposes not be an adequate estimation of ρ for any individual. Calculating separate integrals for the two sexes refines the estimation, because of substantial differences in age-specific mortality and fertility between males and females. Separate integrals for other categorical variables, such as marital status, could further improve the estimation. The fertility functions by age of married and unmarried individuals differ dramatically. In many cultures and other species, polygynous practices and hierarchies of social dominance yield dramatic variance in reproductive success (Daly & Wilson, 1983); where a male has two or more young wives, his ρ value is exceptionally high. An individual's past success or failure in relationships with members of the opposite sex may in many circumstances be a good predictor of future prospects. For example, a young unmarried adult male with repeated rejections from females and poor career prospects might have a very low ρ value, despite his age. Measurements of ρ can thus be derived from careful empirical study and are always stochastic, with greater accuracy of prediction likely to be obtained where more predictive variables are employed.

The b coefficient is a weighting that represents the degree of dependency of ρ_k upon the continued existence of i. This is scaled such that $b_k\rho_k$ equals the increment or decrement in the remaining reproductive potential of k provided by the continued existence of i. This is measurable or at least estimable for many situations, and b for most applications probably has limits such that $-1 \leq b \leq 1$. For example, the ρ value of a nursing infant may be entirely dependent upon the continued existence of the mother, and therefore $b = 1$, at least in conditions prevailing in evolutionary history where adoption of orphans would be improbable. The ρ values of kin that are entirely independent of i would not be determined by i, and for such situations $b = 0$. At the other extreme, one can conceive of situations in which i is so burdensome that he or she entirely precludes k's subsequent reproduction, or alternatively where i kills k, such that in either case $b = -1$. For intermediate degrees of dependency, b may have to be estimated on the basis of empirical evidence from previous comparable instances where the outcome is known, and in any case its value is probabilistic rather than absolute.

The r_k coefficients weight the potential reproductive increment for each k provided by the continued existence of i by the degree to which these relatives share genes with i. The calculation of r is simple and is based on the inheritance of variable genetic material through meiosis and recombination as defined by Wright (1922). The r value between parent and child or between any two siblings is .5; that for grandparent and child or uncle/aunt and nephew/niece is .25; that for first cousins is .125; and so forth, with the value divided by one-half for each further degree of removal.

The value of ψ_i thus represents the summation of all costs of individual's immediate death to the propagation of his or her genes. It is, I believe, a precise formulation of what I have previously (de Catanzaro, 1981, 1984) called the "residual capacity to promote inclusive fitness." This value as defined will vary across individuals, and indeed within any individual over time, as a function of reproductive prospects and interactions with potentially reproducing kin.

Theoretically, the expression of any heritable trait of a self-preserving nature ought to be a function of ψ. Consider that any such trait will be transmitted over generations only insofar as it facilitates the reproduction of self and kin, which is what is quantified in ψ. Conversely, consider the fate of a hypothetical, randomly arising mutation that in any manner predisposed toward self-destructiveness. If such a "suicide gene" were to be expressed when ψ was high, it would be highly deleterious and it would tend to preclude its own replication, being quickly eliminated from the gene pool. However, if we consider the well-established fact that gene expression can vary as a function of age and environmental circumstances, through pleiotropy and varying gene–environment interaction (e.g., see Caspari, 1967; Herskowitz, 1973), circumstances permitting its transmission over generations can be defined. The lower the ψ value with which such expression is associated, the lower its negative impact upon its own propagation. If this gene were held by individuals, being expressed when ψ was low but never when ψ was high, it could be transmitted over generations in that its limited circumstances of expression would never impede its replication. In fact, one need not posit genes favoring self-destructiveness outright to predict an erosion of self-preserving attributes when ψ is low. Rather, one need only consider the many known heritable attributes subserving self-preservation and the fact that there is no pressure of natural selection that would sustain their expression wherever ψ is very low. The cumulative impact of these variable pressures of selection upon multiple such attributes over numerous generations could have been quite significant.

A number of striking conclusions follow from the formula for ψ. First, note that for any species in which there are no interactions among kin (as indeed is probably the case in the majority of species), the $\Sigma b_k = 0$, and therefore $\psi_i = \rho_i$ and $\psi_i \geq 0$. Under these circumstances an animal's ρ, and thus its ψ value, will always be positive or at worst 0. One would predict therefore a weakening of self-preserving tendencies as ρ_i approaches 0, but pressures favoring outright self-destructiveness would never exist. In species where there is any sort of interaction among kin, the second component of the formula for ψ_i assumes importance. The most widespread such interaction in nature is maternal care of young (see Wilson, 1975), which almost always involves positive b_k values. The continued existence of females who are postreproductive ($\rho_i = 0$) but nurturant ($\Sigma b_k \rho_k r_k > 0$) is thus readily accounted for. Wherever more complex social interactions occur, as is especially true of humans, the relevance of ρ_i to ψ_i may diminish as the importance of $\Sigma b_k \rho_k r_k$ increases.

Moreover, the possibility of negative ψ_i values occurs in highly social species, meaning that natural selection could foster the expression of outright self-destructiveness within definable circumstances. Wherever i is burdensome toward k, or at least so overall toward summated k, such that $\Sigma b_k \rho_k r_k < 0$, and ρ_i is negligible, $\psi_i < 0$ and self-destructiveness could be favored. Such burdensomeness would require no more than the consumption of resources such as nutrients, shelter, and so forth that might otherwise be available to potentially reproducing kin, especially when i's own remaining reproductive potential is low. Furthermore, ρ_i need not be low for ψ_i to be negative, if i's summated burdensomeness toward all k is substantial. All that is required for $\psi_i < 0$ is that the absolute value of the negative $\Sigma b_k \rho_k r_k$ be greater than the value of ρ_i. Throughout most of nature we find the tendency to behave beneficially toward kin, such that positive b values and therefore positive ψ values prevail. However, in humans, for example, situations where the elderly or infirm depend on kin, or where an individual's social transgressions are likely to bring shame on kin (among other possibilities), probably merit negative b values. All of this also clearly helps answer questions about the cross-species incidence of self-destructive behavior, and the fact that we see clear instances of such behavior only in the most social of species, such as our own species (of course), certain Hymenopteran insects, and to a lesser extent non-human primates (see de Catanzaro, 1981, Chapter 4; W. J. Hamilton, 1980).

The ψ formula as applied to nonsocial species, where $\psi_i = \rho_i$, is similar to the theory of the evolution of senescence as advanced by Medawar (1957), Williams (1957), and W. D. Hamilton (1966). Those authors have argued that the primary reason for failures of life-preserving physiological attributes with increased age, or senescence, is diminishing probability of gene expression as age increases after sexual maturity. The maximal selective relevance of a gene is said to occur at the onset of reproductive maturity, or the peak of reproductive value as exemplified by Figure 4-1. Thereafter, because some mortality inevitably occurs due to various extrinsic factors, there is a diminishing probability that any gene will be expressed at all as age increases. It accordingly is argued that, through pleiotropy and age-contingent genetic expression, genes with beneficial effects in early adulthood but adverse effects later on can cumulate in the gene pool, since the force of selection is greater at the earlier age. The ψ formula here enhances this logic in a number of ways. In particular, it shows justification for the expression of self-preservation in postreproductive or young nonreproductive individuals who are nonetheless productive toward the welfare of potentially reproducing kin. It predicts circumstances of outright self-destructiveness where negative ψ_i values occur, unlike the theory of senescence, which merely allows for evaporation of self-preservation as reproductive potential diminishes. Also, the concept of ρ as employed here is broader than the strictly age-based predictions of the theory of senescence, allowing the possibility of low ρ_i values at young ages.

Correspondence to Observed Conditions of Self-Destructiveness

The ψ formula presents the evolutionarily optimal degree of self-preservation as would theoretically apply, given current understanding of pressures of natural selection. Such optimality will not necessarily be observed in nature. There are multiple considerations that constrain optimality in adaptation of behavior to selective contingencies (see Barash, 1982, Chapter 4, for an introduction to these considerations). Nevertheless, there is solid reason to believe that contingencies of natural selection summarized by ψ can explain a broad range of behavioral and physiological phenomena related to survival and death.

I have previously reviewed archival evidence (de Catanzaro, 1981, in press) and presented some new data (de Catanzaro, 1984) showing a general correspondence of the social ecology of human suicidal behavior to theoretical selective pressures like those described above. To summarize this only very briefly, it is evident that suicidal behavior has occurred throughout human history, predominantly in individuals experiencing severe coping impasses related to relationships to the opposite sex, health, and social productive behavior. There is long-standing and almost culturally universal evidence that suicide frequency increases with age, is greater in the less nurturant sex, is associated with social isolation (including isolation from kin and the opposite sex), and is high among the unmarried and very low in those with dependent children. Although obvious proximate causes differ considerably across individual cases, in all cultures we see personal factors such as repeated difficulties in heterosexual relationships, ostracism or censure by kin and/or social group, chronically poor health, unemployment, and psychological sense of hopelessness being involved in large numbers of cases. These factors can readily be construed as involving diminished capacities to reproduce and/or to produce toward the welfare of kin (see references and logical development in de Catanzaro, 1981). We need not assume any particular causal model for suicide, be it cultural or biological, to note this ecological correspondence to theoretical conditions of self-preservation failure. We should also keep in mind that this correspondence is only probabilistic and is imperfect, as is discussed below in more detail.

With respect to possible causality underlying this correspondence, let us consider again the many heritable aspects of self-preservation that occur in humans and other animals. In particular, consider the neural and hormonal substrates of our most fundamental drives and emotions. There is growing evidence from physiological psychology, behavioral genetics, and comparative ethology that emotions such as fear, anger, elation, and dysphoria, and drives such as hunger, thirst, pain avoidance, and many others, have inborn physiological components. Appreciation of the evidence supporting this contention cannot be properly conveyed in the space available here, so the reader is referred to the many relevant reviews (e.g., Carlson, 1981; Panksepp, 1982; Plomin, DeFries, & McClearn, 1980; Plutchik & Kellerman, 1980). It seems plausible that all of these factors could have been molded in their expression by the pressures summarized by ψ. In particular, suicide researchers should be interested in the genetics and physiology of dysphoria and elation (see review by de Catanzaro, 1981, Chapter 10), insofar as chronic dysphoria is related to suicide, and given that dysphoria generally accompanies losses to fitness while euphoria accompanies gains to fitness. Any indications that stereotyped physiological systems consistently relate to suicide, as found in other chapters of this volume, may imply that our heritable constitution plays a role in self-destructive behavior.

The assumption that emotional substrates underlying suicidal behavior have heritable biological bases does not preclude roles of learning and culture in determining such behavior. As argued in detail elsewhere (de Catanzaro, 1981, Chapter 6), learning must be involved in the use of any of the common modern methods of suicide, involving firearms, drugs, poisons, automobiles, and so forth. It is totally inconceivable that knowledge of the use of such technologies could be innate. Furthermore, massed suicides, suicide epidemics, and situations where suicide recurs with similar methods and temporal and physical locations (see Hankoff, 1961; Phillips, 1974) probably involve some degree of imitation or observational learning. It is also quite conceivable that some individuals could arrive at a decision to commit suicide through dispassionate cognitive processes.

Empirical study of actual human cases of varying degrees of self-destructiveness in relation to the ψ_i formula is in progress and is not reported here. In Table 4-1, however, I present a small number of contrived, simple, archetypical nonhuman and human individuals with calculated ψ_i values meant to demonstrate the workings of this formula. It should be fairly obvious that positive ψ_i values will generally prevail among extant individuals of any species. The two animal cases are provided to show circumstances in which self-destructive behavior might develop. The first four human cases show how positive ψ_i values can be derived from diverse sorts of individual circumstances. The fifth human case shows an example of a case of $\psi_i = 0$, and assumes that the individual's many past rejections by females mean that it is unlikely that he will ever produce children. Migration away from kin would be

TABLE 4-1. Contrived Archetypical Individuals and the Calculation of Their ψ_i Values

Individuals	ρ_i	$\Sigma b_k \rho_k r_k$	ψ_i
Nonhuman cases			
1. Stinging bee of sterile caste, with any variable benefit to the queen's reproduction equal to x	0	$-x$	$-x$
2. Aging mother bear, two threatened cubs ($b_k = -1$, $\rho_k = 3$, $r_k = .5$)	1	-3	-2
Human cases			
1. Polygynous male, 25, two wives but no nurturant behavior	5	0	5
2. Married female, 20, no children yet	2.5	0	2.5
3. Female, 55, three dependent children ($b_k = .5$, $\rho_k = 2$, $r_k = .5$)	0	1.5	1.5
4. Single female, 37, kind aunt to four children ($b_k = .2$, $\rho_k = 2$, $r_k = .25$)	.2	.4	.6
5. Single male, 32, no kin contact, repeatedly unsuccessful with females	0	0	0
6. Divorced male, 60, bringing shame on kin for social transgression, has three children ($b_k = -.1$, $\rho_k = 2$, $r_k = .5$)	0	$-.3$	$-.3$
7. Infirm female, 75, supported by her financially pressed daughter, who also supports three children ($b_k = -.3$, $\rho_k = 2$, $r_k = .25$)	0	$-.5$	$-.5$

sufficient to produce a value of 0 for the second term in this case, and we might note that any burdensomeness toward kin, no matter how negligible, would make his $\psi_i < 0$. The sixth and seventh archetypical human cases resemble particular recurrent circumstances of suicides in diverse cultures. Although the b_k factors are contrived, the reader should be able to see that any negative b_k factor, no matter what its absolute magnitude, is sufficient to produce a negative ψ_i value.

It might be assumed that any positive ψ_i value, regardless of how small it is, might be sufficient to support carrying on and preserving one's existence. Similarly, any negative ψ_i value could tip the scales toward self-destructiveness. Note that ψ_i may predict suicidal behavior without any direct measure of such behavior.

Qualifications and Imperfections

It is important to consider that over most of our evolutionary history, unlike modern times, an individual's social milieu probably consisted primarily of individuals with whom he or she shared multiple kinship ties (e.g., see Chagnon, 1979). Geographic mobility and cultural change have eroded this, such that there has been a breakdown in the extended family and in some instances even the nuclear family. Individuals now tend to be in regular contact with others from diverse genetic backgrounds, contrary to the situation that prevailed in hunting–gathering groups or agricultural villages. It is of course the ancestral condition and not the modern one that is relevant to the evolution of our psyche and behavior. In ancestral conditions, any socially productive behavior would probably have benefit for the reproduction of kin. This broadens the interpretation of $\Sigma b_k \rho_k r_k$ for modern situations. The human psyche can often function as if it were still in ancestral conditions, with any socially productive behavior being viewed as justification for survival, whereas any social ostracism or censure may be taken as a sign of burdensomeness.

It is essential to note that no specific current behavioral event will necessarily conform to the optimal degree of self-preservation outlined here. The formulations apply strictly to evolutionary pressures prevailing in *past* generations. These pressures are presumed to have shaped current behavioral predispositions, such that within any generation they *probabilistically* conform to this formula. Mutation, novel genetic recombination, and expression of behavior in evolutionarily novel environments all should undermine perfection in such conformation within any particular generation (see de Catanzaro, 1981). It seems quite likely that, given the recent rapid transitions in human culture and technology, psychological vestiges of these pressures of natural selection could misfire in circumstances resembling but not truly involving a reduced capacity to promote inclusive fitness. Accordingly, a mere perception of hopelessness, burdensomeness, or social rejection, for example, as well as true instances of such states, could trigger self-destructiveness.

Another important qualification is the fact that gene expressions in evolutionarily novel environments can also be conducive to self-destructive as well as other nonadaptive behavior. For example, a caged animal is outside of the habitat in which its genes were selected, which means that its behavior may be unpredictable. Humans in modern cultures are out of their natural context in several respects. Not only is this true of contact with kin and individuals from diverse genetic backgrounds as already discussed, it is certainly true technologically. We are now surrounded by a host of technologies, for none of which we could have any biological preparedness, and through which we can readily implement our own deaths. This may have facilitated many impulsive acts of suicide that may truly be maladaptive in a biological context. More broadly, various social and technological transitions can impose coping demands on individuals for which they are not prepared, inducing pathological states that may facilitate self-destructiveness. Therefore, modern instances of self-destructiveness may often relate to pathological conditions that are extraneous to the pressures of natural selection formulated here (see also de Catanzaro, 1981).

Attempted Suicide, Behavior in Warfare, and Risk Taking

The ψ formula can accommodate various self-sacrificing phenomena that we might not necessarily call suicide. In warfare, for example, self-sacrifice is theoretically justified if the summated and weighted benefit to the reproduction of kin exceeds the loss to ρ_i. Maternal defense of young, as observed in many species, follows the same logic. So does the altruistic behavior of social Hymenopteran insects, where death occurs, for example, when a bee stings in colony defense. However, in warfare and maternal defense there may be only a probability of mortality, rather than a certainty. For that matter, the same is true of so-called "attempted suicide" or parasuicide, and indeed of various forms of risk taking. Any such risk of death is biologically adaptive and probabilistically supported by natural selection, insofar as

$$(\psi_l p_l + \psi_d p_d) > \psi_n$$

where ψ_l and ψ_d are the ψ_i values achievable, respectively, if i lives
        or dies as a result of the risk;
        ψ_n is the ψ_i value if i does not take the risk;
        p_l and p_d are the probabilities, respectively, of living and dying
        if the risk is taken.

The interpretation of ψ_d in this context is such that the remaining
capacities to reproduce and benefit kin are calculated just before the
risked death, which makes b_k within that formula interpretable as the
impact of the death itself upon kin. It also accommodates the remote
possibility that ρ_i, which almost always would assume a value of 0 in
the ψ_d formula, could be positive, as for example if death is risked when
a male attempts to fertilize a female. The formula would have to be
elaborated for situations in which there is a risk of being maimed,
which could be accomplished by adding this additional outcome and
its associated probability to the term in brackets.

The extent to which parasuicides and various other risks of death
conform to this biologically optimal formula is an open question that
has not yet been explored. As with the ψ formula for degree of self-
preservation, any conformation would be expected to be imperfect.

The Value of a Macroscopic Approach

I would like to conclude by suggesting that a general theory of self-
destructive behavior has previously eluded researchers of this topic
because they have ignored the full dimensions of the subject matter.
Human suicide has been studied from many perspectives. There have
been several cognitive and psychodynamic approaches, which have
focused on proximate personal antecedents, usually as evidenced in
suicide notes or hearsay from relatives and acquaintances of the deceased.
Generally, these have involved the study of small sample sizes of cases
from modern Western cultures. On the other hand, sociologists since
the work of Durkheim (1897/1951) have focused on larger numbers of
cases, examining social correlates such as sex, marital status, and
degree of integration of individuals into the social network. In Table
4-2 are summaried the various previous forms of study of suicide,
categorizing these forms in terms of their temporal scope (i.e., the
extent to which they look back into the individuals' histories and more
broadly into the species' history) and their spatial scope (i.e., the extent
to which they look across individuals and across cultures and geographic
locations). The vast majority of published studies clearly have been
relatively microscopic in both dimensions. Such microscopic studies

TABLE 4-2. Levels of Analysis of Self-Destructive Behavior

Temporal scope (continuum)	Spatial scope (continuum)			
	Microscopic			Macroscopic
Microscopic	Immediate cognitive and experiential antecedents of cases, suicide notes, methods	Comparison of immediate antecedents, notes, and methods across individuals	Social patterns in immediate antecedents, methods, notes	Cross-cultural patterns in immediate antecedents, methods, notes
	Life history analysis of cases	Comparison of life histories of many cases	Sociological correlates	Cross-cultural comparisons in life histories
	Family histories of cases	Family and intergenerational patterns	Social ecologies of suicide	Cross-species comparisons
		Historical perspectives	Comparisons of primitive and modern cultures	
Macroscopic				Evolutionary perspectives

are invaluable, but a general theory of suicide cannot be derived from a narrow focus. Rather, it is more likely that it would derive from a very broad temporal and spatial perspective—one that takes into account the whole history of self-destructive behavior in the species (and, if necessary, across species), and its frequency, dimensions, and diverse forms across cultures. It must at the same time be able to explain the detail found in research taking more circumscribed approaches. I believe that an evolutionary perspective can satisfy these conditions for a general theory of suicide. There is much empirical research needed before any definitive explanation could be attempted, but there are several consistencies evident in existing data when viewed from this broad perspective.

References

Barash, D. P. *Sociobiology and behavior* (2nd ed.). Amsterdam: Elsevier, 1982.

Carlson, N. R. *Physiology of behavior* (2nd ed.). Boston: Allyn & Bacon, 1981.

Caspari, E. Gene action as applied to behavior. In J. Hirsch (Ed.), *Behavior—genetic analysis*. New York: McGraw-Hill, 1967.

Chagnon, N. A. Mate competition, favoring close kin, and village fissioning among the Yanomamö Indians. In N. A. Chagnon & W. Irons (Eds.), *Evolutionary biology and human social behavior: An anthropological perspective*. North Scituate, Mass.: Duxbury Press, 1979.

Daly, M., & Wilson, M. *Sex, evolution, and behavior* (2nd ed.). Boston: Willard Grant Press, 1983.

de Catanzaro, D. *Suicide and self-damaging behavior: A sociobiological perspective*. New York: Academic Press, 1981.

de Catanzaro, D. Suicidal ideation and the residual capacity to promote inclusive fitness: A survey. *Suicide and Life-Threatening Behavior*, 1984, *14*, 75–87.

de Catanzaro, D. Evolutionary pressures and limitations to self-preservation. In C. Crawford, M. Smith, & D. Krebs (Eds.), *Sociobiology and psychology: Ideas, issues and findings*. Hillsdale, N.J.: Erlbaum, in press.

Durkheim, E. *Suicide*. Glencoe, Ill:. Free Press, 1951. (Originally published, 1897.)

Fisher, R. A. *The genetical theory of natural selection*. New York: Dover, 1958.

Hamilton, W. D. The genetical evolution of social behavior. *Journal of Theoretical Biology*, 1964, *7*, 1–16.

Hamilton, W. D. The moulding of senescence by natural selection. *Journal of Theoretical Biology*, 1966, *12*, 12–45.

Hamilton, W. J. Do nonhuman animals commit suicide? *Behavioral and Brain Sciences*, 1980, *3*, 278–279.

Hankoff, L. D. An epidemic of attempted suicide. *Comprehensive Psychiatry*, 1961, *2*, 294–298.

Herskowitz, I. H. *Principles of genetics*. New York: Macmillan, 1973.

Medawar, P. B. *The uniqueness of the individual*. London: Methuen, 1957.

Panksepp, J. Toward a general psychobiological theory of emotions. *Behavioral and Brain Sciences*, 1982, *5*, 407–467.

Phillips, D. P. The influence of suggestion on suicide: Substantive and theoretical implications of the Werther effect. *American Sociological Review*, 1974, *39*, 340–354.

Plomin, R., DeFries, J. C., & McClearn, G. E. *Behavioral genetics*. San Francisco: W. H. Freeman, 1980.

Plutchik, R., & Kellerman, H. (Eds.). *Emotion: Theory, research, and experience* (Vols. 1 & 2). New York: Academic Press, 1980.
Williams, G. C. Pleiotropy, natural selection, and the evolution of senescence. *Evolution*, 1957, *11*, 398–411.
Wilson, E. O. *The insect societies*. Cambridge, Mass.: Belknap, 1971.
Wilson, E. O. *Sociobiology*. Cambridge, Mass.: Belknap, 1975.
Wright, S. Coefficients of interbreeding and relationship. *American Naturalist*, 1922, *56*, 330–339.

CHAPTER 5

A Stress–Diathesis Theory of Suicide

Donald H. Rubinstein, PhD, MPH
Institute of Culture and Communication, East–West Center

Suicide poses an explanatory problem for an evolutionary theory that assumes all behavior to be oriented toward adaptiveness and toward maximization of biological fitness. From the theoretical perspective of evolutionary biology, self-destruction appears as the "antithesis of almost all other forms of behavior" (de Catanzaro, 1981, p. 47). Regardless, suicide is too widespread throughout nearly all human cultures, too well documented historically, and too frequent in incidence to be explained as a rare, exotic, or aberrant behavior pathology. A biological interpretation of suicidal behavior must address several overlapping questions. Does self-destructive behavior represent a "misfiring" of an otherwise adaptive behavioral capability, such as human cognitive flexibility? Can suicide be ascribed to the stresses of novel evolutionary circumstances, such as rapid sociocultural change, social isolation, aging, instability of nuclear family bonds, and the like? Are there biologically adaptive benefits that accrue to the kin group of a suicide victim— that is, is suicide a form of "altruistic behavior" that removes unfit members from the group? Does the "ecology" of suicide in human groups render this behavior immune to the evolutionary pressure of natural selection?

Denys de Catanzaro has recently brought together a large amount of cultural, psychological, and physiological data that bear upon these questions (de Catanzaro, 1980, 1981). In a paper (de Catanzaro, 1980) that preceded the larger synthesis, de Catanzaro organized the material into four biological interpretations or "models" of suicide. Although

I wish to thank Joanne Sheder of the University of Hawaii Department of Anthropology for her careful reading and suggestions on this chapter. I am also grateful to Andrew Harrison at the East–West Center for his editorial help.

logically separate, the four models build together toward a general theory of stress–diathesis for human suicide. Here I summarize each model, bringing in some recent related data from neuropsychiatry.

Suicide as Learned Behavior

Human cognitive plasticity and behavioral flexibility allow for the transmission of complex, varied cultural repertoires. This permits a fine behavioral adaptation to a wide range of environmental contingencies, which is not possible in species with a more rigid, genetically preprogrammed behavioral repertoire. However, human learning capacity, and our ability at symbolic thought, may be so extensive as to allow for learning of self-destructive behavior. Suicide may thus represent the occasional maladaptive by-product of an otherwise highly adaptive general behavioral flexibility. Therefore, suicide and other self-destructive behaviors would be tolerated by natural selection as a constituent of this flexibility. Evolutionary pressure would act on the general dimension of behavioral flexibility, since the net effect of flexibility would be highly adaptive (de Catanzaro, 1981, p. 73).

Cross-cultural data support the model of suicide as learned behavior. Different cultures show prescribed patterns in the situational determinants for suicide, in the means and staging of the act, in the categories of individuals at risk, and in the local ascriptions of emotions involved (Bohannan, 1960; Farberow, 1975; Headley, 1983). Frequent clustering of suicidal acts in time and space provide evidence for processes of modeling and contagion in suicide behavior.[1] Furthermore, complex belief systems—such as notions of an afterlife, spirit visits or vengeance, or ideas of personal "honor" or "reputation" that persist socially beyond an individual's death—can provide compelling cognitive support and cultural underpinning to suicidal acts.

The question remains, however, whether human learning capacity and cultural or cognitive flexibility can account fully for suicidal acts, or whether there are similarities of environmental stresses or individual predispositions that might underlie cultural variability in suicide patterns. de Catanzaro's position is that there are probably underlying motivational events that are only partly modulated through culturally patterned learning. The other three models address this question.

Suicide as Stress-Induced Pathology

There are several aspects of this model of suicide as pathology. One aspect may be called the "domestic animal hypothesis" (Dawkins, 1980);

this theory contends that animals living in environments outside of the one in which their genes were naturally selected may demonstrate genotypically influenced behavior that is maladaptive. In highly novel or rapidly changing environments, maladaptive behavioral characteristics may appear, which may nevertheless be adaptive within the range of circumstances in which the genes were naturally selected (de Catanzaro, 1981, p. 86). This argument is analogous to the moth-and-flame example—"the very sensible orienting technique of maintaining a fixed compass bearing towards light rays coming from infinity can become suicidal if the moth tries to do the same thing to light rays radiating out from a candle: it describes a neat logarithmic spiral into the flame" (Dawkins, 1980, p. 274).

de Catanzaro invests heavily in the hypothesis that human biological evolution has not caught up to cultural evolution: "Modern human culture frequently places stresses on many individuals by placing them in situations for which they are not genetically prepared" (1980, p. 288). One recent situation that figures importantly in this hypothesis is the increased human longevity within modern society. In light of suicide epidemiology that shows, at least for most modern societies, an increasing rate of suicide with age, the attendant stresses of this evolutionarily novel situation (chronic illness; isolation; cumulative loss of social role, family, and friends; etc.) are significant in the etiology of suicide. The argument is that humans are not genetically adapted to the sorts of aging-related stresses that characterize modern society but that are historically novel for the species.

A second aging-related hypothesis relevant here is the Medawar–Williams theory of senescence. Genes may have multiple effects ("pleiotropy"), and these effects may be expressed at different stages in the life span of the individual. The effects of a single gene or gene combination may be beneficial in youth, yet deleterious in old age. "Senile decay is due to the accumulation in the gene pool of lethal or sublethal genes that have not been removed by natural selection because of beneficial early effects, and because their deleterious effects do not make themselves felt until after the individual has had time to reproduce and pass them on" (Dawkins, 1980, p. 275).

de Catanzaro makes a strong argument that modern suicides are facilitated by stresses of novel environmental conditions: "Human culture and technology have undergone such dramatic changes in the past few centuries that increasingly there should be some lag between genetic evolution and cultural conditions" (1981, p. 87). Although de Catanzaro does not support this argument with comparative suicide data from modern and premodern societies (more is said about this below), he states the notion that "current high rates of suicide reflect the fact that modern society makes excessive demands on many individuals" (1980, p. 268). However, his views are consistent with the general sociological writings on suicide that follow Durkheim's lead (Durkheim, 1897/1965) in ascribing suicide mainly to the anomic conditions of modern society, and the consequent weakening in the bonds (religious, familial, authority, marital, etc.) integrating the individual into the larger groups and shared traditions. Furthermore, role demands of modern occupations are more fragmented, more varied, and often more demanding than earlier in human evolutionary history, and may be considerably stressful for certain individuals (de Catanzaro, 1981, p. 87). This general postulate is supported by some sociological studies of role conflict and status incompatibility, as they are correlated with risk for suicide (Gibbs & Martin, 1964).

Thus, according to this hypothesis—suicide as stress-induced pathology—the broad environmental context for suicide includes social instability leading to role conflict and other stressful conditions; technological innovations such as poison or guns that can facilitate impulsive suicide; and related aspects of historically novel human situations (e.g., old age). At the individual level, the immediate antecedent of the act of suicide is frequently "some exceptionally stressful experience" such as divorce, loss of a loved one, unemployment, illness, alcoholism, or disruption in personal relationships (de Catanzaro, 1980, p. 268). de Catanzaro argues further that under extreme stress, disorganized and maladaptive behavior may develop, and that such behavioral disorganization may facilitate suicide, even though the individual would be genetically predisposed to adaptive behavior under more normal circumstances. Hence, chronic, intractable stress might be associated with evolutionarily novel circumstances, different from those in which the organism's genes were selected, so that there would be no basis for adaptive genetic expression and self-preserving behavior (de Catanzaro, 1980, p. 288).

This social-behavioral model of stress inducement points in the direction of physiological mechanisms. When behavioral means are ineffective for alleviating stress, the burden of coping rests principally on physiological mechanisms (Anisman, 1980, p. 273). Research has indicated that stress will cause an increased demand for central neurotransmitters, such as norepinephrine and serotonin. When demand exceeds the rate at which these neurotransmitters can be synthesized, a depletion of these brain neurotransmitters will result, especially when the organism has no control over the stress (Anisman, 1980). Data also indicate that the monoamines most affected by stress are those linked to clinical depression (Murphy, Campbell, & Costa, 1978). Before discussing recent research on central neurotransmitter "triggers" for suicide, however, it is necessary to digress in order to review generally the biogenic-amine hypothesis.

Amine Metabolism and Amine Tracts

A series of steps are involved in neurotransmission across the synapse separating two neurons. Thus, disruption at any step can result in malfunction of the general process by which neurons communicate with each other. At the nerve ending, precursor amino acids are synthesized into the transmitter substance (e.g., tyrosine is the precursor for dopamine [DA] and norepinephrine [NE]). A nerve impulse causes the transmitter substance to be released into the synaptic cleft. Once released, the transmitter substance is chemically broken down mainly in two ways— through reuptake inactivation at the nerve ending where it was released, or through action at the postsynaptic receptor. The breakdown (catabolism) of catecholamines is accomplished by a particular enzyme, monoamine oxidase (MAO).

Psychoactive drugs and antidepressant medication appear to act selectively on different steps in amine metabolism across the synapse. Phenothiazine, for example, which is used in treating schizophrenics, seems to accelerate the synthesis of DA from its precursor tyrosine, perhaps through its action of blocking postsynaptic DA receptors. Researchers posit an interneuron feedback system to the DA cells; blockade of the receptor site causes a message to the DA cells that "we aren't receiving enough DA, send more!" (Snyder, 1975, p. 111). Tricyclic antidepressants, similar in chemical structure to phenothiazines, are potent inhibitors of the reuptake inactivation mechanism of catecholamines and serotonin (5-HT). By blocking reuptake, these medications increase the level of neurotransmitter compounds in the synaptic cleft. Another group of antidepressants works by inhibiting the action of MAO, the enzyme that breaks down the monoamine neurotransmitters. This causes an accumulation of NE, DA, and 5-HT within nerve terminals; at some point the amines begin leaking out into the synaptic cleft. Thus, both types of antidepressant drugs—tricyclics and MAO inhibitors—facilitate the action of the monoamines, but through effects at different steps along the metabolic pathway. Electroconvulsive therapy (ECT) appears to derive its antidepressive effect by somehow causing the release of NE at the nerve endings. Lithium, used in treating manic–depressive disorders, has the opposite action: It diminishes the release of NE and increases the reuptake of the amine at nerve endings.

It is important to point out that these amino acid transmitters—

acetylcholine, the catecholamines NE and DA, and the indoleamine 5-HT—are quantitatively only minor transmitters in the brain, although they have particular importance in the areas of the brain concerned with emotional behavior. In the peripheral system these compounds are much more important, especially acetylcholine and NE. However, this causes difficulties in using gross measurement techniques, such as urinalysis, for detecting changes in monoamine levels in the brain.

It is also important to appreciate the specificity of this transmitter system in the central nervous system. Uptake systems are highly efficient and specific for the different neurotransmitter compounds NE, DA, 5-HT, and so on (Snyder, 1975, p. 108). Thus, some neural pathways use one particular transmitter compound, while other pathways use a different compound. When the course of these pathways in the brain is known, it is possible to speculate on their function.

Neurotransmitters and Depression

The biogenic-amine hypothesis holds that some depressions may be associated with an absolute or relative deficiency of catecholamines, particularly NE, at functionally important receptor sites in the brain, while manias are associated with an excess of such monoamines (Kety, 1975, p. 181). This hypothesis "has come to be regarded as the central dogma of biological psychiatry, even though it is largely based on indirect evidence" (Kaplan, Sadock, & Freeman, 1975, p. 163). The intricate and complex relationships among catecholamines and other elements of body chemistry still remain to be elucidated. The most consistent behavioral correlate of brain catecholamine function may be level of psychomotor activity, rather than depressive symptoms (Kaplan *et al.*, 1975).

There may also be complex reciprocal effects between neurotransmitter functions. Thus, the role of 5-HT may be to stabilize the NE system by exerting a damping effect on synapses, including those associated with mood. Clinical evidence shows a reduction in 5-HT or its activity in the brain of patients with affective disorders, regardless of whether the state of their illness is depressive, manic, or in remission. This suggests that a 5-HT deficiency could be a genetic or constitutional predisposition for affective disorders, by allowing otherwise normal and adaptive changes in NE levels (and their associated moods or emotional states) to swing out of homeostatic bounds and produce depressive or manic states. "The symptomatic extremes of depression and mania would thus be attributable to high or low synaptic activity, and the predisposition to them or the extent to which those changes overrun their adaptive bounds would depend upon a constitutional deficit in serotonin activity" (Kety, 1975, p. 184).

There may also be some reciprocal or balanced activity between DA and NE. DA is an intermediate step in the metabolic process of synthesizing NE. Suppression of the enzyme (DA-B-hydroxylase of "DBH") that converts DA to NE could produce a release of DA at the expense of NE (Kety, 1975, p. 186).

A corollary of the biogenic-amine hypothesis involves genetic aspects of depression. There is some evidence for single-gene dominant transmission of bipolar depression—depressive disease characterized by cyclic swings between manic and depressive states. In such disease, the morbidity risk for offspring of manic–depressives approaches 50%, if alcoholic, sociopathic, and cyclothymic personality is included (Rainer, 1975, p. 101). However, other evidence points in the direction of multiple-gene transmission. The question of whether depressive disease has a genotypic substrate remains unresolved. Family studies have shown a differentiation of depressive illness from schizophrenia (Rainer, 1975), but depression per se is still a problematic disease entity in psychiatry. Although suicidal depression "is the single most important category in emergency psychiatry" (Linn, 1975, p. 1787), it is not certain that psychotic depression is a clinical entity, or how psychiatric diagnosis can differentiate along the spectrum from mild depressed mood, to neurotic depressive states, to psychotic depression with its attendant risk to the patient or others (Huston, 1975, p. 1051). In regard to this, some psychiatric researchers infer a particular genotype underlying the predispositions to manic–depressive psychosis. The psychological characteristics of individuals so predisposed include a tendency to "emotional overreaction since infancy, persistent alimentary dependent state, a strong craving to gratification from without, and an intolerance to pain" (Rainer, 1975, p. 101).

Since the biogenic-amine hypothesis—the involvement of neurotransmitters in depression—is crucial to the stress–diathesis model of suicide under discussion here, it is important to emphasize the conjectural nature of this hypothesis. Cole and Davis (cited in Coppen, 1972, p. 1953) point out that neurotransmitters are implicated in depression by a number of lines of circumstantial evidence, but the evidence remains indirect.

The amine hypothesis, in its simplest form, is that depression is associated with low levels of biogenic amines in the brain, and mania is associated with high levels. It is certainly heuristically useful to have explicit hypotheses about depression; however, alternate views exist. . . . Conceivably, there could be a defect in one or more places in the chain of events that make up the functioning of biogenic amines. The defect could be in the synthesis of amines, storage, release, neuronal reuptake, axonal transport, or the receptor site. It could involve norepinephrine, serotonin, dopamine, acetylcholine, or possibly other amines or neurotransmitter substances. It need not be a disturbance of any one amine; it could be a disturbance of another of a family of amines or of the balance between different amines. (Coppen, 1972, p. 1953)

Neurotransmitters and Suicide

Having made this digression to discuss the biogenic-amine hypothesis in general, we can consider specific research linking neurotransmitter malfunction with suicide.

Although recent research has been headlined in both the scientific and the lay press, the possible correlation between 5-HT levels and suicide was pointed out at least 10 years ago (Coppen, 1972; Kety, 1975, p. 184). Brain postmortems of suicide victims showed a consistent diminution in 5-HT or its metabolite, with no consistent pattern for the catecholamines. The recent research has focused on binding sites for [³H]imipramine (tritiated imipramine), which is closely associated with the neuronal uptake mechanism for 5-HT. Brain samples from suicide victims and matched controls were analyzed through a technique involving homogenization of the samples from brain (frontal cortex), centrifugation, and incubation in a solution of tritiated imipramine, which marked the binding sites. The homogenate samples were then filtered through glass filters, and the binding sites were counted by examination of the filters. The results showed that the mean number of binding sites in suicides was about 45% lower than in controls (Stanley, Virgilio, & Gershon, 1982). Very similar results have been reported by other researchers (Brown, Ebert, Goyer, Jimerson, Klein, Bunney, & Goodwin, 1982; Greenberg, 1982; "Serotonin Malfunction May Trigger Suicide," 1982).

The significance of these studies is that they suggest a particular neurochemical substrate in suicide. Since binding properties appear not to be correlated with measures of depression, and appear unaltered by treatment outcome, these research findings suggest that binding characteristics are a biological marker for a diagnostic category (affective disorder), rather than for clinical status or mood (Stanley et al., 1982, p. 1337). Furthermore, since receptor sites for [³H]imipramine in the brain and in the platelets possess virtually identical binding charac-teristics (Stanley et al., 1982), measurements of binding levels in blood tissue could possibly be useful in screening individuals predisposed to suicidal depression ("Serotonin Malfunction ... , " 1982). However, these studies should be interpreted with caution. Given the complexity of the neurochemical substrate for affective disorders and depressive disease, it is unwarranted to assume, as some researchers have done, that these brain studies have pinpointed 5-HT as the key factor in suicide (Greenberg, 1982). Rather, they have only reinforced the link between affective disorder, which carries some neurochemical markers, and risk for suicide. This is a link that clinical psychiatrists have appreciated long before they could identify a biological or genetic basis for depression. More is said about this in the critique below.

This digression into the biogenic-amine hypothesis and some recent research on neurochemical links with suicide should have brought the stress–diathesis model into better perspective. The diathesis is polygenic in nature, and involves the system of mood maintenance that regulates affective states of depression, dysphoria, and despondency. Hence, multiple genes could subtly contribute to the motivational predisposition toward depression and suicide. The stressor, on the other hand, may consist of any of a number of common but serious life crises. The stress can also be equated with exposure to evolutionarily novel circumstances.

Suicide as Altruistic Behavior

The first two models of suicide concern the pathological aspects of the self-destructive act—whether suicide is a pathological adjunct of the normally adaptive flexibility of human behavior, or whether suicide is an outcome of novel and stressful events paired with some individual predisposition toward affective disorder. The second two models suggest adaptive aspects of suicide, and provide some rationale for suicide from the perspective of sociobiology.

Assuming that there is some subtle, multiple-gene combination that subserves the cognitive–affective predisposition toward suicide, why would the pressures of natural selection permit this gene combination to persist? Both of the remaining two models address this question. For the purpose of this article, I pass over these two models rather quickly. Although they bear upon a general stress–diathesis theory of suicide, they lead beyond the scope of this discussion, into arguments concerning sociobiological theory.

The model of suicide as altruistic behavior suggests that self-destruction may occur because it has beneficial effects for individuals other than the suicidal individual. This model involves the sociobiological concept of inclusive fitness and capacity to reproduce, for the fitness of related, reproducing individuals who share many of their genes through common descent (de Catanzaro, 1981, p. 4). The concept of kin selection has been offered as an explanation for the transmission of homosexual behavior, or for parenting behaviors that might reduce the life span of the parent while promoting the fitness of offspring (Trivers, 1972; Wilson, 1978). In cases of suicide, kin selection may occur when the loss of one individual supports the survival of close relatives. de Catanzaro suggests that prosuicidal genetic factors may be expressed when the individual is or perceives that he or she is a burden to relatives: "Individuals may be motivated to act for the benefit of kin" (1980, p. 296). Furthermore, in cases of individuals who, through coping inabilities or other serious life failures, lack the capacity to reproduce and work toward the benefit of kin, the only opportunity they have to propagate their genes may lie in behavior promoting the welfare of their group or subpopulation. de Catanzaro suggests that self-destruction may be such a behavior (1981, p. 120). This suggestion leads into the fourth model.

Evolutionary Tolerance of Suicide

Aside from the model of suicide as altruism, de Catanzaro offers another explanation for why suicide might be tolerated by, or immune to the pressures of, natural selection. This explanation lies in the social epidemiology of the suicide act. Basically, the argument is that the risk for suicide varies inversely with an individual's reproductive potential or success: Suicide is more common among single and divorced individuals, individuals without dependent children, and those with unstable marriages than it is among those with stable marriages and young children. The frequency of suicide increases as a direct function of age, especially in men. Furthermore, as de Catanzaro argues (1980, p. 276), suicide is an act of desperation that occurs in extreme circumstances, especially among individuals who feel incapable of coping with present circumstances and expect little improvement in the future; their acceptable life conditions are seriously and permanently threatened. Accordingly, suicide is common not only among the elderly but among the terminally ill, among those with severe physical disability, and among those who have suffered economic hardship and see little chance for recovery. Assuming that adaptive coping behavior (e.g., proper eating, sleeping, sexual behavior, grooming, and working habits) promotes the individual's genes, then difficulty in coping would seem to entail difficulty in advancing one's genes (de Catanzaro, 1980). Among well-adapted individuals, selective pressure should act against self-destructive behavior. However, when individuals lose biological fitness and the capacity to further their genes—during old age or terminal illness, for example—

selective pressures would no longer operate. "A low capacity to promote one's genes, thus, appears to account well for all the best predictors of suicide" (de Catanzaro, 1981, p. 27).

Discussion and Critique

An evolutionary, biological perspective on suicide behavior is important in establishing a wider framework for analyzing the adaptive significance of stressors and the human response they engender. de Catanzaro's work is useful in this regard.[2] He has suggested how proximate mechanisms of chronic inescapable stress and coping failure interact with central neurotransmitter catecholamines and 5-HT. This neurochemical substrate, in certain individuals, may be genetically predisposed toward imbalance or deficit that is associated with suicidal or aggressive behavior. The predisposition or diathesis may, as recent research suggests, be a genetic or constitutional *flaw*, or, as de Catanzaro suggests, may be part of an *adaptive genetic mechanism* by which individuals with low capacity to further their genes undergo a disruption or throttling of self-promoting behavior. If we knew that certain individuals have a special liability or predisposition for suicide—whether owing in part to their individual genetic endowment or to their reproductive potential— this would allow us a more balanced assessment of the precise function of environmental stresses that trigger suicide in the predisposed individual.

However, de Catanzaro's study is open to criticism on a number of issues. First of all, his argument for the evolutionary tolerance of suicide rests on epidemiological data primarily from Western Europe and the United States, which show a fairly consistent increase in suicides with age. From these data, de Catanzaro infers that risk of suicide increases as reproductive potential decreases. Yet these data probably reflect, in large part, the negative cultural attitudes towards the aged and the social–environmental hardships that accompany aging in Western societies. Cross-cultural data do not consistently support the association of suicide frequency with increasing age. There are, for example, at least two well-documented counterexamples. One comes from rural Taiwan during the Japanese Colonial Administration (1895–1940). Early in this period, the suicide rate was highest among young married women, who were facing the dislocation stress, social isolation, and domestic conflict that accompanied their postmarital entrance into their husbands' households and their traditional domination by their mothers-in-law (Wolf, 1975, p. 111). With modernization, urbanization, and changes in family authority patterns, suicides among young females declined over two generations, while suicides among elderly women increased sharply. Here is at least one case showing that elderly suicide is associated with culture change and modernization.

Another example comes from recent research on Micronesian adolescent suicide (Rubinstein, 1983). In association with rapid sociocultural change during the past 25 years, suicide has reached epidemic proportions among young men. The onset for high risk of suicide occurs at about the age of sexual maturity (i.e., at age 15), which directly contradicts the hypothesis that suicide risk varies inversely with reproductive potential. de Catanzaro appears to have overgeneralized upon a modern, Western culture-specific suicide pattern, and to have assumed that this pattern is species-wide. By contrast, cross-cultural data indicate that the age and sex incidence of suicide is highly variable, and suicide behavior is thus more thoroughly shaped by culturally patterned environmental or social stresses than de Catanzaro's model allows.

Related to this claim that suicide nearly everywhere increases with age is the argument that suicide is most common in developed countries (de Catanzaro, 1980, p. 270). de Catanzaro attributes this to social isolation: The family unit has become relatively less stable and smaller, and thus individuals have less opportunity to promote the welfare of relatives sharing their genes. This argument is simply not supported by cross-cultural data. The comparability of suicide data between small tribal groups and modern nations is highly problematic, for one thing. Furthermore, scattered ethnographic evidence suggests that suicide rates may be highly variable in small traditional human groups living in a more or less "natural" condition. No global association is apparent between incidence of suicide and degree of modernization. This again argues for more culturally patterned and culturally specific frequencies and forms of suicide than de Catanzaro's model suggests. Hence, the first point of criticism with de Catanzaro's thesis is that he has not seriously considered much cross-cultural variability in suicide incidence, which challenges his main argument that suicide frequency increases as a function of age and declining reproductive potential.

A second point of criticism, somewhat related to the first, is that de Catanzaro probably overstates considerably the severity and permanence of the stressful conditions triggering suicides, and the degree of hopelessness and failure of the suicidal individual. This overstatement is important to the sociobiological model, since only individuals who have permanently lost their biological fitness should be candidates for self-destruction. de Catanzaro refers to the "chronic, intractable stress," the "serious, permanent threat to acceptable life-conditions," and the "extreme difficulties in coping" that motivate individuals to suicide (1980, p. 270). However, the general experience of workers in suicide and crisis centers refutes this characterization. Only a tiny percentage (about 2%) of suiciders who were "saved" or interrupted in seriously lethal acts afterwards expressed regret that they had not been allowed to die (Stengel, 1964). If they were indeed experiencing chronic stress and irreversible life conditions, one would expect them to complete the interrupted act at the first opportunity. de Catanzaro's characterization of the suicide victim seems drawn primarily from a clinical population of psychiatrically impaired individuals, institutionalized patients, terminally ill people, and so forth. For the purpose of an evolutionary hypothesis for suicide, it would be important to assess just how adaptively impaired the suicidal individual is and how significantly reduced his or her capacity to achieve biologically relevant goals is (McGuire & Essock-Vitale, 1981, 1982; McGuire, Essock-Vitale, & Polsky, 1981). The ambitious high school student who commits suicide after scoring low on a college entrance exam is certainly not experiencing "permanent intractable stress," yet such cases can be a frequent, culturally patterned occurrence. The point here is that suicide should not be analyzed as an indication of permanent coping failure or unremitting chronic stress, but as a transient, situationally organized, acute psychiatric crisis.[3] We might then speculate as to a plausible biological model for episodic disorders leading to breakdowns of normally adaptive, self-protective behavior.

A third point of criticism concerns the presumed connection between depression and suicide. In American folk theorizing on psychology, depression is an amorphous, widely encompassing category of mood or mental state, which can be used as an explanatory principle for innumerable deviant behaviors: from suicide to overeating (or undereating); from passive withdrawal to extreme hyperactivity; and even for bizarre behaviors such as borrowing gopher-like into a hole in the ground.[4] The psychiatric entity of clinical depressive disease is also an ill-defined category, difficult to diagnose differentially from other affective disorders. The diagnosis is partly definitional; disorders that respond successfully to antidepressant medication are diagnosed as depression. American and Western European folk theories of suicide commonly explain the act in terms of popular concepts about depression (Atkinson, 1978). Yet cross-cultural surveys show a wide variation in the association between depression and suicidal thinking: In some cultures more than two-thirds of depressed individuals reported suicidal ideation, while in other cultures no depressed individuals indicated suicidal thoughts (Jablensky, Sartorius, Gulbinat, & Ernberg, 1981). Thus, in arguing that 5-HT or some other neurotransmitter imbalance implicated in depressive disorders may "trigger" suicide, researchers are trading upon folk theories of suicide that attribute the act to depression. The linkages from stressor to physiological state (e.g., 5-HT deficit) to affective mood ("depression") to behavioral response (e.g., suicide) need to be elucidated much more thoroughly. Clearly these linkages, in the case of suicide, are heavily influenced by cultural conditioning.

Conclusions

The most valuable aspect of de Catanzaro's stress–diathesis theory of human suicide is the attempt to understand self-destructive behavior from a perspective of evolutionary adaptation. This situates suicide in a wider biological perspective, while intersecting with recent research on possible genetic or neurochemical bases for predisposition toward suicide. However, the sociobiological argument (i.e., that suicide is associated with reduced reproductive potential) seems to have little explanatory value and to misrepresent the variability in cross-cultural patterning of suicidal behavior.

If one accepts the assumption that suicidal behavior is often a fairly sudden, stress-induced, but transient psychiatric crisis or behavioral disorder in otherwise normal, potentially productive individuals—and not the last resort of hopeless, chronically stressed, and permanently impaired sufferers—then the question of the biological adaptiveness of suicidal behavior must be reconsidered. de Catanzaro's first two models (suicide as learned behavior, among predisposed individuals experiencing particular life stresses) could be expanded toward a more specific biocultural theory of suicide. It would be useful to consider suicide not simply as the by-product of human flexibility in learned behavior, but in particular association with adaptive human capacities for symbolic goal-setting and goal-seeking behavior, identity formation and maintenance, and superego development. In this sense, suicide occurs in situations of perceived failure, in situations involving loss of identity supports, or as self-punishment for perceived transgressions. The adaptive emotional system that subserves suicide is also the basis for attachment to symbolic goals, values, and ideals of self, and for close social bonding. Hence, a useful biocultural theory of suicide would address both the specific situational stressors and the categories or predisposing factors of vulnerable individuals in a given culture. It should also consider how individuals apprehend these situational stressors in terms of their cultural notions of shame, guilt, self-worth, and social identity. In order to understand the dynamics of the behavior, as well as perhaps to deal with the problem, this approach would be more productive than sociobiological speculation on altruism and reproductive potential.

Notes

1. This is especially so in small-scale communities with high levels of shared information, mutual identification, and face-to-face communication. Pacific Islands suicide data show clear modeling effects among suicides (see Bowles, 1985; Firth, 1961; Poole, 1985; Rubinstein, 1983).
2. For a good discussion of the potential usefulness of de Catanzaro's sociobiological perspective, see the review by Ayres (1982).
3. A good argument for situationally induced suicide and context-dependent personality is a study by Reynold and Farberow (1976).
4. The Honolulu *Advertiser* (Sept. 13, 1982) carried the following story under the headline "Burrowing Man Dies": "Police say a man . . . apparently believed he was a gopher, burrowed into a hole and suffocated. . . . His mother said he first started digging holes in April, staying in them for up to two weeks at a time. 'Last July, they dug him out of the same hole,' she said. 'I know he was depressed. He couldn't get a job.'"

References

Anisman, H. Depression and suicide: Stress as a precipitating factor. *Behavioral and Brain Sciences*, 1980, *3*, 272.

Atkinson, J. M. *Discovering suicide: Studies in the social organization of sudden death.* Pittsburgh: University of Pittsburgh Press, 1978.

Ayres, B. Review of *Suicide and self-damaging behavior: A sociobiological perspective* by D. de Catanzaro. *American Anthropologist*, 1982, *84*, 654.

Bohannan, P. (Ed.). *African homicide and suicide.* Princeton, N.J.: Princeton University Press, 1960.

Bowles, J. R. Suicide and attempted suicide in contemporary Western Samoa. In F. X. Hezel, D. H. Rubinstein, & G. W. White (Eds.), *Culture, youth and suicide in the Pacific: Papers from an East–West Center Conference.* Honolulu: Pacific Islands Studies Program Working Papers, University of Hawaii, 1985.

Brown, G. L., Ebert, M. H., Goyer, P. F., Jimerson, D. C., Klein, W. J., Bunney, W. E., & Goodwin, F. K. Aggression, suicide and serotonin: Relationships to CSF amine metabolites. *American Journal of Psychiatry*, 1982, *139(6)*, 741–746.

Coppen, A. Indoleamines and affective disorders. *Journal of Psychiatric Research*, 1972, *9*, 163.

Dawkins, R. Domesticity, senescence, and suicide. *Behavioral and Brain Sciences*, 1980, *3*, 274.

de Catanzaro, D. Human suicide: A biological perspective. *Behavioral and Brain Sciences*, 1980, *3*, 265.

de Catanzaro, D. *Suicide and self-damaging behavior: A sociobiological perspective.* New York: Academic Press, 1981.

Durkheim, E. *Suicide: A study in sociology* (G. Simpson, Ed.). Glencoe, Ill.: Free Press, 1965. (Originally published, 1897.)

Farberow, N. L. *Suicide in different cultures.* Baltimore: University Park Press, 1975.

Firth, T. Suicide and risk-taking in Tikopia society. *Psychiatry*, 1961, *24*, 1.

Gibbs, J. P., & Martin, W. T. *Status integration and suicide.* Eugene, Oregon: University of Oregon Books, 1964.

Greenberg, J. Suicide linked to brain chemical deficit. *Science News*, May 29, 1982, p. 355.

Headley, L. *Suicide in Asia and the Near East.* Berkeley: University of California Press, 1983.

Huston, P. E. Psychotic depressive reaction. In A. M. Freedman, H. I. Kaplan, & B. J. Sadock (Eds.), *Comprehensive textbook of psychiatry* (2nd ed.). Baltimore: Williams & Wilkins, 1975.

Jablensky, A., Sartorius, N., Gulbinat, W., & Ernberg, G. Characteristics of depressive patients contacting psychiatric services in four cultures: A report from the WHO Collaborative Study on the Assessment of Depressive Disorders. *Acta Psychiatrica Scandinavica*, 1981, *63*, 367.

Kaplan, H. I., Sadock, B. J., & Freedman, A. M. The brain and psychiatry. In A. M. Freedman, H. I. Kaplan, & B. J. Sadock (Eds.), *Comprehensive textbook of psychiatry* (2nd ed.). Baltimore: Williams & Wilkins, 1975.

Kety, S. S. Biochemistry of the major psychoses. In A. M. Freedman, H. I. Kaplan, & B. J. Sadock (Eds.), *Comprehensive textbook of psychiatry* (2nd ed.). Baltimore: Williams & Wilkins, 1975.

Linn, L. Other psychiatric emergencies. In A. M. Freedman, H. I. Kaplan, & B. J. Sadock, (Eds.), *Comprehensive textbook of psychiatry* (2nd ed.). Baltimore: Williams & Wilkins, 1975.

McGuire, M. T., & Essock-Vitale, S. M. Psychiatric Disorders in the context of evolutionary biology: A functional classification of behavior. *Journal of Nervous and Mental Disease*, 1981, *169(11)*, 672.

McGuire, M. T., & Essock-Vitale, S. M. Psychiatric disorders in the context of evolutionary biology: The impairment of adaptive behaviors during the exacerbation and remission of psychiatric illness. *Journal of Nervous and Mental Disease*, 1982, *170(1)*, 9.

McGuire, M. T., Essock-Vitale, S. M., & Polsky, R. H. Psychiatric disorders in the context of evolutionary biology: An ethological model of behavioral changes associated with psychiatric disorders. *Journal of Nervous and Mental Disease*, 1981, *169(11)*, 687.

Murphy, D. L., Campbell, I., & Costa, J. L. Current status of the indoleamine hypothesis of the affective disorders. In M. A. Lipton, A. DiMascio, & K. F. Killam (Eds.), *Psychopharmacology: A generation of progress*. New York: Raven Press, 1978.

Poole, F. J. P. Among the boughs of the hanging tree: Male suicide among the Bimin-Kuskusmin of Papua New Guinea. In F. X. Hezel, D. H. Rubinstein, & G. W. White (Eds.), *Culture, youth and suicide in the Pacific: Papers from an East–West Center Conference*. Honolulu: Pacific Islands Studies Program Working Papers, University of Hawaii, 1985.

Rainer, J. D. Genetics and psychiatry. In A. M. Freedman, H. I. Kaplan, & B. J. Sadock (Eds.), *Comprehensive textbook of psychiatry* (2nd ed.). Baltimore: Wlliams & Wilkins, 1975.

Reynold, D. K., & Farberow, N. L. *Suicide inside and out*. Berkeley: University of California Press, 1976.

Rubinstein, D. Epidemic suicide among Micronesian adolescents. *Social Science and Medicine*, 1983, *17(10)*, 657–665.

Serotonin malfunction may trigger suicide. *The NIH Record*, August 31, 1982, p. 9.

Snyder, S. H. Basic science of psychopharmacology. In A. M. Freedman, H. I. Kaplan, & B. J. Sadock (Eds.), *Comprehensive textbook of psychiatry* (2nd ed.). Baltimore: Williams & Wilkins, 1975.

Stanley, M., Virgilio, J., & Gershon, S. Tritiated imipramine binding sites are decreased in the frontal cortex of suicides. *Science*, 1982, *216*, 1337–1339.

Stengel, E. *Suicide and attempted suicide*. Baltimore: Penguin Books, 1964.

Trivers, R. L. Parental investment and sexual selection. In B. Campbell (Ed.), *Sexual selection and the descent of man*. Chicago: Aldine, 1972.

Wilson, E. O. *On human nature*. Cambridge, Mass.: Harvard University Press, 1978.

Wolf, M. Women and suicide in China. In M. Wolf & R. Witke (Eds.), *Women in Chinese society*. Stanford, Calif.: Stanford University Press, 1975.

CHAPTER 6

Electroconvulsive Therapy and Suicide

Bryan L. Tanney, MD, FRCP (C)
University of Calgary

Electroconvulsive therapy (ECT) is an established and effective biological treatment modality for some mental disorders. If there is a specific biological disorder that is either a cause or a mechanism for suicidal behaviors, the possibility of using ECT as a specific treatment should be considered. Little support for either specific effectiveness of ECT for suicidal behaviors or a specific biological disorder that characterizes suicidal behaviors has been found. Clinical experience suggests a further exploration involving those disorders in which ECT has been found to be an effective treatment modality and in which suicidal behaviors are a recognized complication. In the syndromes of the affective disorders, the effectiveness of ECT in diminishing, reducing, and preventing suicidal behavior has been confirmed. This activity is assumed to be a consequence of the treatment's effectiveness for only some types or presentations of these disorders. When the effectiveness and mortality–morbidity of ECT are compared with those of drug therapies, it appears that ECT is an effective and preferred treatment strategy. It remains underutilized as a modality of suicide prevention. The controversies that presently limit the use of this treatment are briefly addressed.

An Introduction to ECT

Definition

ECT is a biological treatment procedure involving the application of measured amounts of electrical energy to specific dysfunctional parts of the human brain under controlled conditions. The procedure must be repeated a number of times before it is effective. There is no specific anatomically dysfunctional site of brain function that is targeted by the treatment procedure.

Description

The electrical stimulus is applied to the exterior of the skull, with specific attention to anatomical placement of the electrodes and to interelectrode distance. Electrode placement is usually over the hemispheres, either bilaterally or unilaterally. Though some controversy remains, both placements are accepted as therapeutically effective. The unilateral placement appears to reduce the transient memory impairment and organic confusional state that are side effects of the procedure (Fontaine & Young, 1985).

Electrical energy is introduced with careful attention to a number of parameters. At present, Cronholm and Ottosson's (1960) contention that sufficient energy to induce a "convulsive" seizure is required remains the therapeutic standard. Recently, the assertion that a threshold exists for therapeutic effectiveness has generated concern that more electrical energy is being applied than is required (Sackheim, Decina, Prohounik, Portnoy, Kanzler, & Malitz, 1985). There is increasing sophistication in the specification of these electrical parameters: current and voltage; polarity and direction of the stimulus waveform; pulse duration specifying the individual pulse width, interpulse interval, pulse frequency, and total stimulus duration. The energy and total energy applied during treatments can be calculated. At present, there are at least five commercially available devices that can provide for these modifications in the type and amount of electrical energy required.

The patient experiences the treatment under controlled, comfortable, and safe conditions. These include brief anesthesia with loss of consciousness; oxygenation; adequate muscular relaxation that is drug-induced; and specific measurement of cardiovascular and brain electrical functions. In most treatment programs, experienced teams are responsible for the procedure, including psychiatrists, anesthesiologists, respiratory technologists, and nurses.

The treatment procedure is usually repeated two or three times weekly for an average total of 7 to 10 individual applications. Efforts to shorten this time frame by multiple applications of electrical energy during one anesthetic, or more closely spaced treatments, have not provided significant treatment advantages. There is no apparent development of tolerance to the procedure, and it can be successfully reapplied during recurrent episodes of the index condition, or for other indications as required.

History

ECT was introduced during the 1930s and has been used continuously since that time throughout the world. Insulin-coma therapy and psychosurgery are other biological treatment modalities that were introduced in that same decade. Their use has since been abandoned or occurs under extremely specific conditions. As with any newly introduced treatment, the effectiveness of ECT was explored in a wide variety of disorders. The results of open trials, open comparative trials, open controlled trials, and partially controlled trials are well documented. There have been two major periods in which simulated or sham ECT was used in "placebo-controlled," double-blind studies.

Mechanisms of Action

Although no specific biological mechanism to explain ECT's effectiveness has yet been demonstrated, there are changes in brain biology as a result of the treatment (Table 6-1). With respect to effects on neurochemical transmission in the brain, ECT does not appear to produce any changes in affinity between neurotransmitters and their specific receptors. It does induce changes in the number and/or density of available receptor sites for particular neurotransmitters. The most important effects on receptor density are believed to involve the down-regulation of beta-1-noradrenergic receptors (Pandey, Heinze, Brown, & Davis, 1979) and an increase in receptor binding activity at the serotonin, Type 2 (5-HT$_2$) binding sites (NYAS, 1985). The changes in receptor density are believed to result from stabilization of the cell membrane, which alters the internalization of the receptor for the purposes of storage or breakdown, or simply withdraws the receptor from availability to the neurotransmitters found in the external cellular environment.

TABLE 6-1. The Effects of ECT on Brain Biology

Parameter or function	Effect
EEG low-frequency power index	Increased
Seizure threshold	Increased
Regional cerebral blood flow	Decreased
Glucose utilization	Decreased (postictal)
Hormones: Prolactin	Spike
Electrostimulation	Increased synaptogenesis (D2 fraction)
Membrane "stabilization"	—
Receptor density of neurotransmitters	Altered

Tricyclic antidepressant drugs are noted to affect the same receptor sites, although they decrease 5-HT$_2$ receptor activity.

As the origin of many of the disorders for which ECT is effective is still unknown, it is difficult to specify which of these many changes in biological function are primary in the therapeutic process. Though there remains some diminishing resistance to the idea, it is generally accepted that the mechanisms of therapeutic efficacy result from some change in biological parameters, and not from some psychological meanings (pain, punishment, or shock) attributed to the treatment on the part of the patient (Ottosson, 1968).

ECT and Suicidal Behaviors

Suicidal behaviors represent a broad and possibly discontinuous spectrum of human thoughts, feelings, and behaviors. These range from threats through indirect self-destructive behaviors to gestures, attempts, and completed self-destruction. Their origin is understood to be both multi-determined and multidimensional.

There has been some effort to identify deliberate self-harm activity as a specific disorder within the descriptive framework of DSM-III (Kahan & Pattison, 1984). Among possible etiologies for this disorder, there is some evidence for a genetic, not familial, basis to suicidal behaviors (Schulsinger, Kety, Rosenthal, & Wender, 1979) that is independent of the transmission of depression or another major mental disorder. This genetic effect might be mediated through a diminished function of the 5-HT neurotransmitter system (see Chapter 10, this volume). Six postmortem reports and the consistent, but not universal, findings of a decreased level of 5-HT and its metabolite 5-HIAA in the cerebrospinal fluid of "violent" and seriously intent suicidal attempters and completers (Asberg, Traskman, & Thoren, 1976) support this possibility. If ECT is specifically effective in diminishing suicidal behaviors, its action to increase 5-HT$_2$ receptor activity offers more support for diminished 5-HT function as a specific biological indicator of suicidal predisposition.

Suicidal behaviors are best appreciated as a symptom complex arising as a final common pathway or solution to a large variety of biological, psychological, and sociocultural stressors. Since the condition can prove fatal, there is every justification for the use of and search for specific treatment modalities that might alleviate the danger without necessarily solving or curing the disorder.

One approach to assessing the value of ECT as a specific treatment that reduces the likelihood of suicidal behaviors is to study the response of suicidal ideas, intent, and behaviors to its use. Suicidal ideation and/ or a history of suicide attempts were included as variables in a series of studies that sought to develop predictors of the outcome of ECT. Suicidal behaviors did not appear as a feature that would predict or be associated with the outcome of ECT in any of the five studies (Carney, Roth, & Garside, 1965; Hamilton & White, 1960; Hobson, 1953; Mendels, 1965; Roberts, 1959).

Abrams, Fink, and Feldstein (1973) found the response to ECT to be unrelated to any symptom pattern, but they included suicidal symptoms as a measure of the treatment response and not as a possible predictor. In analyzing the results of the Northwick Park ECT trial, their Factor 1, which defined severity of depression to include suicidal risk, did not relate to improvement with real versus simulated ECT (Crow, Deukin, Johnstone, MacMillan, & Owens, 1984).

In this series of studies on factors predicting ECT response, some variant of multiple or stepwise regression was the most common statistical tool. If suicidal behaviors were appearing at a quite low base rate of frequency within the study samples, it would have been most unlikely for them to appear as an important predictive variable when these techniques were used. Depressed patients, in whom suicidal behavior is a commonly recognized complication, were the focus in all of the studies. This makes it unlikely that this methodological defect would have accounted for the failure to discover a relationship between suicidal inclination and ECT responsiveness.

Avery and Winokur (1977) suggest that those with a history of suicide attempts or suicide thoughts are more likely to be markedly improved at discharge when treated with ECT (56% and 54% for those with attempts and thoughts, respectively) compared to no treatment (26% and 29%) or to adequate antidepressant drug therapy (23% and 14%). Avery and Lubrano's (1979) analysis of the data of DeCarolis, Gibert, Roccatagliata, *et al.* (1964) suggests that severely depressed patients (defined as those with suicide ideation and psychomotor activity changes) respond well to ECT, if they are unresponsive to antidepressant treatment. These two studies offer comparative data. They cannot be regarded as strong support for a specific effectiveness of ECT in the presence of suicide ideation, because numerous studies have reported a poor response to antidepressant drug treatments in those with suicide ideation, suicide tendencies, or suicide attempts (Bielski & Friedel, 1976; Kiloh, Ball, & Garside, 1962; Paykel, 1972; Robin & Langley, 1964).

As no study could be found in the English-language literature directly measuring the effectiveness of ECT in persons with suicidal behaviors, it was surprising to find that the presence of suicidal behaviors is regarded as a strong symptomatic indication for this therapy in most textbooks of psychiatry. No fewer than 13 of 16 North American and 6 of 9 British texts specifically mention suicide as an indication for ECT (references are available from me). On further examination of the textbook indications for ECT, it is important to note that 16 of the 19 texts that point out the effectiveness of ECT for suicidal behaviors do so in sections discussing the overall treatment of affective disorders. Only 2 of the total of 25 texts prescribe ECT for the "symptomatic relief" of suicidal ideation or intent. This implies that the effectiveness of ECT in suicidal behaviors is not a direct, specific action, but is mediated through the treatment's impact in relieving affective disorders. This is a similar argument to that advanced by Barraclough (1972), and others for lithium. Lithium decreases the occurrence of completed suicide in persons with bipolar affective disorders by effectively relieving the disordered affective–cognitive–behavioral state. Suicidal behaviors are not specifically affected by the treatments with lithium or ECT, but are noted to occur less frequently because the disorders for which suicide represents a particularly serious and fatal complication are being effectively relieved by the biological therapies. For example, the decrease in suicidal ideation with imipramine and ECT in the British Medical Research Council's trial (Medical Research Council, 1965) is accounted for as part of the general improvement in depressive symptomatology that occurs with these therapies, and not with placebo or phenelzine.

To determine the strength and usefulness of this derivative or indirect helping effect of ECT on suicidal behaviors, the entire range of disorders that are complicated by suicidal behavior should be examined. If there are specific therapeutic effects of ECT in these disorders, the contention for a helping effect of ECT as a treatment modality in reducing the frequency of suicidal behaviors will be reinforced.

Medical–Mental Disorders Complicated by Suicide

Several recent studies have argued for a very high frequency of completed suicide as a complication of the schizophrenic disorders (Johns, 1985; Roy, 1982).Other medical disorders that have been noted to be complicated by the presence of suicidal behaviors include personality disorders (antisocial, hysterical, borderline); epilepsy; pain syndromes; and mental handicap. Affective disorders and substance abuse (alcohol and drugs) are the psychological states noted prior to death in the majority of completed suicides (Barraclough, Bunch, Nelson, *et al.*, 1974; Murphy, Wilkinson, Robins, *et al.*, 1959). Juel-Nielsen (1979) reviews the Scandinavian evidence for high suicide risk in recurrent affective disorders. Goodwin and Jamison's (in press) review, supplementing Guze and Robin's (1970) classic paper for a total of 27 studies, supports an important relationship between the presence of affective disorders and completed suicide. The remainder of the present review of the potential value of ECT focuses on the largest diagnostic group in which suicidal behaviors are most commonly found—the affective disorders.

The Effectiveness of ECT in Affective Disorders

The studies to be reviewed encompass a half-century of scientific study. It is important to realize that much progress has been made during this time in understanding the origins of the affective disorders. With this knowledge have come efforts to subgroup and to classify this extremely common group of mental disorders in numerous ways. This has created a tremendous complexity of overlapping terminologies, which reflect both different theories and different eras. Some of the major terms used during the past half century in North America and Europe to name those affective disorders accompanied by a significant biological disturbance include "involutional melancholia"; "involutional psychosis"; "depressive psychosis"; "manic–depressive disorder, depressed stage"; "bipolar depression"; "unipolar depression" (some); "endogenous depression"; and "psychotic depression."

There is clear agreement concerning the indications for ECT in surveys of the psychiatrists who might use it. ECT is "appropriate" or "the treatment of choice" for the following:

- Major affective disorders (Pankratz, 1978)
- Depressive psychoses (Pippard & Ellam, 1981)
- Depressive disorders: psychotic; involutional; postpartum; manic–depressive, depressed (Asnis, Fink, & Saferstein, 1978)
- Depressive psychosis, depressive mood state, and depressive delusions (Gill & Lambourn, 1979)
- Manic–depressive/depressed (American Psychiatric Association, 1978)

Other endorsed indications that have achieved some agreement across surveys include manic excitement, catatonia, and some types of schizophrenic (schizoaffective) disorders.

Scovern and Kilmann (1980) summarize outcome studies with ECT: "The most sophisticated of the studies from a methodologic viewpoint . . . are remarkably consistent in demonstrating the superiority of ECT for depression" (p. 281). Double-blind and controlled studies, conducted in two different eras over the past quarter century, have confirmed the effectiveness of ECT in the treatment of depressive disorders. All six studies in the period 1978–1985 (Brandon, Cowley, McDonald, Neville, Palmer, & Wellstood-Eason, 1984; Freeman, Basson, & Crichton, 1978; Gregory, Shawcross, & Gill, 1985; Johnstone, Deakin, Lawler, Frith, Stevens, McPherson, & Crow, 1980; Lambourn & Gill, 1978; West, 1981) included a control, placebo, or "sham" ECT group, in which patients received all of the components of the procedure except the application of electrical energy sufficient to produce convulsive seizure activity.

The use of ECT is also suggested for affective disorders of the bipolar (manic–depressive) type during the manic phase. In the early era of open comparative trials, five studies documented the effectiveness of ECT for manic patients McCabe (1976) reported results favoring ECT in a comparison of manic patients, who received an average of 17 treatments, with a group of manic controls from an early era. Small, Milstein, Klapper, Kelkems, Miller, and Small (1985) found that 8 out of 10 non-rapid-cycling, bipolar, manic patients who received bilateral ECT improved, compared to 6 of 11 on lithium. As part of a rebirth in awareness of its effectiveness, Roy-Byrne, Gerner, Liston, and Robertson (1981) have called attention to ECT as a "forgotten treatment modality" for acute mania.

ECT has also been reported as an effective treatment for schizoaffective disorders (Tsuang, Dempsey, & Fleming, 1979).

The Effect of ECT on Suicidal Behavior in Affective Disorders

Several different methods have been used to investigate the impact of ECT on the frequency of suicidal behaviors in affective disorders. A number of studies (Table 6-2) have compared the number of suicidal deaths in different treatment eras. Although information about diagnosis is not specified in these studies, it is most likely that the majority of the ECT was used on the affectively disordered patients for whom it is demonstrably most effective. Three of four studies reported a decreased frequency of suicides during the years when ECT treatment was available for affective disorders, although Levy and Southcombe (1953) did not attribute the decrease to a specific treatment effect.

Although interesting, these studies are not as valuable as investigations concerning the response of individual patients, in the presence of an appropriate control group (Table 6-3). Five of the six controlled studies have supported a role for ECT in reducing suicidal behaviors in depressed patients. The most recent study (Babigian & Guttmacher, 1984) found no advantage to ECT in preventing suicide within 5 years

TABLE 6-2. The Effect of ECT on Suicidal Behaviors: Comparing Different Treatment Eras

Study	Study location	Total number of suicides	Frequency of suicidal behaviors in ECT era	Comment
Pre-ECT versus (electro)convulsive therapies				
Levy & Southcombe (1953)	Washington	58	Decreased	Result not attributed to treatment effect.
Impastato (1961)	New York	—	Decreased	
Beisser & Blanchette (1961)	California	75	No change	
Lonnquist, Niskanen, Rinta-Manty, Achte, & Karha (1974)	Finland (1841–1971)	47	Decreased	
ECT versus Tricyclic Antidepressant Pharmacotherapy				
Impastato (1961)	New York	—	Decreased	Result not attributed to treatment effect.
Lonnquist (1974)	Finland (1841–1971)	—	Decreased	
Beisser & Blanchette (1961)	California	—	Decreased	Comparison to era of "tranquilizers."

Study	Location (period)		Result	Comments
Kline (1959)	Northeastern USA	—	No change	Surveys of clinical populations in predrug era.
Hussar (1962)	New York (1952–1955/1956–1959)	15	Decreased	Compared groups of similar size.
Chapman (1965)	Kansas (1946–1962)	18	No change	Results not attributed to treatment effect, as suicide increased in general population during (later) drug era.
Krieger (1966)	California (1955–1959/1960–1964)	38	Decreased	
Flatten (1975)	Norway	—	Decreased	Suicide attempts only; treatments mixed in each era.
Hesso & Retterstol (1975)	Norway (1950–1954/1960–1964)	78	Decreased	
Avery & Winokur (1978)	Iowa (1959–1963/1964–1968)	17	Decreased	

TABLE 6-3. The Effect of ECT on Suicide Outcome in Affective Disorders: Controlled Studies

Study	Study population Diagnosis	n's	Follow-up duration (years)	Treatment	Suicide outcome (%)	Comment
Ziskind, Somerfeld-Ziskind, & Ziskind (1945)	Affective psychoses: involutional melancholia; manic–depressive, depressed	109 88	3.3 3.3	— ECT	8.3 1.1	
Huston & Locher (1948a)	Involutional psychoses— melancholic	93 61	6.5 3.0	— ECT	13 1.6	Three-fourths of controls who committed suicide did so within 2 years.
Huston & Locher (1948b)	Manic–depressive, depressed	80 74	6.8 3.0	— ECT	7.5 1.4	Five-sixths of controls who committed suicide did so within 2 years.
Avery & Winokur (1976)	Depression—mixed subtypes	70 135 122	3.0 3.0 3.0	— ECT ECT + TCA	2.9 0.7 2.5	No-treatment group consisted of younger females with neurotic depression.
Avery & Winokur (1978)	Depression—mixed subtypes	71 257	0.5 0.5	TCA ECT ± TCA	4.2 0.8	Outcome figure represents suicide attempts.
Babigian & Guttmacher (1984)	Depression	3111 818	5.0 5.0	— ECT	1.4 1.6	
Seager (1958a)	Depression	206	2.0	ECT	3.9	
Seager (1958b)	Depression	118	0.5	ECT	1.7	Both of the 2 suicides were in neurotic depression subgroup.

of first psychiatric hospitalization for depression in patients followed through the Psychiatric Case Register of Monroe County, New York. This study includes patients treated from 1961 to 1975 when antidepressants and other psychotropic drugs were available for inpatient as well as continuation and maintenance therapies. More information about the range of treatments employed in both ECT and non-ECT patients both during and after hospitalization is needed before interpreting this finding. The works of Avery and Winokur (1976, 1978) reported different outcomes (completions vs. attempts) and different follow-up periods, but they used the same population of patients in both studies. They found an advantage to ECT in preventing suicide even when TCA's were available. Two additional studies (Seager, 1958a, 1958b) have provided data on the suicide rate at follow-ups of 2 years and 6 months, respectively, for a total of 324 depressions of mixed subtypes treated with ECT.

Karagulla (1950) and Bond (1954) combined the two approaches in retrospective studies with depressed patients from different treatment eras (Table 6-4). Their 5-year follow-ups found no advantage for ECT in altering suicide outcomes, although only 7 out of 14 suicidal deaths in Bond's "convulsive therapies" group had actually received ECT. Karagulla's overall findings of no advantages for the ECT group over the control group stand virtually alone in the literature from the pre-ECT era, and they have been refuted by Slater (1951).

The weight of evidence from these three groups of studies suggests a beneficial effect of ECT in decreasing the outcome of suicide or suicidal behaviors in patients with depressive disorders.

With respect to suicide in manic–depressive or bipolar patients in the manic phase, Robins et al. (1959) and Winokur, Clayton, and Reich (1969) both suggest that suicidal outcomes are uncommon. McCabe (1976) does not mention suicidal behaviors in his study of manic patients who received ECT. The presentation of a mixed state may increase the risk of suicide in a manic–depressive patient.

Tsuang et al. (1979) reported on the mortality at more than 25 years of follow-up for a group of 74 schizoaffective patients. Three of the 19 deaths were regarded as suicide or undetermined. All 3 were from the group ($n = 50$) who had not been treated with ECT.

This decrease in suicide outcome noted in affective disorders of several types is most often attributed to the rapid response of the disorder to ECT. With a more rapid response, the period of risk for suicidal behavior is correspondingly decreased. As reflected by a decreased period of hospitalization, ECT shortened the duration of the illness episode in five of seven reports (Table 6-5). Four of the six 1978–1985 studies of sham/simulated versus real ECT mention the rapid response of depressive

TABLE 6-4. The Effect of ECT on Suicide Outcome in Affective Disorders: Comparing Different Treatment Eras

| Study | Study population | | Follow-up duration (years) | Treatment | Suicide outcome (%) | Comment |
	Diagnosis	n's				
Karagulla (1950)	Depressive states	Pre-1940: 489	5	No ECT	1.4	64% of no-ECT suicides occurred during hospitalization
		1940–1948: 256	5	No ECT	2.7	
		1940–1948: 178	< 5	ECT	3.9	
Bond (1954)	Involutional psychoses	1925–1934: 123	5	No ECT	5.6	Only 7 out of 14 suicides in convulsive therapy group had had ECT.
		1940–1946: 90	5	Convulsive therapies	5.5	

TABLE 6-5.   The Effect of ECT on Duration of Hospital Stay for Affective Disorders

Study	Duration of hospital stay or % discharged	
	Control	ECT
Huston & Locher (1948a)	21 months (median 7)	6 months (median 1.5)
Huston & Locher (1948b)	21.1 months (median 15)	12.6 months (median 9)
Oltman & Friedman (1950)	18% at 2 months	70% at 2 months
Karagulla (1950)[a]	Group 1: 20% F, 23% M at 2 months; Group 2: 33% F, 37% M at 2 months	18% F, 7% M at 2 months
Bond (1954)[b]	4.5 months	2.3 months
Medical Research Council (1965)	25% at 5 weeks	42% at 5 weeks
Babigian & Guttmacher (1984)	17.8 days	32.3 days

[a] Study used two control groups and divided groups into males (M) and females (F).
[b] Treatment group in this study received insulin coma or ECT.

symptomatology to the real procedure (Brandon *et al.*, 1984; Freeman *et al.*, 1978; Gregory *et al.*, 1985; Johnstone *et al.*, 1980). In the Leicestershire trial (Brandon *et al.*, 1984), the rapid treatment response has been specifically mentioned as a reason to use ECT in suicidally depressed patients, perhaps because the only reported suicide in the studies using a sham ECT group occurred in a patient who was part of the simulation/control group.

Mortality and Morbidity with ECT

Mortality

In assessing the effectiveness of any treatment, it is important to assess both benefits and relative risks. In a review of 20 reported studies from 1942 through 1977, excluding isolated case reports, the mortality due to ECT has remained remarkably low, and has decreased with the use of improved procedures (references are available from me). A mortality rate of approximately 5 deaths per 100,000 treatments has been calculated, on average, over the past quarter century. Assuming that the average course of treatments during this era has consisted of fewer than 10 per patient, the death of less than 1 patient in every 2,000 who received ECT must be considered remarkably safe. A large number of the deaths in the initial era of use were attributed to cardiovascular collapse or complications (Impastato, 1957; Maclay, 1953) although an increased mortality from cardiovascular disease had already been noted in patients with affective disorders (those most likely to receive ECT).

In the modern era, almost all deaths during an ECT procedure can be attributed to anesthesia complications or misadventures. The mortality rate with ECT is similar to, or less than, the mortality rate due to general anesthesia given for nonspecific procedures.

Morbidity

Early Relapse.   The affective disorders that respond to ECT are often those with a course of recurrent episodes. With no further treatment following ECT, Thomas (1954) found a 23% recurrence rate of endogenous depressions at a 1-year follow-up, and Herrington, Bruce, Johnstone, and Lader (1974) had 15% of their patients with severe depressions relapse within 6 months of discharge. Salzman (1947) stated that the use of ECT shortened the interval between recurrences in his study group of manic–depressives and schizophrenics, with more relapses and faster readmissions. Ziskind *et al.* (1945), Huston and Locher (1948a, 1948b), Oltman & Friedman (1950), Fetterman, Victoroff, and Horrocks (1951), and Avery and Winokur (1978) did not confirm this observation. Kiloh, Child, and Latner (1960) reported an increased incidence of relapses with ECT, compared to the "active placebo" iproniazid. This is probably due to the large difference in the initial improvement rate of ECT versus iproniazid (89% vs. 11%), for there were more members in the group of ECT-improved patients who might experience subsequent relapse. There appears to be no evidence that ECT either hastens recurrence or predisposes subsequent depressions.

Increased Seizure Activity.   Early work, suggesting the use of ECT in epilepsy, supported the view that ECT did not increase the frequency of later seizure activity. Blackwood, Cull, Freeman, Evans, and Maudsley (1980) found 4 of 166 patients treated with ECT who had seizures in the 2 years following therapy. In 2 of these patients, seizure activity was attributed to ECT as a likely cause, but the authors indicated that the convulsive activity rarely persisted for greater than 1 year. Devinsky and Duchowny (1983) surveyed 19 studies for a total sample of 81 patients treated with ECT and followed for more than 18 months. They found that the age-adjusted incidence of seizure activity was eight times that of nontreated patients. They were particularly impressed by the possibility of "kindling" as an etiology for this increase in seizure activity in the ECT group.

Brain Damage. Breggin (1979) has asserted a causative relationship between shock treatment and brain damage. His data are drawn from experimental animals and from older reports or individual case studies, with the majority of these from the era of uncontrolled and unmodified ECT. This concern about the safety of ECT was a major stimulus to the sham/simulation studies of ECT that are now available to confirm it as a rapid and effective treatment procedure.

In a monumental review, Weiner (1984) has stated, "For the typical individual receiving ECT, no detectable correlates of irreversible brain damage appear to occur" (p. 1), although quickly admitting that selected patients might have a possible defect in autobiographical memory function. Meldrum (1985) reviewed studies in cats, rats, monkeys, and baboons, concluding that there was no evident damage to brain cells during or resulting from ECT. He found that a period of 90–120 minutes of sustained seizure activity was required in rats before changes of structure and function in regions susceptible to anoxia were demonstrable. These changes were often reversible within a short time. In their study of 98 patients with status epilepticus, Aminoff and Simon (1980) found that 5 of the 6 patients with outcomes of permanent neurological damage or death and in whom the duration of seizure activity was known had had continuous seizure activity for longer than 2 hours. The usual duration of seizure activity during ECT is less than 1 minute, and most clinicians curtail seizure activity continuing for more than 4 minutes with intravenous diazepam.

Memory Loss. There has been no demonstration that the ability to learn new material, verbal or nonverbal, is impaired with ECT (Weiner, 1984). ECT does produce a transient organic confusional state, characterized as a disorientation delirium, which appears to affect the brain's ability to transfer retained memories from short-term to long-term storage. Clinically, this creates a definable memory defect, apparently permanent, for the days or weeks surrounding the treatment (Squire, Slater, & Miller, 1981). This adverse affect appears to involve both verbal and nonverbal memory storage, but the duration of the transfer-to-storage defect is limited and clearly resolves within days or weeks of the end of treatment. Duration is effected by electrode placement (unilateral or bilateral), waveform characteristics, and the number and spacing of treatment applications (Fontaine & Young, 1985). New ECT devices, with their ability to deliver measurable and defined amounts of electrical energy, minimize the extent of memory complaints.

There is little objective evidence for a loss of remote personal memories. The issue, however, is not entirely settled. There are individuals willing to provide personal descriptions of the long-term, seemingly permanent, adverse consequences of the treatment upon their memory. Freeman, Kendell, and Week (1985) reported the presence of differences ($p <$ .05) on several measures, including reaction time and verbal learning, among normal controls and those who received ECT with or without later complaints of memory loss. As differences on the Wakefield Depression Scale were also found, it is important to recall that one of the more common and distressing findings in depressive disorders is a measurable as well as a subjectively perceived memory deficit.

Alternative Therapies: Comparisons of ECT and Antidepressant Drug Treatments

Affective Disorders

Pharmacotherapy for affective disorders was widely introduced during the 1960s and targeted the groups of affective disorders that had previously been widely and successfully treated with ECT. Over the next 20 years, these drug treatments, usually employing tricyclic antidepressants (TCAs) or monoamine oxidase inhibitors (MAOIs), largely replaced ECT. This is surprising, because extensive reviews of the effectiveness of these two treatment modalities have been unable to document any well-designed study in which the antidepressant medications were more effective than the ECT on measures including rapidity of response, discharge rate, degree of improvement, and duration of hospitalization (Barton, 1977; Fink, 1978; Scovern & Kilmann, 1980; Turek & Hanlon, 1977). The two largest and best-designed trials comparing drug therapies and ECT (Greenblatt, Grosser, & Wechsler, 1964; Medical Research Council, 1965) reported a clear advantage in short-term outcome to those patients who received ECT, although the Medical Research Council's trial found it only for women. One of the most common criticisms directed against these comparative studies involves the possible use of inadequate or nontherapeutic doses of the TCA medications. In a number of studies that have examined this variable, either the clear advantage in treatment effectiveness (for properly selected affective disorders), remains in favor of ECT (Avery & Winokur, 1977; Wilson, Vernon, Guinn, & Sandifer, 1963), or no significant difference has been found between the treatments (Hordern, Burt, & Holt, 1965). Coryell (1978) used an innovative treatment design comparing the response of the same patient to ECT and TCAs during different episodes of the patient's recurrent affective illness. Of the 18 episodes of ECT, 17 resulted in complete recovery (94%). When the same patient received TCA therapy for a later depressive episode, complete recovery was noted in only 8 of 15 episodes (53%).

Suicidal Behaviors

Despite the apparent advantages for ECT over antidepressant drug treatment, it is important to look for a possible differential effectiveness of these two treatments on the likelihood of suicidal behaviors. In the studies that have compared ECT and TCA drug therapy by comparing numbers of suicides across different treatment eras (see the bottom portion of Table 6-2), there is again a clear advantage in decreased frequency of suicides for the ECT era. Avery and Winokur (1976) did not find a difference in suicide mortality at a 3-year follow-up between ECT (1 suicide in 135 cases) and adequate treatment with antidepressants (1 suicide in 71 patients). In a later study documenting suicide attempts within 6 months of discharge in the same patient populations (Avery & Winokur, 1978), those receiving ECT with or without antidepressants had a suicide attempt rate of 0.9% in contrast to 6.8% in the adequately treated antidepressant group. Hordern et al. (1965) had no suicides at a 6-month follow-up in 34 women treated with ECT, but reported 2 in the 84 patients treated with antidepressants (2.4%). Bratfos and Haug (1965) reported no suicides in a 3-month follow-up of manic–depressive depressed patients treated with either ECT or one of several antidepressant drug therapies. Both of the suicides in the Medical Research Council (1965) trial occurred in the ECT group during the course of treatment. With this exception, there is little justification for the apparent preference for antidepressant drug therapy over ECT in the treatment of affective disorders, whether overall outcome or effect on decreasing suicidal behaviors is the criterion variable.

The advantage for ECT in decreasing suicidal behaviors in affective disorders might be explained by a more rapid onset of action. Studies have been found that documented a decreased length of stay (Avery & Winokur, 1977; Bratfos & Haug, 1965; Jaaskelainen & Viukari, 1976; Medical Research Council, 1965) or a faster immediate response of depression to ECT as compared to TCA drug treatments (Ball & Kiloh, 1959; Bruce, Crone, Fitzpatrick, Fewins, Gillis, Lascelles, Levene, & Merskey, 1960). Hordern et al. (1965) found no difference in mean length of stay when antidepressant and ECT responders were compared. Only with the use of parenteral TCA was the speed of response found equal to that of ECT (Fahy, Imlah, & Harrington, 1963). On the basis of this more rapid response, Glassman, Kantor, and Shostak (1975) indicate that ECT is the treatment of choice to decrease the time during which there is a high risk of suicidal behaviors.

Mortality–Morbidity

Some increased risk associated with ECT might explain the apparent clinical preference for antidepressant drugs. Avery and Winokur (1978) and Bratfos and Haug (1965) did not find a difference in risk of relapse or rehospitalization, although follow-up periods were only 6 and 3 months, respectively. The value of prophylactic or maintenance use of TCAs following remission of an acute episode using either ECT or drug therapy is not addressed in this review. Freeman and Kendell (1980) indicate that some 4% of patients receiving ECT experience a push into a period of mania or elated mood, but this side effect is also a well-recognized consequence of TCA therapy. Although the newer antidepressant drug treatments argue for a different and lessened profile of serious cardiovascular and other side effects, the TCAs that remain in widest use in North America have the potential for dangerous effects on the cardiovascular system. These are mediated through the adrenergic and cholinergic systems, as well as through direct effects on cardiac conduction. Almost all of the TCA drugs lower the threshold for convulsive seizures, and the tetracyclic maprotiline is felt by some to have so narrow a therapeutic index in regard to its potential for induction of seizure activity as to be clinically contraindicated.

The potential for death by overdose of antidepressant drugs is a major concern. Antidepressant drug therapies are used in persons at definite risk of suicidal behavior. For unknown reasons, they require several weeks before lifting the depressive affect. The suicidal risk remains high while the patients are awaiting this onset of therapeutic activity, and the medications themselves are often chosen as the method of suicide. Data from the Drug Abuse Warning Network (DAWN) (1983) reflect the seriousness of this problem. TCAs were the fourth most common class of drug employed in overdoses presenting to emergency rooms in the United States during 1982 and were the third most common cause of drug-related deaths. While the vast majority of patients with TCA overdoses treated in emergency rooms do survive, the availability of these medications clearly contributes to suicidal behaviors.

Again, it is difficult to offer any suitable explanation for the preference for antidepressant drug therapies over ECT in the treatment of affective disorders when the possible risks and dangers of the respective treatment modalities are considered.

Delusional Depressions

The Northwick Park (Johnstone et al., 1980) and Leicestershire (Brandon et al., 1984) trials point directly to the presence of delusions as a symptom feature that responds better to real than to simulated ECT. Depressed patients with delusions respond significantly better to ECT than to TCA's (Avery & Lubrano, 1979; DeCarolis et al., 1964; Glassman et al, 1975). Roose, Glassman, Walsh, Woodring, and Vital-Herne (1983) retrospectively studied 22 suicides in patients with major affective disorders. They concluded that their 14 patients with delusional unipolar depressions were 5.3 times as likely to complete suicide as their unipolar depressed patients without delusions. Despite the possibility that this relationship between completed suicide and the presence of delusional symptoms in depressed patients may be explained by the covariable severity of depression, this important finding that links a specific symptom to the outcome of suicide deserves further attention. If confirmed, depressed patients with delusions may represent a group at high risk of suicide for whom ECT is a specific and effective treatment agent.

The Prejudice against ECT

Despite the evidence favoring ECT in the treatment of affective disorders and suggesting a consequent reduction in suicidal behaviors with its use, there remains significant resistance to the increased use of this treatment modality. Much of this derives from the persistent reports of those who maintain that they have experienced some significant and permanent deterioration in their memory functions following ECT (Breggin, 1979; Freeman & Kendell, 1980; Hughes, Barraclough, & Reeve, 1981). From the opposite viewpoint, 78% and 83% respectively, of the patients in the latter two studies indicated that the treatment had helped, and 64% and 81% said that they would have it again if it were recommended by their physician. Kalayam and Steinhart (1981) find surprisingly little support in the general public for the efforts of some media to discredit ECT. From the potential of prospective deliverers of the treatment, only 1% and 2% of British and American psychiatrists surveyed indicated that they opposed any and all use of ECT (American Psychiatric Association, 1978; Pippard & Ellam, 1981). Weiner (1984) suggests that several areas of professional responsibility may underlie the resistance to ECT. These include historical issues of unsophisticated technique and patient selection, along with a disparaging and biased approach to ECT within the professional literature by those who oppose its use.

Conclusions

ECT has demonstrated its effectiveness in preventing suicide. This is attributed to the rapid amelioration of depressive (and particularly delusionally depressive) disorders of biological origin, which are conditions often accompanied by the complication of suicidal behavior. No specific biological mechanisim to explain this effectiveness of ECT has been demonstrated. With the alterations in 5-HT quantities, metabolites, activities, and receptors noted in some persons exhibiting suicidal behaviors, the effects of ECT on beta-adrenergic and on $5\text{-}HT_2$ receptors offer a direction for further study of specific antisuicidal activity.

In the American Psychiatric Association (1978) survey, 72% of the responding psychiatrists indicated that ECT was the "safest, least expensive and most effective treatment for many patients." As an effective suicide prevention agent in patients with melancholia, endogenous depression, or the syndrome of hypothalamic hypofunction, the description of ECT as a "life-saving" treatment can appropriately be added to that description.

References

Abrams, R., Fink, M., & Feldstein. Prediction of clinical response to ECT. *British Journal of Psychiatry*, 1973, *122*, 457–460.

American Psychiatric Association. *Electroconvulsive therapy* (Task Force Report 14). Washington, D.C.: Author, 1978.

Aminoff, M. J., & Simon, R. P. Status epilepticus: Causes, clinical features and consequences in 98 patients. *American Journal of Medicine*, 1980, *69(5)*, 657–666.

Asberg, M., Traskman, L., & Thoren, P. 5-HIAA in the cerebrospinal fluid—a biochemical suicide predictor? *Archives of General Psychiatry*, 1976, *33*, 1193–1197.

Asnis, G. M., Fink, M., & Saferstein, S. ECT in metropolitan New York hospitals: A survey of practice, 1975–76. *American Journal of Psychiatry*, 1978, *135*, 479.

Avery, D., & Lubrano, B. A. Depression treated with imipramine and ECT: The DeCarolis study reconsidered. *American Journal of Psychiatry*, 1979, *136*, 559–562.

Avery, D., & Winokur, G. Mortality in depressed patients treated with electroconvulsive therapy and antidepressants. *Archives of General Psychiatry*, 1976, *33*, 1029–1037.

Avery, D., & Winokur, G. The efficacy of electroconvulsive therapy and antidepressants in depression. *Biological Psychiatry*, 1977, *12(4)*, 507–523.

Avery, D., & Winokur, G. Suicide, attempted suicide, and relapse rates in depression. *Archives of General Psychiatry*, 1978, *35*, 749–753.

Babigian, H. M., & Guttmacher, L. B. Epidemiologic considerations in electroconvulsive therapy. *Archives of General Psychiatry*, 1984, *41*, 246–253.

Ball, J. R. B., & Kiloh, L. G. A controlled trial of imipramine in treatment of depressive states. *British Medical Journal*, 1959, *2*, 1052–1055.

Barraclough, B. M. Suicide prevention, recurrent affective disorder, and lithium. *British Journal of Psychiatry*, 1972, *121*, 391–392.

Barraclough, B. M., Bunch, J., Nelson, B., Sainsbury, P. A hundred cases of suicide: Clinical aspects. *British Journal of Psychiatry*, 1974, *125*, 355–373.

Barton, J. L. ECT in depression: The evidence of controlled studies. *Biological Psychiatry*, 1977, *12*, 687–695.

Beisser, A. R., & Blanchette, J. E. A study if suicides in a mental hospital. *Diseases of the Nervous System*, 1961, *22*, 365–369.

Bielski, R. J., & Friedel, R. O. Prediction of tricyclic antidepressant response. *Archives of General Psychiatry*, 1976, *33*, 1479–1489.

Blackwood, D. H. R., Cull, R. E., Freeman, C. P. L., Evans, U. I., & Mawdsley, C. A study of the incidence of epilepsy following ECT. *Journal of Neurology, Neurosurgery and Psychiatry*, 1980, *43*, 1098–1102.

Bond, E. D. Results of treatment in psychoses—with a control series. *American Journal of Psychiatry*, 1954, *110*, 881–887.

Brandon, S., Cowley, P., McDonald, C., Neville, P., Palmer, R., & Wellstood-Eason, S. Electroconvulsive therapy: Results in depressive illness from the Leicestershire trial. *British Medical Journal*, 1984, *288*, 22–25.

Bratfos, O., & Haug, J. O. ECT and antidepressant drugs in manic–depressive disease. *Acta Psychiatrica Scandinavica*, 1965, *41*, 588–596.

Breggin, P. R. *Electroshock: Its brain-disabling effects*. New York: Springer, 1979.

Bruce, E. M., Crone, N., Fitzpatrick, G., Fewins, S. J., Gillis, A., Lascelles, C. F., Levene, L. J., & Merskey, H. A comparative trial of ECT and Tofranil. *American Journal of Psychiatry*, 1960, *117*, 76.

Carney, M. W. P., Roth, M, & Garside, R. F. The diagnosis of depressive syndromes and the prediction of ECT response. *British Journal of Psychiatry*, 1965, *111*, 659–674.

Chapman, R. F. Suicide during psychiatric hospitalization. *Bulletin of the Menninger Clinic*, 1965, *29*, 35–44.

Coryell, W. Intrapatient responses to ECT and tricyclic antidepressants. *American Journal of Psychiatry*, 1978, *135*, 1108–1110.

Cronholm, B., & Ottosson, J. O. Experimental studies of the therapeutic action of electroconvulsive therapy in endogenous depression. *Acta Psychiatrica Scandinavica*, 1960, *35*(suppl. 145), 69–101.

Crow, T. J., Deukin, J. F. W., Johnstone, E. C., MacMillan, J. F., & Owens, D. G. C. The Northwick Park ECT trial: Predictors of response to real and simulated ECT. *British Journal of Psychiatry*, 1984, *144*, 227–237.

Drug Abuse Warning Network (DAWN). *Annual data report* (Series 1, No. 2). Rockville, Md.: Department of Health and Human Services, National Institute on Drug Abuse, 1983.

DeCarolis, V., Gibert, F., Roccatagliata, G., *et al*. Imipramine and electroshock in the treatment of depression: A clinical statistical analysis of 437 cases. *Sistema Nervoso*, 1964, *1*, 29–42.

Devinsky, O., & Duchowny, M. S. Seizures after convulsive therapy: A retrospective case survey. *Neurology*, 1983, *33*, 921–925.

Fahy, P., Imlah, N., & Harrington, J. A controlled comparison of electroconvulsive therapy, imipramine and thiopentone sleep in depression. *Journal of Neuropsychiatry*, 1963, *4*, 310–314.

Fetterman, J. L., Victoroff, V. M., & Horrocks, J. A ten-year followup study of electrocoma therapy. *American Journal of Psychiatry*, 1951, *108*, 264–270.

Fink, M. Efficacy and safety of induced seizures (EST) in man. *Comprehensive Psychiatry*, 1978, *19*, 1–18.

Flatten, O. Should ECT be reevaluated? *Tidsskrift for den Norske Laegeforening*, 1975, *95*, 1571–1574.

Fontaine, R., & Young, T. Unilateral ECT: Advantages and efficacy in the treatment of depression. *Canadian Journal of Psychiatry*, 1985, *30*, 142–147.

Freeman, C. P. L., Basson, J. V., & Crichton, A. Double-blind controlled trial of electroconvulsive therapy (ECT) and simulated ECT in depressive illness. *Lancet*, 1978, *i*, 738–740.

Freeman, C. P. L., & Kendell, R. E. ECT: Patients' experiences and attitudes. *British Journal of Psychiatry*, 1980, *137*, 8–16.

Freeman, C. P. L., Kendell, R., & Week, D. *Patients' experiences to and attitudes about ECT*. Paper presented at International Conference on Electroconvulsive Therapy (ECT): Clinical and basic research issues, New York Academy of Sciences, 1985.

Gill, D., & Lambourn, J. Indications for electroconvulsive therapy and its use by senior psychiatrists. *British Medical Journal*, 1979, *1*, 1169–1171.

Glassman, A. H., Kantor, S. H., & Shostak, M. Depression, delusions and drug response. *American Journal of Psychiatry*, 1975, *132*, 716–719.

Goodwin, F. K., & Jamison, K. R. *Manic–depressive illness*. London: Oxford University Press, in press.

Gregory, S., Shawcross, C. R., & Gill, D. The Nottingham ECT study—a double-blind comparison of bilateral, unilateral and simulated ECT in depressive illness. *British Journal of Psychiatry*, 1985, *146*, 520–524.

Greenblatt, M., Grosser, G. H., & Wechsler, H. Differential response of hospitalized depressed patients to somatic therapy. *American Journal of Psychiatry*, 1964, *120*, 935–943.

Guze, S. B., & Robins, E. Suicide and primary affective disorders. *British Journal of Psychiatry*, 1970, *117*, 437–438.

Hamilton, M., & White, J. Factors related to the outcome of depression treated with ECT. *Journal of Mental Science*, 1960, *106*, 1031–1041.

Harris, J. A., & Robin, A. A. A controlled trial of phenelzine in depressive reactions. *Journal of Mental Science*, 1960, *106*, 1432–1437.

Herrington, R. N., Bruce, A., Johnstone, E. C., & Lader, M. H. Comparative trial of L-tryptophan and ECT in severe depressive illness. *Lancet*, 1974, *ii*, 731–734.

Hesso, R., & Retterstol, N. T. *Norske psykiatriske sykehas Nor Laegeforen*, 1975, *95*, 1571.

Hobson, R. F. Prognostic factors in electric convulsive therapy. *Journal of Neurology, Neurosurgery and Psychiatry*, 1953, *16*, 275–281.

Hordern, A., Burt, C. G., & Holt, N. F. *Depressive states*. Springfield, Ill.: Charles C Thomas, 1965.

Hughes, J., Barraclough, B. M., & Reeve, W. Are patients shocked by ECT? *Proceedings of the Royal Society of Medicine*, 1981, *74*, 283–285.

Hussar, A. E. Effect of tranquilizers on medical morbidity and mortality in a mental hospital. *Journal of the American Medical Association*, 1962, *179*, 682–686.

Huston, P. E., & Locher, L. M. Involutional psychosis: Course when untreated and when treated with electric shock. *Archives of Neurology and Psychiatry*, 1948, *59*, 385–394. (a)

Huston, P. E., & Locher, L. M. Manic–depressive psychosis: Course when treated and untreated with electric shock. *Archives of Neurology and Psychiatry*, 1948, *60*, 37–48. (b)

Impastato, D. Prevention of fatalities in electroshock therapy. *Diseases of Nervous System*, 1957, *18*, 34–75.

Impastato, D. Electric and chemical convulsive therapy in psychiatry. *Diseases of the Nervous System*, 1961, *22*, 91–96.

Jaaskelainen, J., & Viukari, N. M. A. Do tricyclic antidepressants work? *Lancet*, 1976, *i*, 424.

Johns, C. A. *Suicide and schizophrenia*. Paper presented at Conference on Psychobiology of Suicidal Behavior, New York Academy of Sciences, 1985.

Johnstone, E. C., Deakin, J. F. W., Lawler, P., Frith, C. D., Stevens, M., McPherson, K., & Crow, T. J. The Northwick Park ECT trial. *Lancet*, 1980, *ii*, 1317–1320.

Juel-Nielsen, N. Suicide risk in manic–depressive disorders. In M. Schou & E. Stromgren (Eds.), *Origin, prevention and treatment of affective disorders*. New York: Academic Press, 1979.

Kahan, J., & Pattison, E. M. Proposal for a distinctive diagnosis: The deliberate self-harm syndrome. *Suicide & Life-Threatening Behavior*, 1984, *14*, 17–35.

Kalayam, B., & Steinhart, M. J. A survey of attitudes on the use of electroconvulsive therapy. *Hospital and Community Psychiatry*, 1981, *32*, 185–188.

Karagulla, S. Evaluation of electric convulsive therapy as compared with conservative methods of treatment in depressive states. *Journal of Mental Science*, 1950, *96*, 1060–1091.

Kiloh, L. G., Ball, J., & Garside, R. Prognostic factors in treatment of depressive states with imipramine. *British Medical Journal*, 1962, *2*, 1225–1227.

Kiloh, L. G., Child, J. P., & Latner, G. Endogenous depression treated with iproniazid—a followup study. *Journal of Mental Science*, 1960, *106*, 1425–1428.

Kline, N. S. Psychopharmaceuticals: Effects and side-effects. *Bulletin of the World Health Organization*, 1959, *21*, 397–410.

Krieger, G. Suicides, drugs and the open hospital. *Hospital and Community Psychiatry*, 1966, *17*, 196–199.

Lambourn, J., & Gill, D. A controlled comparison of simulated and real ECT. *British Journal of Psychiatry*, 1978, *133*, 514–519.

Levy, S., & Southcombe, R. H. Suicide in a state hospital for the mentally ill. *Journal of Nervous and Mental Disease*, 1953, *117*, 504–514.

Lonnquist, J., Niskanen, P., Rinta-Manty, R., Achte, K., & Karha, E. Suicides in psychiatric hospitals in different therapeutic eras: A review of literature and own studies. *Psychiatria Fennica*, 1974, 265–273.

Maclay, W. S. Death due to treatment. *Proceedings of the Royal Society of Medicine*, 1953, *46*, 13–20.

McCabe, M. S. ECT in the treatment of mania: A controlled study. *American Journal of Psychiatry*, 1976, *133*, 688–691.

Medical Research Council. Clinical trial of the treatment of depressive illness. *British Medical Journal*, 1965, *5439*, 881–886.

Meldrum, B. S. *Neuropathological consequences of chemically and electrically induced seizures*. Paper presented at International Conference on Electroconvulsive Therapy (ECT): Clinical and Basic Research Issues, New York Academy of Sciences, 1985.

Mendels, J. Electroconvulsive therapy and depression: The prognostic significance of clinical factors. *British Journal of Psychiatry*, 1965, *111*, 675–682.

Oltman, J. E., & Friedman, S. Analysis of temporal factors in manic–depressive psychosis, with particular reference to the effect of shock therapy. *American Journal of Psychiatry*, 1950, *107*, 57–68.

Ottosson, J. O. Psychological or physiological theories in ECT. *International Journal of Psychiatry*, 1968, *5*, 170–174.

Pandey, G. N., Heinze, W. J., Brown, B. D., & Davis, J. M. Electroconvulsive shock treatment decreases beta adrenergic receptor sensitivity in rat brains. *Nature*, 1979, *280*, 234–235.

Pankratz, W. J. *Position paper on electroconvulsive therapy*. Ottawa: Professional Standards and Practice Council, Canadian Psychiatric Association, April 1978.

Paykel, E. S. Depressive typolgies and responses to amitryptiline. *British Journal of Psychiatry*, 1972, *120*, 147–156.

Pippard, J., & Ellam, L. Electroconvulsive treatment in Great Britain. *British Journal of Psychiatry*, 1981, *139*, 563–568.

Roberts, J. M. Prognostic factors in the electroshock treatment of depressive states: Clinical features from testing and examination. *Journal of Mental Science*, 1959, *105*, 693–713.

Robin, A. A., & Langley, G. E. A controlled trial of imipramine. *British Journal of Psychiatry*, 1964, *110*, 419–422.

Robins, E., Murphy, G. E., Wilkinson, R. H. Jr., Gassner, S., Kayes, J. Some clinical considerations in the prevention of suicide based on a study of 134 successful suicides. *American Journal of Public Health*, 1959, *49*, 888–899.

Roose, S. P., Glassman, A. H., Walsh, B. T., Woodring, S., & Vital-Herne, J. Depression, delusions, and suicide. *American Journal of Psychiatry*, 1983, *140*, 1159–1162.

Roy, A. Risk factors for suicide in psychiatric patients. *Archives of General Psychiatry*, 1982, *39*, 1089–1095.

Roy-Byrne, P., Gerner, R. H., Liston, E. H., & Robertson, A. G. ECT for acute mania: A forgotten treatment modality. *Journal of Psychiatric Treatment and Evaluation*, 1981, *3*, 83–86.

Sackheim, H. A., Decina, P. Prohounik, I., Portnoy, S., Kanzler, M., & Malitz, S. *Dosage, seizure threshold and efficacy.* Paper presented at International Conference on Electroconvulsive Therapy (ECT): Clinical and Basic Research Issues, New York Academy of Sciences, 1985.

Salzman, L. An evaluation of shock therapy. *American Journal of Psychiatry*, 1947, *103*, 669–679.

Schulsinger, F., Kety, S. S., Rosenthal, D., & Wender, P. H. A family study of suicide. In M. Schou, & E. Stromgren, (Eds.), *Origin, prevention and treatment of affective disorders.* New York: Academic Press, 1979.

Scovern, A. W., & Kilmann, P. R. Status of ECT: A review of the outcome literature. *Psychological Bulletin*, 1980, *87*, 260–303.

Seager, C. P. A comparison between the results of unmodified and modified electro-plexy. *Journal of Mental Science*, 1958, *104*, 206–220. (a)

Seager, C. P. Controlled trial of straight and modified electro-plexy. *Journal of Mental Science*, 1958, *105*, 1022–1028. (b)

Slater, E. T. O. Evaluation of electric convulsion therapy as compared with conservative methods of treatment in depressive states. *Journal of Mental Science*, 1951, *97*, 567–569.

Small, J. G., Milstein, V., Klapper, M. H., Kelkems, J. J., Miller, M. J., & Small, F. *ECT in the treatment of manic episodes.* Paper presented at International Conference on Electroconvulsive Therapy (ECT): Clinical and Basic Research Issues, New York Academy of Sciences, 1985.

Squire, L. R., Slater, P. C., & Miller, P. L. Retrograde amnesia and bilateral ECT. *Archives of General Psychiatry*, 1981, *38*, 89–95.

Thomas, D. L. L. Prognosis of depression with electrical treatment. *British Medical Journal*, 1954, *ii*, 950.

Tsuang, M. T., Dempsey, G. M., & Fleming, J. A. Can ECT prevent premature death and suicide in schizoaffective patients? *Journal of Affective Disorders*, 1979, *1*, 167–171.

Turek, I. S., & Hanlon, T. E. The effectiveness and safety of electroconvulsive therapy (ECT). *Journal of Nervous and Mental Disease*, 1977, *164*, 419–431.

Ulett, G. A., Smith, K., & Gleser, G. C. Evaluation of convulsive and subconvulsive shock therapies utilizing a control group. *American Journal of Psychiatry*, 1956, *112*, 795–802.

Weiner, R. D. Does ECT cause brain damage? *Behavioral and Brain Sciences*, 1984, *7*, 1–53.

West, E. Electric convulsion therapy in depression: A double-blind controlled trial. *British Medical Journal*, 1981, *282*, 355–357.

Wilson, I. C., Vernon, J. T., Guinn, T., & Sandifer, M. G. A controlled study of treatments of depression. *Journal of Neuropsychiatry*, 1963, *4*, 331–337.

Winokur, G., Clayton, P., & Reich, T. *Manic–depressive illness.* St. Louis: C. V. Mosby, 1969.

Wolff, G. E. Electroconvulsive treatment: A help for epileptics. *American Practitioner*, 1956, *7(11)*, 1791–1793.

Ziskind, E., Somerfeld-Ziskind, E., & Ziskind, L. Metrazol and electroconvulsive therapy of the affective psychoses. *Archives of Neurology and Psychiatry*, 1945, *53*, 212–217.

CHAPTER 7

Human Aggression and Suicide

Gerald L. Brown, MD, and Frederick K. Goodwin, MD
National Institute of Mental Health

Both aggression and suicide have been studied independently for a great while, from sociopsychological points of view. In some cases they have also been written about as being integrally concerned with each other, the most famous example probably being that of Freud's quote: "We have long known, it is true, that no neurotic harbours thoughts of suicide which he has not turned back upon himself from murderous impulses against others, but we have never been able to explain what interplay of forces can carry such a purpose through to execution" (1917/1953, p. 252).

Animal Models of Self-Destructive Behaviors

It is problematic to discuss animal counterparts for suicidal behavior, since suicide may certainly involve high levels of cognitive and, apparently, intentional mental processes. Though cognition and intention surely play important roles in many instances of suicidal behavior, it would be an assumption necessarily to ascribe basic etiological roles to cognition and intention. Whether a behavior is self-destructive or "suicidal" in animals can be as difficult to discriminate as making that human clinical distinction. Jones (1982, p. 148) writes, "[W]hile it is commonly assumed in human self-injury that thought initiates the act, the order may, in fact, be reversed, with thought being used to elaborate and transform, rather than to initiate, and no doubt also deferring or inhibiting the act altogether on occasions." He proposes that it is an "impulse to injure" that is induced by a stressful environment, and that it is transformed in its expression by the addition of cognitive and affective elements that shape the resulting behaviors. We might add to his views that the etiology of the "impulse" may be basically biological (with different individuals having differing propensities for such impulses) and that the "amount" of environmental stress that might induce such impulses could be different from time to time in the same individual.

One might construct a model in which certain basic biological characteristics, such as the level of excitation–inhibition in critical areas of the central nervous system (CNS) (influenced by internal and external biological stimuli) thought to interact with the laying down of short-term memory, the transformation of short-term memory to long-term memory, and the retrieval of the latter all together forms a system from which behavior originates (Brown & Goodwin, 1984a). Manifest behavior, then (e.g., suicide), would be influenced by both basic biological characteristics and predispositions (genetic or acquired) interacting with cognitive processes stimulated by environmental experience. Such an interactional model could explain, first, the repeatedly impulsive individual (perhaps with a family history of impulsivity) who manifests suicidal behavior triggered by seemingly mild to moderate environmental stress as an example of an individual with a "biological predisposition" toward suicidal behaviors. The model could also, by contrast, explain the patriotic kamikaze pilot as an example of an individual, who, at the very least, demonstrates a considerable cognitive contribution to suicidal behavior. Human pathology can either affect the biological structure in which such processes (emotional, memory, and cognitive) are effected, and/or can provide another "external" stress decreasing the resiliency of the individual in coping with other stresses.

Certain advantages accrue in looking at self-destructive behaviors in animals, in that one might come to view possible evolutionary and genetic contributions to the "proneness" to suicide in humans that one might otherwise overlook. Certain kinds of animal behaviors that often lead to the animals' demise from causes other than a "disease" or accident have been carefully reviewed (Crawley, Sutton, & Pickar, 1985). Among these general categories are altruistic behaviors, dispersal behaviors, stress-related behaviors, and laboratory models. Though each model has its relative advantages and disadvantages in providing comparisons and contrasts to human self-destructive behavior, the controlled laboratory model lends itself most readily to the investigation of a possible understanding of biological bases and/or accompanying changes to self-destructive behaviors. Among such behaviors are "learned helplessness" in rats (Maier & Seligman, 1976; Overmier & Seligman, 1976; Sherman, Sacquitne & Petty, 1982); animals trained for "learned helplessness" have been found to have lower CNS serotonin (5-HT) release and lower 5-hydroxyindoleacetic acid (5-HIAA) levels in comparison with naive controls (Petty & Sherman, 1983).

Another such potentially self-destructive laboratory-induced behavior is that of the separation model in primates (Harlow, 1959; McKinney, Suomi & Harlow, 1971; McKinney, Moran & Kraemer, 1984; Suomi, Harlow & McKinney, 1972; Suomi, Eisele, Grady, 1975). Such animals would not long survive in a natural habitat; this is not unlike, perhaps, the relatively poor "survivability" of humans afflicted with significant psychopathology, especially without the "protective" elements of society (i.e., family and other care providers, institutions, etc.). Suomi and associates have noted that "prolonged psychopathology is rarely observed among free-ranging animals other than man for a very elementary reason: Animals so afflicted are not apt to survive very long" (Suomi et al., 1972, p. 927). We have alluded to the protest–despair model in earlier papers (Brown, Goodwin, Ballenger, Goyer & Major, 1979b; Brown Ebert, Goyer, Jimerson, Klein, Bunney & Goodwin, 1982a) as roughly analogous to the aggressive rage (protest), sometimes followed by depressive affect (despair), that can be seen in humans. Furthermore, the "despair" in such animals can often be therapeutically modified by those medications effective in the treatment of human depression (McKinney et al., 1984). Not only does this primate model have an analogy in the "anaclitic depression" described by Spitz in infants (Spitz, 1947; Spitz & Cobliner, 1965), which can lead to their death; but infants who have experienced such social deprivation have also been reported to show CNS changes related to the hypothalamic–pituitary axis and its regulation of hormones that influence glucose metabolism. (These changes may or may not be entirely reversible with a restoration of the caretaker (see Powell, Brasel & Blizzard, 1967; Powell, Brasel, Raiti & Blizzard, 1967.)

Perhaps of more interest is not the simple fact that such CNS changes have been reported. In order to pursue indications of a genetic contribution to suicidal behavior (Kety, 1979; Schulsinger, Kety, Rosenthal, & Wender, 1979), there would need to be a further understanding of the relative vulnerability of different infants to such environmentally induced stresses. For example, a recent report (Salk, Lipsitt, Sturner, Reilly & Levat, 1985) linking adolescent suicide to perinatal respiratory distress and problem pregnancies not only indicates the possibility of an interaction between biological and socioeconomic variables; it also raises questions as to whether a biological variable predisposing individuals toward suicidal behavior is simply acquired (e.g., is provoked by medical events) or whether certain individuals may be more genetically vulnerable to specific medically stressful conditions. That there has been a large increase in the number of adolescent suicides

in the last 20 years (though the rate is disputed) might appear super-
ficially to support the idea that some noxious changes in the cultural
or socioeconomic environment, and/or some unique changes in the psychology of adolescents, have occurred. On the other hand, biological
influences, especially those of a genetic nature, may be assumed to
have occurred at a very slow rate, if at all. However, it is possible that
the kind of individual who would have been biologically vulnerable to
suicide all along is now interacting with different nonbiological conditions
in such a way as to result in a more lethal outcome.

Animal Models of Aggressive Behaviors

Aggressive behaviors among animals, according to Moyer (1968, 1976),
may fall into seven categories: predatory, intermale, fear-induced, irritable, territorial, maternal, and instrumental. Reis (1974) grouped
animal aggressive behaviors into two major categories: predatory and
affective. Certain CNS neurotransmitters (i.e., 5-HT, gamma-butyric
acid [GABA]) and dopamine (DA) that are largely inhibitory, and norepinephrine (NE), largely excitatory, as well as others, such as acetylcholine (ACh), have been associated with aggressive behaviors in
animals (West, 1981). Other biochemical compounds found in the CNS
and periphery (i.e., the cyclic nucleotides) have also been sometimes
associated with aggressive behaviors in animals (Angel, Deluca & Murphree, 1976; Orenberg, Renson, Eliott, Barchas & Kessler, 1975). Further,
various pharmacological compounds that induce changes in the CNS,
particularly the neurotransmitters, have also been shown to alter aggressive behaviors in animals and humans (Leventhal, 1984; Luchins,
1983; Sheard, 1971 & Sheard, 1975). Reviews of the animal literature
have been provided by Eichelman (1979) and Valzelli (1981).

Authors perhaps point more frequently to the obvious differences
between humans and animals than to some of their behavioral similarities. Most laboratory-controlled animal studies focus on a highly
controlled "state," whereas human studies that are associated with
cerebrospinal fluid (CSF) neurotransmitter metabolites and aggressive
behavior have largely focused on "trait." However, those studies that
have distinguished "violent" versus "nonviolent" suicide attempts in
relationship to CSF 5-HIAA (a major metabolite of 5-HT), 3-methoxy-
4-hydroxyphenylglycol (MHPG, a major metabolite of NE), and homovanillic acid (HVA, a major metabolite of DA) are not so easily categorized
with regard to "state" or "trait,"; longitudinal behavioral history is
usually not reported in these studies. As both suicide (Pokorny, 1983)
and aggression (Robins, 1966; Robins, 1978) are best predicted by a

history of similar behavior, one might wonder if those individuals who make a "violent" suicidal attempt have not generally been more repetitively impulsive individuals in other destructive behaviors. The fact that suicide not associated with violence has not been so consistently associated with decreased CSF 5-HIAA as that associated with violence might indicate that aggression/impulsivity is a more basic and primitive response than depression and suicide (45–85% of suicides are associated with depression as a syndrome or symptom (Beskow, 1979).

Another important difference between animal and human studies is the greater memory capacity of humans. A human, for example, may show less aroused, less aggressive, and sometimes less self-destructive behavior when exposed to a novel environment than is often the case for animals (Christmas & Maxwell, 1970), particularly those with experimentally depleted CNS 5-HT. Possibly, with a greater store of memory and a greater cognitive capacity to search and utilize such a store, the human is more likely to be able to make some association between the new environment and past experience to ameliorate the adjustment process. In any case, muricidal behavior in rats with decreased CNS 5-HT is attenuated by prior exposure to mice (Marks, O'Brien, & Paxinos, 1977). How likely a proneness to act on "impulse" is influenced by prior experience is surely variable in humans (perhaps more so) as it is in animals. Decreases in CNS 5-HT in animals have also been associated with the inability to delay before acting (Sanger & Blackman, 1976) (differential reinforcement of low rates, a behavioral suppression under nonreward conditions), as well as with release of inhibition of "punished behaviors" (Tye, Everitt, & Iversen, 1977; Tye, Iversen, & Green, 1979). A clinical analogy may be the relative incapacity of some aggressive/ violent individuals, and most impulsive individuals by definition, to "delay gratification." The animal data certainly would be consistent with the notion that, in general, CNS biochemistry may be more related to patterns of behavior than to psychiatric diagnoses, as has been discussed in an earlier review (Brown, Goodwin, & Bunney, 1982b).

Two Studies of Human Aggressive/Impulsive/Suicidal Behavior

In large part because of such animal data, we initiated one study reported in 1979 (Brown et al., 1979b), and we reported a replication in 1982 (Brown et al., 1982a). These studies may be summarized as follows. The two independent studies were a joint effort between the National Naval Medical Center and the National Institute of Mental Health, both in Bethesda, Maryland. The individuals studied were inpatient, active-duty military men of normal intelligence; the first study was comprised of 26 subjects and the second of 12 (more subjects were not available for the second study). For both studies, ages ranged from 17 to 32 years (mean + SD = 22.1 + 3.6 and 22.0 + 5.2, respectively), and height ranged from 68 to 73 inches (70.6 + 1.4) for the second study. All were nonpaid volunteers from whom informed consent was obtained. Patients were excluded from both studies if medical disorders were present, or if there was evidence of past or current primary affective disorder or schizophrenia, or if other than transient organic brain syndrome had ever been observed (according to DSM-II and DSM-III, respectively).

Both studies were comprised of individuals with personality disorders. An important clinical distinction between the two studies was that any presence or history of psychotic symptomatology was a basis for exclusion from the first study, whereas, in some of the patients from the second study, a history of "brief, reactive psychosis" (DSM-III, #301.20) as a secondary diagnosis was present. Such a disturbance is often present in young military populations and confounds the differentiation between severe personality disorder and mild psychotic disorder (DSM-III) (Strange, 1974; Spitzer, Endicott, & Gibbon, 1979). Those personality disorder categories within both groups, along with further descriptions of their clinical symptomatology, have been further detailed elsewhere (Brown et al., 1979a,b; Brown et al., 1982a; Brown & Goodwin, 1984b). Clinical diagnoses and clinical history assessments were made independently of the biochemical investigations.

Further exclusion criteria were the ingestion of any drug, prescribed or illicit, within 10 days of the lumbar puncture, and heavy use of alcohol (a score of more than 6 on the Michigan Alcoholism Screening Test) (Selzer, 1971; Zung & Charalampous, 1975). None of the patients had a history of heavy drug abuse, nor had any been prescribed a psychoactive drug except for transient symptomatic episodes. Methods to increase the likelihood of drug history veracity were described in previous studies (Brown et al., 1979a, 1979b).

Material available for evaluating each patient included the full medical–psychiatric history, physical examination, and job performance assessments. Because a purpose of admission was evaluation of suitability for further military service, emphasis was placed on a life history of aggression, particularly in response to authority. Most of the subjects were not returned to full active duty after the medical–psychiatric assessment. The categories of behavior used to determine a measure of aggression history, the scoring of the measure, its reliability, and its use in a normal, age-matched, sex-matched control group have been previously described (Brown et al., 1979a,b). The Buss–Durkee Inventory (BDI) for aggression (Buss, 1961; Buss & Durkee, 1957; Buss, Durkee

& Baer, 1957), and the Minnesota Multiphasic Personality Inventory (MMPI) (Lanyon, 1961; Welsh & Dahlstrom, 1956) were also available in the second study. Individual items of the psychopathic deviate (*PD*) scale of the MMPI approximate behaviors reflected in the measure of aggression history. A patient self-administered questionnaire containing subsections to score childhood behaviors and relationships, childhood school experience, childhood medical experience, similar items of adulthood behaviors and relationships, and similar items of adult medical experience was collected on all subjects and is further described elsewhere (Brown, Kline, Goyer, Minichello, Krevsi, & Goodwin, 1985).

CSF was obtained, as previously described (Goodwin, Post, Dunner, & Gordon, 1973) between 8 and 9 A.M. after 8 hours of bed rest and after postmidnight fasting. For 48 hours before the procedure, foods in the diet that might affect 5-HT, NE, or DA metabolism or the assay itself were restricted by means of a low-monoamine diet; coffee, tea, and cigarettes were also restricted. None of the patients was acutely symptomatic during this period. Details of diet, specimen handling, assay methodology, and statistical methods and results have been discussed elsewhere (Brown et al., 1979b; Brown et al., 1982a).

Within the initial group of subjects, aggression scores showed a significant negative correlation with CSF 5-HIAA, a significant positive correlation with MHPG, and no correlation with HVA. The prediction formula obtained from multiple-regression analysis indicated that 85% of the variance in aggression scores was accounted for by the combination of 5-HIAA and MHPG. The major contribution came from 5-HIAA, which alone accounted for 80% of the variance in aggression scores. When subjects with aggression scores above the median were compared with those below the median, 5-HIAA levels of the more aggressive group were significantly lower, but there was no significant difference with regard to MHPG levels. Those subjects who had been given personality diagnoses more closely associated with behavioral impulsivity (antisocial, explosive, immature, and hysterical) had a significantly higher mean aggression score, lower 5-HIAA, and no difference in MHPG when compared with the group with less impulsive personality disorders (passive–aggressive, passive–dependent, schizoid, obsessive–compulsive, and inadequate). Independent of both the aggression scores and the metabolite data, a Navy Medical Board judged 16 of the 26 subjects to be unsuitable for further military service. Compared with those who were not discharged, the discharged subjects had a significantly higher mean aggression score, lower 5-HIAA, and higher MHPG. Of particular interest was an association among mean aggression score, a history of suicidal behavior, and CSF 5-HIAA, MHPG & HVA, in these subjects. The 11 subjects with a prior history of at least one suicide attempt had a significantly higher mean aggression score, a lower 5-HIAA, and higher MHPG than the 15 subjects with no history of suicide attempts; no difference was observed for HVA.

In the second study, the *PD* scores were negatively correlated with CSF 5-HIAA; the lower 5-HIAA subjects scored significantly higher on the *PD* scale. Furthermore, a negative correlation between aggression history and 5-HIAA was again observed: Subjects with lower 5-HIAA (by median split) showed higher aggression history scores than subjects with higher 5-HIAA. Although lower 5-HIAA subjects had higher BDI scores on both behavioral and total aggression, these differences were not significant. Only the "irritability" score of the BDI showed a significant negative correlation with CSF 5-HIAA, though all other categories except "guilt" were negatively correlated (Brown & Goodwin, 1984b). *PD* scores, aggression history, and BDI scores were not significantly related to MHPG or HVA. None of the relationships between age and height and metabolite data was significant, though the expected negative correlation was observed for height.

In the initial study, a history of suicidal behavior was associated with life histories characterized by higher levels of aggression, and both behavior patterns were associated with decreased CSF 5-HIAA. The second study re-examined the relationship between aggression and suicide, as well as the relationships of both behavior patterns to neurotransmitter metabolites. Significantly higher aggression history scores were found among those subjects with a suicidal history versus those without such a history in both studies (see Figure 7-1). The trivariate relationship among aggression, suicidal history, and CSF 5-HIAA is readily apparent (see Figure 7-2). A relationship between a history of suicide attempts and CSF 5-HIAA was confirmed; those with such a history had significantly lower 5-HIAA than those without such a history in both studies (see Figure 7-3). No relationships between suicidal behaviors and CSF MHPG or HVA were observed.

Aggression history correlated significantly with BDI scores for total aggression, behavioral aggression, and hostility, and with the *PD* scale of the MMPI as well. The *PD* scale score did not correlate significantly with the BDI scores for total aggression or behavioral aggression, but did correlate with the score for hostility.

Literature Review

Though suicide for many years was largely considered a sociopsychological phenomenon, several lines of studies began to converge in the 1960s and 1970s to indicate a possible biological contribution to such

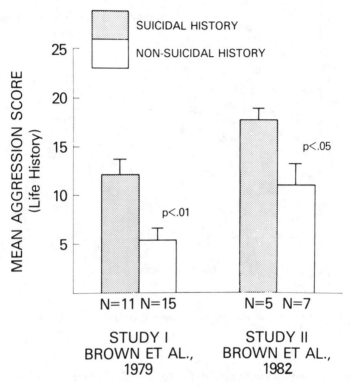

Figure 7-1. The relationship between suicidal history and aggression history in our two studies.

behaviors. The studies of Bunney, and colleagues (Bunney & Fawcett, 1965; Bunney, Fawcett, Davis, & Gifford, 1969) indicated the possibility of increased urinary steroid metabolites in depressed patients who made a suicidal attempt. Several follow-up studies provided conflicting results (Fink & Carpenter, 1976; Levy & Hansen, 1969; Rockwell, Winget, Rosenblatt, Higgins, & Hetherington, 1978; Ostroff, Giller, Bonese, Ebersole, Harkness, & Mason, 1982; Prasad, 1985). In three studies, plasma cortisol appears to correlate with suicidal behavior (Platman, Plutchik, & Weinstein, 1971; Krieger, 1974; Meltzer, Perline, Tricou, Lowry & Robertson, 1984); A single study of CSF cortisol (Traskman, Tybrings, Asberg, Bertilsson, Lantto & Schalling, 1980)

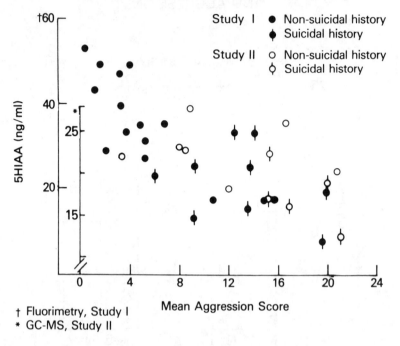

AGGRESSION, SUICIDAL HISTORY AND CSF 5HIAA

† Fluorimetry, Study I
* GC-MS, Study II

Figure 7-2.   The trivariate relationship among aggression history, suicidal history, and
CSF 5-HIAA in our two studies.

found no relationship with suicidal behavior. Earlier (1957–1976) autopsy
studies (Beskow, Gottfries, Roos, & Winblad, 1976; Bourne, Bunney,
Colburn, Davis, Shaw, & Coppen, 1968; Pare, Yeung, Price, & Stacey,
1969; Shaw, Camps, & Eccleston, 1967; Lloyd, Farley, Deck, & Hornykiewicz, 1974; Cochran, Robins, & Grote, 1976) of completed suicides,
usually in patients who were primarily depressed, indicated that either
5-HT or 5-HIAA might be decreased. Other neurotransmitters (NE and
DA) or their metabolites showed either inconsistent results or none at
all. More recent autopsy studies have indicated changes in certain CNS
neurotransmitter receptors, particularly with regard to 5-HT, and to
a lesser extent ACh, as being related to suicide (Crow et al., 1984;
Meyerson, Wennogle, Abel, Coupet, Lippa, Rau, & Beer, 1982; Perry,
Marshall, Blessed, Tomlinson, & Perry, 1983; Stanley & Mann, 1983,
1984; Stanley, Virgilio, & Gershon, 1982), though there have been
conflicting data. The first *in vivo* reports linking suicide to 5-HT metabolism to suicidal behavior were those of Asberg and colleagues in

SUICIDAL HISTORY AND CSF 5HIAA

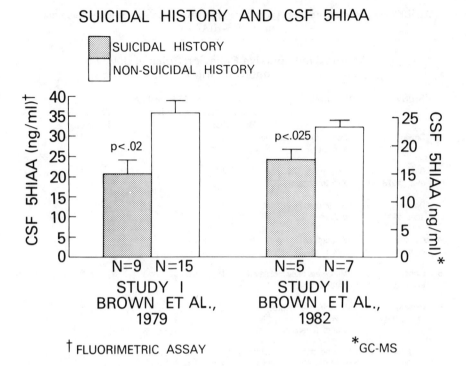

Figure 7-3. The relationship between suicidal history and CSF 5-HIAA in our two studies.

Sweden (Asberg, Thoren, Traskman, 1976; Asberg, Traskman, & Thoren, 1976), in which depressed patients were shown to have a bimodal distribution of CSF 5-HIAA. Those who had made suicidal attempts were largely in the lower-level mode, particularly those who had made violent attempts. These studies linked a concept of aggressive behavior (viz., violent suicidal attempts) with suicidal behavior.

Since these initial clinical and biological studies linking aggression (our own work, described in the preceding section) and suicide (the studies of Asberg's group in 1976) there have been five additional studies published relating aggressive/impulsive behavior, suicidal behavior, and CSF 5-HIAA (see Table 7-1) (Bioulac, Benezech, Renaud, Roche, & Noel, 1978; Bioulac, Benezich, Renaud, Noel, & Roche, 1980; Lidberg, Asberg, & Sundguist-Stensman, 1984; Lidberg, Tuck, Asberg, Scalia-Tomba, & Bertilsson, 1985; Linnoila, Virkkunen, Scheinin, Nuutila, Rimon, & Goodwin, 1983). CSF MHPG and HVA have yielded inconsistent results. The studies of Bioulac's group, from France, reported

TABLE 7-1.   Studies Linking Aggressive/Impulsive Behavior, Suicidal Behavior, and CSF 5-HIAA

Aggressive/Impulsive Behavior, Suicidal Behavior and CSF 5HIAA

Study	Diagnosis	CSF 5HIAA Aggressive/Impulsive Behavior	Suicidal Behavior
1. Brown et al., 1979	Personality Disorders (military)	↓	↓
2. Bioulac et al., 1978, 80	Personality Disorders XYY (prisoners)	↓[a]	?
3. Brown et al., 1982	Borderline Disorders (military)	↓	↓
4. Linnoila et al., 1983	Personality Disorders (prisoners)	↓	↓
5. Lidberg et al., 1984	Murderers of own children (forensic)	↓[b]	↓
6. Lidberg et al., 1985	Murderers --- depression anxiety, Personality Disorders (forensic)	↓[b,c]	↓

a = post-probenecid; b = not necessarily a history of aggressivity/impulsivity
c = only if victims were sexual partners and subjects were not alcoholics
1 of 4 studies in which CSF HVA was examined found it lower in more aggressive subjects;
1 of 3 studies in which CSF MHPG was examined found it higher in more aggressive subjects
↓ = decrease; ? = not reported (see study for details)

Branchey et al., 1984 (alcoholics) -- ↓ plasma tryptophan/neutral amino acids in more aggressive subjects

decreased CSF 5-HIAA turnover (via the probenecid method) in 47-chromosome, XYY institutionalized criminals; though the history of aggression was not quantified in these reports, descriptions of aggressive behaviors were provided. Linnoila and associates (1983) studied incarcerated murderers in Finland. Of particular interest, it was noted that those personality disorder diagnoses associated particularly with impulsivity (i.e., antisocial and explosive) had the lowest levels of CSF 5-HIAA. These more specific clinical findings replicated our earlier work (Brown *et al.*, 1979a,b). Lower CSF 5-HIAA was also associated with a history of suicidal behavior in the Finnish group.

Lidberg and associates, in Sweden, have recently (1984) published reports of three suicidal individuals who killed their own children; all three individuals had quite low levels of CSF 5-HIAA. Lidberg and associates have more recently (1985) reported a larger group of murderers in whom suicide was related to lower CSF. However, only those in this group who murdered sexual partners (and were not alcoholics) had lower levels of CSF 5-HIAA, contrasted to nonemotional or nonviolent murderers (e.g., a murderer who had killed a number of patients in a nursing home because of a belief in euthanasia). All of these studies taken together tend to lend credence to the idea that some form of impulsivity, disinhibition, or dyscontrol is the behavioral variable linked to CSF 5-HIAA, and not antisocial acts in and of themselves.

Following the initial reports of Asberg's group, nine other studies have assessed the relationship between CSF 5-HIAA and violent versus nonviolent suicidal behavior (Table 7-2) (Banki & Arato, 1983a, 1983b; Bank, Arato, Papp, & Kurcz, 1984; Oreland, Widberg, Asberg, Traskman, Sjostrand, Thoren, Bertilsson, & Tybring, 1981; Roy, Ninan, Mazonson, Pickar, van Kammen, Linnoila, & Paul, 1985; Roy-Byrne, Post, Rubinow,

TABLE 7-2. Studies Examining the Relationship between Violent versus Nonviolent Suicidal Behavior and CSF 5-HIAA

Violent and Non-Violent Suicidal Behavior and CSF 5HIAA

Study	Diagnosis	CSF 5HIAA	
		Violent Suicide	Non-Violent Suicide
1. Asberg et al., 1976 (2)	Unipolar depression	↓↓	NS
2. Oreland et al. 1981; Traskman et al., 1981	Depression and controls (anxiety; personality disorders)	↓↓	↓
3. Van Praag, 1982	Depression	↓↓	↓
4. Van Praag, 1983	Schizophrenia	↓↓	↓
5. Roy-Byrne et al., 1983	Unipolar depression Bipolar depression	NS[a] NS	NS NS
6. Banki et al. 1983 (2), 1984	Depression, schizophrenia, alcoholism, adjustment disorder	↓	NS
7. Roy et al., 1985	Schizophrenia	NS	NS

a = non-significantly lower in unipolar depressives
1 of 3 studies in which CSF HVA was examined found it lower in violent attempts;
CSF MHPG was examined in 2 studies and was lower in neither
↓ = decrease; ↓↓ = greater decrease; NS = nonsignificant change (see study for details)

Linnoila, Savard, & Davis, 1983; Traskman, Asberg, Bertilsson, & Sjostrand, 1981; van Praag, 1982, 1983). CSF MHPG and HVA have yielded inconsistent results. Five of seven groups reported that groups of patients with lower CSF 5-HIAA also had a history of violent suicidal attempts; three of the seven groups also reported patients having lower (but less so) CSF 5-HIAA, if they had had a history of suicidal behavior by nonviolent means. Two studies showed no relationship between low CSF 5-HIAA in those with histories of violent or nonviolent suicidal attempts (Roy et al., 1985; Roy-Byrne et al., 1983). In general, the distinction between violent and nonviolent suicide has been that of the use of guns, knives, and hanging for the former, and minor cuts and drug overdoses for the latter. Among those studies in Table 7-1, the diagnoses were primarily personality disorders; among those in Table 7-2, the diagnoses were primarily major affective disorders and schizophrenia.

Nine studies (Table 7-3) (Agren, 1980, 1983; Banki, Molnar, & Vojnik, 1981; Berrettini et al., 1985; Leckman et al., 1981; Montgomery & Montgomery, 1982; Ninan, van Kammen, Scheinin, Linnoila, Bunney, & Goodwin, 1984; Palaniappan et al., 1983; Vestergaard, Sørenson, Hoppe, Rafaelson, Yates, & Nicolaou, 1978) have reported observations of suicidal behavior and CSF 5-HIAA, MHPG, and HVA in which the aggressivity or violent nature of the suicidal behavior was not reported, nor was any life history of the subjects' aggressivity/impulsivity. Among these studies, seven have reported a lower level of CSF 5-HIAA and suicidal behavior. Again, among these studies, CSF MHPG and HVA have yielded inconsistent results. These studies have primarily examined major affective disorders. The subjects in all previously cited CSF 5-HIAA–aggression–suicide studies have been either European or American, but one study in this last group (Palaniappan et al., 1983) reported decreased CSF 5-HIAA in depressive Indian patients with a history of suicidal behavior (though no biochemical findings were related specifically to subtypes of depression). The fact that a similar behavioral–biochemical association has been found in such diverse social, cultural, and national backgrounds could be some evidence for a biological contribution in some suicidal behaviors that is more basic than environmental or social variables. Of particular interest is that a relationship between suicidal behavior and CSF 5-HIAA has not been observed in any of five studies in Tables 7-2 and 7-3 in which bipolar affective illness has been studied.

Though relatively little has been published that pertains to the behavioral interactions of aggression/impulsivity, suicide, and 5-HIAA in alcoholics, several studies are of interest. Early studies (Major, Ballenger, Goodwin, & Brown, 1977; Takahaski, Yamane, Kondo, & Tani,

TABLE 7-3. Studies Examining the Relationship between Suicidal Behavior and
Various CSF Amine Metabolites

Suicidal Behavior and CSF Amine Metabolites

	Study	Diagnosis	CSF Amine Metabolites		
			5HIAA	HVA	MHPG
l.	Vestergard et al., 1978	Unipolar depression Bipolar depression	NS	____	____
2.	Agren, 1980	Unipolar depression Bipolar depression	↓ NS	NS NS	↓ NS
3.	Leckman et al., 1981	Affective and schizo- phrenic psychoses	↓a	NS	NS
4.	Banki et al., 1981	Major depression	↓	NS	____
5.	Montgomery et al., 1982	Depression and Personality Disorder	↓	↓	____
6.	Agren, 1983	Unipolar depression Bipolar depression	↓ NS	NS NS	↓ NS
7.	Palaniappan et al., 1983	Depression	↓	↓	NS
8.	Ninan et al., 1984	Schizophrenia	↓	____	____
9.	Berrettini et al., 1985	Euthymic bipolar depression	NS	NS	____

a = suicidal ideation
↓ = decrease; NS = nonsignificant change; ____ = not measured (see study for details)

1974) showed no difference between alcoholics and personality disordered nonalcoholic controls during an abstinent state with regard to CSF 5-HIAA. However, the same group of investigators later showed that CSF 5-HIAA decreased with the interval of time between acute intoxication and a period of "drying out" (Ballenger, Goodwin, Major, & Brown, 1979). More recently, Branchey, Branchey, Shaw, and Lieber (1984) have shown the ratio of tryptophan to neutral amino acids in plasma to be lower in alcoholics, particularly those with a history of aggressive/impulsive behaviors and suicidal behaviors. The ratio of tryptophan to neutral amino acids is important, in that it is directly related to the amount of tryptophan (the dietary precursor of 5-HT) that is transported across the blood–brain barrier for the synthesis of 5-HT in the CNS (Gessa, Bigglio, Fadda, Corsini, & Tagliamonte, 1974).

Furthermore, this group showed a statistically significant relationship between aggressive behavior and suicidal behavior, much like that reported in our two studies (Brown et al., 1979b, 1982a). Of further interest, the murderers reported by Lidberg et al. (1985), who were also alcoholics, tended to have normal levels of CSF 5-HIAA. Though more studies need to be done, particularly in alcoholics, the studies thus far reported suggest the hypothesis that some alcoholics may be drinking excessively as an attempt to treat themselves for depressive, aggressive, and suicidal affects.

The central question appears to be that of a necessary, but not a sufficient, role for both aggression and serotonin in suicide. In that sense, an affect of aggressive rage may be critical for the development of depression and, in some instances, suicide; thus, aggression may be a more primitive affective response to the environment than depression. Such a construct appears consistent with the fact that aggression is found at all ages in all species (and probably in all individuals), but significant depression and suicide are not. Furthermore, since a small number of "normal" subjects (i.e., those that do not report a history of either aggressive or impulsive behavior) have also been shown to have lower CSF 5-HIAA, one would question whether the former group might be different in some ways other than CSF 5-HIAA from other "normals." If so, what kind of "compensating" mechanisms—biological, psychological, or social—might be coming into play? Of equal interest, how many individuals with histories of aggressive/impulsive and/or suicidal behaviors have high levels of CSF 5-HIAA? Since many new data have been added to the literature in recent years regarding the possible biological contributions to aggressive/impulsive and suicidal behavior, now would appear to be an important time to reassess some of the nonbiological questions that might be further studied. For example, if a certain propensity for self-destructive behavior exists in certain individuals "waiting for the right kind of environmental stress," what new clinical studies might be done to assess the families and childhood of such individuals? The biological data seem to suggest the strong possibility of a trait, just as the earlier studies of Schulsinger et al. (1979) and Kety (1979) indicated the strong possibility of a genetic contribution toward suicide.

In summary, there have now been a substantial number of scientific reports indicating that CNS 5-HT may be altered in aggressive/impulsive and suicidal behaviors in humans. These reports are largely consistent with the animal data, and they constitute one of the most highly replicated set of findings in biological psychiatry. That CNS 5-HT has been associated with animal aggression prior to its hypothesized relationship to suicidal behavior in humans might suggest that some suicidal behavior may be a special kind of aggressive behavior in humans, though perhaps not absolutely unique to humans.

References

Agren, H. Symptom patterns in unipolar and bipolar depression correlating with mono-amine metabolites in the cerebrospinal fluid: II. Suicide. *Psychiatry Research*, 1980, *3*, 225–236.

Agren, H. Life at risk: Markers of suicidality in depression. *Psychiatric Developments*, 1983, *1*, 87–104.

Angel, C., Deluca, D. C., Murphree, O. D. Probenecid induced accumulation of cyclic nucleotides, 5-hydroxyindoleacetic acid, and homovanillic acid in cisternal spinal fluid of genetically nervous dogs. *Biological Psychiatry*, 1976, *11*, 743–753.

Asberg, M., Thoren, P., Traskman, L., "Serotonin depression"—biochemical subgroup with the affective disorders? *Science*, 1976, *191*, 478–480.

Asberg, M., Traskman, L., & Thoren, P. 5-HIAA in the cerebrospinal fluid: A biochemical suicide predictor? *Archives of General Psychiatry*, 1976, *33*, 1193–1197.

Ballenger, J. C., Goodwin, F., Major, L., & Brown, G. Alcohol and central serotonin metabolism in man. *Archives of General Psychiatry*, 1979, *36*, 224–227.

Banki, C. M., & Arato, M. Amine metabolites and neuroendocrine responses related to depression and suicide. *Journal of Affective Disorders*, 1983, *5*, 223–232. (a)

Banki, C. M., & Arato, M. Amine metabolites, neuroendocrine findings, and personality dimensions as correlates of suicidal behavior. *Psychiatry Research*, 1983, *10*, 253–261. (b)

Banki, C. M., Arato, M., Papp, Z., & Kurcz. Biochemical markers in suicidal patients. Investigations with cerebrospinal fluid amine metabolites and endocrine tests. *Journal of Affective Disorders*, 1984, *6*, 341–350.

Banki, C. M., Molnar, G., & Vojnik, M. Cerebrospinal fluid amine metabolites, tryptophan and clinical parameters in depression, Part 2. *Journal of Affective Disorders*, 1981, *3*, 91–99.

Berrettini, W. H., Nurnberger, J. I. Jr., Scheinin, T., Seppala, M., Linnoila, M., Narrow, W., Simmons-Alling, S., & Gershon, E. S. Cerebrospinal fluid and plasma monoamines and their metabolites in euthymic bipolar patients. *Biological Psychiatry*, 1985, *20*, 257–269.

Beskow, J. Suicide and mental disorder in Swedish men. *Acta Psychiatrica Scandinavica*, 1979, *277*, 85–88.

Beskow, J., Gottfries, C. G., Roos, B. E., & Winblad, B. Determination of monoamine and monoamine metabolites in the human brain: Post mortem studies in a group of suicides and in a control group. *Acta Psychiatrica Scandinavica*, 1976, *53*, 7–20.

Bioulac, B., Benezech, M., Renaud, B., Roche, D., & Noel, B. Biogenic amines in 47, XYY syndrome. *Neuropsychopharmacology*, 1978, *4*, 366–370.

Bioulac, B., Benezich, M., Renaud, B., Noel, B., & Roche, D. Serotoninergic dysfunction in the 47, XYY syndrome. *Biological Psychiatry*, 1980, *15*, 917–923.

Bourne, H. R., Bunney, W. E., Jr., Colburn, R. W., Davis, J. M., Shaw, D. M., & Coppen, A. J. Noradrenaline, 5-hydroxytryptamine, and 5-hydroxyindole-acetic acid in hind-brains of suicidal patients. *Lancet*, 1968, *ii*, 805–808.

Branchey, L., Branchey, M., Shaw, S., & Lieber, C. S. Depression, suicide, and aggression in alcoholics and their relationship to plasma amino acids. *Psychiatry Research*, 1984, *12*, 219–226.

Brown, G. L., Ballenger, J. C., Minichiello, M. D., & Goodwin, F. K. Human aggression and its relationship to cerebrospinal fluid 5-hydroxyindoleacetic acid, 3-methoxy-4-hydroxyphenylglycol and homovanillic acid. In M. Sandler (Ed.), *Psychopharmacology of aggression*. New York: Raven Press, 1979a.

Brown, G. L., Goodwin, F. L., Ballenger, J. C., Goyer, P. F., & Major, L. F. Aggression in humans correlates with cerebrospinal fluid amine metabolites. *Psychiatry Research*, 1979b, *1*, 131–139.

Brown, G. L., Ebert, M. E., Goyer, P. F., Jimerson, D. C., Klein, W. J., Bunney, W. E., & Goodwin, F. K. Aggression, suicide, and serotonin: Relationships to CSF amine metabolites. *American Journal of Psychiatry*, 1982a, *139*, 741–746.

Brown, G. L., Goodwin, F. K., & Bunney, W. E., Jr. Human aggression and suicide: Their relationship to neuropsychiatric diagnoses and serotonin metabolism. In B. T. Ho, E. Usdine, & E. Costa (Eds.), *Advances in biochemical psychopharmacology* (Vol. 34, *Serotonin in biological psychiatry*). New York: Raven Press, 1982b.

Brown, G. L., & Goodwin, F. K. Aggression, adolescence, and psychobiology. In C. R. Keith (Ed.), *The aggressive adolescent: Clinical perspectives*, New York: Free Press, 1984. (a)

Brown, G. L., & Goodwin, F. K. Diagnostic, clinical, and personality characteristics of aggressive men with low 5-HIAA. *Clinical Neuropharmacology*, 1984, *7*, 756–757. (b)

Brown, G. L., Kline, W. J., Goyer, P. F., Minichiello, M. D., Kreusi, M. J. P., & Goodwin, F. K. *Relationship of childhood characteristics to cerebrospinal fluid 5-hydroxyindoleacetic acid in aggressive adults.* Paper presented at the IV World Congress of Biological Psychiatry, Philadelphia, September 1985.

Bunney, W. E., Jr., & Fawcett, J. A. Possibility of a biochemical test for suicidal potential. *Archives of General Psychiatry*, 1965, *13*, 232–239.

Bunney, W. E., Jr., Fawcett, J., Davis, J., & Gifford, S. Further evaluation of urinary 17-hydroxycorticosteroids in suicidal patients. *Archives of General Psychiatry*, 1969, *21*, 138–150.

Buss, A. H., Durkee, A., & Baer, M. The measurement of hostility in clinical situations. *Journal of Abnormal Psychology*, 1957, *21*, 343–348.

Buss, A. H. *The psychology of aggression.* New York: Wiley, 1961.

Buss, A. H., & Durkee, A. An inventory for assessing different kinds of hostility. *Journal of Consulting and Clinical Psychology*, 1957, *21*, 343–348.

Christmas, A. J., & Maxwell, D. R. A comparison of the effects of some benzodiazepines and other drugs on aggressive and exploratory behavior in mice and rats. *Neuropharmacology*, 1970, *9*, 17–29.

Cochran, E., Robins, E., & Grote, S. Regional serotonin levels in brain: A comparison of depressive suicides and alcoholic suicides with controls. *Biological Psychiatry*, 1976, *11*, 283–294.

Crawley, J. N., Sutton, M., & Pickar, D. Animal models of self-destructive behavior and suicide. *Psychiatric Clinics of North America*, 1985, *8*, 299–310.

Crow, T. J., *et al.* Neurotransmitter receptors and monoamine metabolites in the brains of patients with Alzheimer-type dementia and depression and suicide. *Neuropharmacology*, 1984, *23*, 1561–1569.

Eichelman, B. Role of biogenic amines in aggressive behavior. In M. Sandler (Ed.), *Psychopharmacology of aggression.* New York: Raven Press, 1979.

Fink, E. B., & Carpenter, W. T. Further examination of a biochemical test for suicide potential. *Diseases of the Nervous System*, 1976, *37*, 341–343.

Freud, S. Mourning and melancholia. In J. Strachey (Ed.), *Standard edition of the complete psychological works of Sigmund Freud* (Vol. 14). London: Hogarth Press, 1953. (Originally published, 1917.)

Gessa, G. L., Bigglio, G., Fadda, F., Corsini, C. V., & Tagliamonte, A. Effect of the oral administration of tryptophan-free amino acid mixtures on serum tryptophan, brain tryptophan, and serotonin metabolism. *Journal of Neurochemistry*, 1974, *22*, 869–870. (Now in paper)

Goodwin, F. K., Post, R. M. Dunner, D. L., & Gordon, E. K. Cerebrospinal fluid amine metabolites in affective illness: The probenecid technique. *American Journal of Psychiatry*, 1973, *130*, 73–79.

Harlow, H. F. Love in infant monkeys. *Scientific American*, 1959, *200*, 68–74.

Jones, I. H. Self-injury: Toward a biological basis. *Perspectives in Biological Medicine*, 1982, *26*, 137–150.

Kety, S. S. Disorders of the human brain. *Scientific American*, 1979, *241*, 202–214.

Krieger, G. The plasma level of cortisol as a predictor of suicide. *Diseases of the Nervous System*, 1974, *35*, 237–240.

Lanyon, R. L. *A handbook of MMPI group profiles*. Minneapolis: University of Minnesota Press, 1961.

Leckman, J. F., Charney, D. S., Nelson, C. R., Heninger, G. R., Bowers, M. B., Jr. CSF tryptophan, 5-HIAA and HVA in 132 psychiatric patients categorized by diagnosis and clinical state. In B. Angrist *et al.* (Eds.), *Recent advances in neuropsychopharmacology*. New York: Pergamon Press, 1981.

Leventhal, B. L. The neuropharmacology of violent and aggressive behavior. In C. R. Keith (Ed.), *The aggressive adolescent: Clinical perspectives*. New York: Free Press, 1984.

Levy, B., & Hansen, E. Failure of the urinary test for suicidal potential. *Archives of General Psychiatry*, 1969, *20*, 415–418.

Lidberg, L., Asberg, M., & Sundquist-Stensman, U. B. 5-Hydroxyindoleacetic acid levels in attempted suicides who have killed their children. *Lancet*, 1984, *ii*, 928.

Lidberg, L., Tuck, J. R., Asberg, M., Scalia-Tomba, G. P., & Bertilsson, L. Homicide, suicide and CSF 5-HIAA. *Acta Psychiatrica Scandinavica*, 1985, *71*, 230–236.

Linnoila, M., Virkkunen, M., Scheinin, M., Nuutila, A., Rimon, R., & Goodwin, F. K. Low cerebrospinal fluid 5-hydroxyindoleacetic acid concentration differentiates impulsive from nonimpulsive violent behavior. *Life Sciences*, 1983, *33*, 2609–2614.

Lloyd, K. G., Farley, I. J., Deck, J. H. N., & Hornykiewicz, O. Serotonin and 5-hydroxyindoleacetic acid in discrete areas of the brainstem of suicide victims and control patients. *Advances in Biochemical Psychopharmacology*, 1974, *11*, 387–397.

Luchins, D. J. Carbamazepine for the violent psychiatric patient. *Lancet*, 1983, *i*, 766.

Maier, S. F., & Seligman, M. E. P. Learned helplessness: Theory and evidence. *Journal of Experimental Psychology*, 1976, *1*, 3–46.

Major, L. F., Ballenger, J. C., Goodwin, F. K., & Brown, G. L. Cerebrospinal fluid homovanillic acid in male alcoholics: Effects of disulfiram. *Biological Psychiatry*, 1977, *12*, 635–642.

Marks, P., O'Brien, M., Paxinos, G. 5,7-DHT-induced muricide: Inhibition as a result of exposure of rats to mice. *Brain Research*, 1977, *135*, 383–388.

McKinney, W. T., Moran, E. C., & Kraemer, G. W. Separation in nonhuman primates as a model for human depression: Neurobiological implications. In R. M. Post & J. C. Ballenger, (Eds.), *Neurobiology of mood disorders*. Baltimore: Williams & Wilkins, 1984.

McKinney, W. T., Jr., Suomi, S. J., & Harlow, H. F. Depression in primates. *American Journal of Psychiatry*, 1971, *127*, 1313–1320.

Meltzer, H. Y., Perline, R., Tricou, B. J., Lowry, M., & Robertson, A. Effect of 5-hydroxytryptophan in serum cortisol levels in major affective disorders: II. Relation to suicide, psychoses, and depressive symptoms. *Archives of General Psychiatry*, 1984, *41*, 379–390.

Meyerson, L. R., Wennogle, L. P., Abel, M. S., Coupet, J., Lippa, A. S., Rau, C. E., & Beer, B. Human brain receptor alterations in suicide victims. *Pharmacology, Biochemistry and Behavior*, 1982, *17*, 159–163.

Montgomery, S. A., & Montgomery, D. B. Pharmacological prevention of suicidal behavior. *Journal of Affective Disorders*, 1982, *4*, 291–298.

Moyer, K. E. Kinds of aggression and their pathological basis. *Communications in Behavioral Biology* (Part A), 1968, *2*, 65–87.

Moyer, K. E. *The psychobiology of aggression*. New York: Harper & Row, 1976.

Ninan, P. T., van Kammen, D. P., Scheinin, M., Linnoila, M., Bunney, W. E., & Goodwin, F. K. Cerebrospinal fluid 5-HIAA levels in suicidal schizophrenic patients. *American Journal of Psychiatry*, 1984, *141*, 566–569.

Oreland, L., Widberg, A., Asberg, M., Traskman, L., Sjostrand, L., Thoren, P., Bertilsson, L., & Tybring, G. Platelet MAO activity and monoamine metabolites in cerebrospinal fluid in depressed and suicidal patients and in healthy controls. *Psychiatry Research*, 1981, *4*, 21–29.

Orenberg, E. K., Renson, J., Eliott, G. R., Barchas, J. D., & Kessler, S. Genetic determination of aggressive behavior and brain cyclic AMP. *Communications in Psychopharmacology*, 1975, *1*, 99–107.

Ostroff, R., Giller, E., Bonese, K., Ebersole, E., Harkness, L., & Mason, J. Neuroendocrine risk factors of suicidal behavior. *American Journal of Psychiatry*, 1982, *139*, 1323–1325.

Overmier, J. B., & Seligman, M. E. P. Effects of inescapable shock upon subsequent escape and avoidance learning. *Journal of Comparative Physiology and Psychology*, 1967, *63*, 28–33.

Palaniappan, V., Ramachandran, V., & Somasundaram, D. Suicidal ideation and biogenic amines in depression. *Indian Journal of Psychiatry*, 1983, *25*, 286–292.

Pare, C. M. B., Yeung, D. P. H., Price, K., & Stacey, R. S. 5-Hydroxytryptamine, noradrenaline and dopamine in brain stem, hypothalamus and caudate nucleus of controls and of patients committing suicide by coal-gas poisoning. *Lancet*, 1969, *ii*, 133–135.

Perry, E. K., Marshall, E. F., Blessed, G., Tomlinson, B. E., & Perry, R. H. Decreased imipramine binding in the brains of patients with depressive illness. *British Journal of Psychiatry*, 1983, *142*, 188–192.

Petty, F., & Sherman, A. D. Learned helplessness induction decreases *in vivo* cortical serotonin release. *Pharmacology, Biochemistry, and Behavior*, 1983, *18*, 649–650.

Platman, J. R., Plutchik, R., & Weinstein, B. Psychiatric, physiological, behavioral, and self-report measures in relation to a suicidal attempt. *Journal of Psychiatric Research*, 1971, *8*, 127–137.

Pokorny, A. D. Prediction of suicide in psychiatric patients: Report of a prospective study. *Archives of General Psychiatry*, 1983, *40*, 249–257.

Powell, G. F., Brasel, J. A., & Blizzard, R. M. Emotional deprivation and growth retardation simulating idiopathic hypopituitarism: I. *New England Journal of Medicine*, 1967, *276*, 1271–1278.

Powell, G. F., Brasel, J. A., Raiti, S., & Blizzard, R. M. Emotional deprivation and growth retardation simulating idiopathic hypopituitarism: II Endocrinologic evaluation of the syndrome. *New England Journal of Medicine*, 1967, *276*, 1279–1283.

Prasad, A. J. Neuroendocrine differences between violent and nonviolent parasuicides. *Neuropsychobiology*, 1985, *13*, 157–159.

Reis, O. J. Central neurotransmitters in aggression. *Research Publications, Association for Research in Nervous and Mental Disease*, 1974, *52*, 119–148.

Robins, L. N. *Deviant children grown up: A sociological and psychiatric study of sociopathic personality*. Baltimore: Williams & Wilkins, 1966.

Robins, L. N. Sturdy childhood predictors of adult antisocial behavior: Replications for longitudinal studies. *Psychological Medicine*, 1978, *8*, 611–622.

Rockwell, D. A., Winget, C. M., Rosenblatt, L. S., Higgins, E. A., & Hetherington, N. W. Biological aspects of suicide. *Journal of Nervous and Mental Disease*, 1978, *166*, 851–858.

Roy, A., Ninan, P., Mazonson, A., Pickar, D., van Kammen, D., Linnoila, M., & Paul, S. CSF monoamine metabolites in chronic schizophrenic patients who attempt suicide. *Psychological Medicine*, 1985, *15*, 335–340.

Roy-Byrne, P., Post, R. M., Rubinow, D. R., Linnoila, M., Savard, R., & Davis, D. CSF 5-HIAA and personal and family history of suicide in affectively ill patients: A negative study. *Psychiatry Research*, 1983, *10*, 263–274.

Salk, L., Lipsitt, L. P., Sturner, W. Q., Reilly, B. M., & Levat R. H. Relationship of maternal and perinatal conditions to eventual adolescent suicide. *Lancet*, 1985, 624–627.

Sanger, D. J., & Blackman, D. E. Effects of chlordiazepoxide, ripazepam and d-amphetamine on conditioned acceleration timing behavior in rats. *Psychopharmacology*, 1976, *48*, 209–215.

Schulsinger, F., Kety, S. S., Rosenthal, D., & Wender, P. H. A family study of suicide. In M. Schou & E. Stromgren (Eds.), *Origin, prevention and treatment of affective disorders*. New York: Academic Press, 1979.

Selzer, M. L. The Michigan Alcoholism Screening Test: The quest for a new diagnostic instrument. *American Journal of Psychiatry*, 1971, *127*, 1653–1658.

Shaw, D. M., Camps, F. E., & Eccleston, D. E. 5-Hydroxytryptamine in the hindbrain of depressive suicides. *British Journal of Psychiatry*, 1967, *113*, 1407–1411.

Sheard, M. H. Effect of lithium on human aggression. *Nature*, 1971, *230*, 113–114.

Sheard, M. H. Lithium in the treatment of aggression. *Journal of Nervous and Mental Disease*, 1975, *100*, 108–117.

Sherman, A. D., Sacquitne, J. L., & Petty, F. Specificity of the learned helplessness model of depression. *Pharmacology, Biochemistry and Behavior*, 1982, *16*, 449–454.

Spitz, R. Anaclitic depression: An inquiry into the genesis of psychiatric conditions in early childhood. II. *Psychoanalytic Study of the Child*, 1947, *2*, 313–342.

Spitz, R. L., & Cobliner, W. G. *The first year of life: A psychoanalytic study of normal and deviant development of object relations.* New York: International Universities Press, 1965.

Spitzer, R. L., Endicott, J., & Gibbon, M. Crossing the border into borderline personality and borderline schizophrenia. *Archives of General Psychiatry*, 1979, *36*, 17–24.

Stanley, M., & Mann, J. J. Increased serotonin-2 binding sites in frontal cortex of suicidal victims. *Lancet*, 1983, *i*, 214–216.

Stanley, M., & Mann, J. J. Suicide and serotonin receptors. *Lancet*, 1984, *i*, 349.

Stanley, M., Virgilio, J., & Gershon, S. Tritiated imipramine binding sites are decreased in frontal cortex of suicides. *Science*, 1982, *216*, 1337–1339.

Strange, R. E. Personality disorders in the military service. In J. R. Lion (Ed.), *Personality disorders—diagnosis and management.* Baltimore: Williams & Wilkins, 1974.

Suomi, S. J., Eisele, C. D., & Grady, S. A. Depressive behavior in adult monkeys following separation from family environment. *Journal of Abnormal Psychology*, 1975, *84*, 576–578.

Suomi, S. J., Harlow, H. F., & McKinney, W. T. Monkey psychiatrists. *American Journal of Psychiatry*, 1972, *128*, 927–932.

Takahaski, Yamane, H., Kondo, H., & Tani, N. CSF monoamine metabolites in alcoholism: A comparative study with depression. *Folia Psychiatrica Neurologica Japan*, 1974, *28*, 347–354.

Traskman, L., Asberg, M., Bertilsson, L., & Sjostrand, L. Monoamine metabolites in CSF and suicidal behavior. *Archives of General Psychiatry*, 1981, *38*, 631–636.

Traskman, L., Tybring, G., Asberg, M., Bertilsson, L., Lantto, O., & Schalling, G. Cortisol in the CSF of depressed and suicidal patients. *Archives of General Psychiatry*, 1980, *37*, 761–767.

Tye, N. C., Everitt, B. J., Iversen, S. O. 5-Hydroxytryptamine and punishment. *Nature*, 1977, *268*, 741–743.

Tye, N. C., Iversen, S. D., Green, A. R. The effects of benzodiazepines and serotonergic manipulations on punished responding. *Neuropharmacology*, 1979, *18*, 689–695.

Valzelli, L. *Psychobiology of aggression and violence.* New York: Raven Press, 1981.

van Praag, H. M. Depression, suicide and metabolism of serotonin in the brain. *Journal of Affective Disorders*, 1982, *4*, 275–290.

van Praag, H. M. CSF 5-HIAA and suicide in nondepressed schizophrenics. *Lancet*, 1983, *ii*, 977–978.

Vestergaard, P., Sørenson, T., Hoppe, E., Rafaelson, O. J., Yates, C. M., & Nicolaou, N. Biogenic amine metabolites in cerebrospinal fluid of patients with affective disorders. *Acta Psychiatrica Scandinavica*, 1978, *58*, 88–96.

Welsh, G. S., & Dahlstrom, W. B. (Eds.). *Basic readings on the MMPI in psychology and medicine.* Minneapolis: University of Minnesota Press, 1956.

West, L. J. Studies of aggression in animals and man. *Psychopharmacological Bulletin*, 1977, *13*, 14–25.

Zuckerman, M. A biological theory of sensation seeking. In M. Zuckerman (Ed.), *Biological bases of sensation seeking, impulsivity, and anxiety*, Hillsdale, N.J.: Erlbaum, 1983.

Zung, B. J., & Charalampous, K. D. Item analysis of the Michigan Alcoholism Screening Test. *Journal of Studies on Alcohol*, 1975, *36*, 127–132.

CHAPTER 8

Alcoholism and Suicide

Alec Roy, MD and Markku Linnoila, MD, PhD

National Institute on Alcohol Abuse and Alcoholism

The purpose of this chapter is to review knowledge about suicide in alcoholism: how commonly suicide among alcoholics occurs; which alcoholics commit suicide and why; suicide among alcoholic women and alcoholic physicians; possible predisposing biological factors; possible linkages with depression, adverse life events, and personality disorder; and future research directions.

Suicide Risk among Alcoholics

Information about how often alcoholics commit suicide is derived in two ways—first, by examining follow-up studies of alcoholics that report mortality to determine how many of the deaths were due to suicide, and second, by examining studies on suicides in the general population to find out how many alcoholics were among the suicide victims.

Kessel and Grossman (1961) estimated that the risk of a completed suicide among male alcoholics was 75- to 85-fold higher than that in the general population; Kendell and Staton (1966) arrived at a figure of 58-fold, and Gillis (1969) at 60- to 70-fold. In 1977, Miles reviewed 15 follow-up studies that reported the incidence of suicide among alcoholics. He estimated that 15% of alcoholics die by committing suicide. He also estimated that the suicide rate for alcoholics is 270 per 100,000 per year, and that in the United States there are between 6,900 and 13,000 alcoholic suicides each year.

The number of follow-up studies on alcoholics that report mortality and/or suicide has now increased to 21; they are reviewed in Table 8-

1. These studies come from different countries, en.
up methods, have varying follow-up times, report
drawn from different types of institutions, and use
for the diagnosis of alcoholism. They report on a total of .
The number of alcoholics reported in these studies t.
committing suicide ranges from 2% to 56%, with a mea.

Six of these follow-up studies have also compared the   of
deaths by suicide against the number of suicides that might   .e been
expected to occur, using either normative data (derived from the vital
statistics of the country in which the study was performed) or controls.
Interestingly, the ratio of the observed number of deaths of alcoholics
to the number of deaths that might have been expected was raised in
all six studies by a factor of 2 to 3. However, the ratio of the observed
number of suicides to the expected number of suicides was not only
raised in all six studies; it was *substantially* raised in four of the six,
with a range from 2 to 25 and a mean of 10.5 (Table 8-2). The largest
ratio, of 25, was derived from a 10- to 15-year follow-up study of alcoholics
drawn from four psychiatric hospitals (Nicholls, Edwards, & Kyle,
1974) and probably reflects the long follow-up time and accurate criteria
used by the coroners for death certifications.

There have been five carefully carried out studies, from four countries,
reporting large series of suicides in the general population. These studies
have all examined suicides reported as such by the respective coroners'
offices and have retrospectively assigned psychiatric diagnoses to the
suicide victims by the method of psychological autopsy after interviews
with relatives, friends, coworkers, and physicians, and after scrutiny
of all available medical and hospital records. The percentage of alcoholic
suicides in these five studies ranges from 15% to 26.9%. The total
number of suicide victims is 748, of whom 158 were determined to be
alcoholic, or 21.1% (Table 8-3). It is also of interest that in all but one
of these studies, a primary diagnosis of alcoholism was the second most
common diagnosis among the suicide victims, while in the study of
Dorpat and Ripley (1960) alcoholic suicide victims formed the largest
subgroup.

It is estimated that between 0.5% and 1% of the general population
die by committing suicide (Sainsbury, 1986). It is also estimated that
up to 5% of the general population are alcoholics (Efron, Keller, &
Gurioli, 1972). As the mean percentage of deaths from suicide among
the 21 follow-up studies of alcoholics was 17.6%, and as a mean 21.1%
of the suicide victims in the five general population studies were alcoholic,
we can conclude not only that the suicide rate is substantially raised
among alcoholics, but that suicide is also the cause of death for a
significant percentage of alcoholics.

TABLE 8-1. Suicide in 21 Follow-Up Studies of Alcoholics

Study	Origin of study	Number of alcoholics for whom data were available	Mean years of follow-up	Number of deaths	Number of suicides	% dead by suicide
Gabriel (1935)	Vienna, Austria	1,109	Not given	148	30	20
Dahlgren (1945)	Lund, Sweden	174	Not given	Not given	Not given	20
Lemere (1953)	Seattle, Washington	500	Not given	100	55	11
Norvig & Nielsen (1956)	Copenhagen, Denmark	181	2¾ to 5¼	42	15	33
Meir, Breyinova, & Vondracek (1956)		103	Not given	103	27	27
Selzer & Holloway (1957)	Michigan	98	6	18	1	6
Hastings (1958)	Minneapolis, Minnesota	22	6 to 12	6	1	16
Kessel & Grossman (1961)	London, England	218	5	23	13	56
Tashiro & Lipscomb (1964)	California	1,692	1 to 4	124	6	5

Study	Location				
Helgason (1964)	Reykjavik	163	Not given	57	9	16
Battegay (1965)		213	Not given	Not given	6	Not known
Kendell & Staton (1966)	London	62	6.7	11	5	45
Sundby (1967)	Oslo, Norway	1,722	22 minimum	1,061	54	5
Ritson (1968)	Edinburgh, Scotland	300	¾ to 2	Not given	8	Not known
Gillis (1969)	Cape Town, South Africa	802	1 to 7	95	15	10
Gorwitz, Bahn, Warthen, & Casper (1970)	Maryland	6,432	Not given	Not given	Not given	3
Schmidt & deLint (1972)	Toronto, Canada	6,478	1 to 14	738	51	7
Pell & D'Alonzo (1973)	Delaware	871	5 years	102	2	2
Nicholls, Edwards, & Kyle (1974)	London	935	10 to 15	309	46	15
Schuckit & Gunderson (1974)	San Diego, California	4,750	6½	70	16	23
Berglund (1984)	Lund, Sweden	1,312	18	537	88	16

Note. Total n = 27,956. Mean % dead by suicide = 17.7.

TABLE 8-2. Studies of Alcoholic Mortality Reporting Ratio of Observed Deaths
to Expected Age-Adjusted Deaths or to Death in Controls

Study	Deaths in total sample	Observed: expected	Percentage of deaths due to suicide	Observed: expected
Sundby (1967)	1,061	2	5	8
Schmidt & deLint (1972)	738	2	7	6
Pell & D'Alonzo (1973)	102	3	2	2
Nicholls et al. (1974)	309	2.7	15	25
Polich, Armor, & Braiker (1981)	111	3	12	20
Vaillant (1983)	20	2	15	2

Note. Adapted from Vaillant (1983). Used by permission of the author and Harvard University Press.

Which Alcoholics Commit Suicide and Why?: Social Risk Factors

Sex Ratio among Alcoholic Suicides

Many more alcoholic suicide victims are men than women. In all 12
studies that reported sex distribution, there was a clear overrepresen-
tation of men among the suicide victims (Table 8-4). Among the total
number of 349 suicide victims in these 12 studies, 87.4% were men.
Rushing (1969) argues that the association between suicide and alcoholism should be weaker in women, as many alcoholic women drink

TABLE 8-3. Alcoholism among Suicide Victims in Studies of Suicide
in the General Population

Study	Place	Number of suicides	Number and percent of suicides with a primary diagnosis of alcoholism
E. Robins, Murphy, Wilkinson, Gassner, & Kayes (1959)	St. Louis	134	31 (23.1%)
Dorpat & Ripley (1960)	Seattle	108	29 (26.9%)
Barraclough, Bunch, Nelson, & Sainsbury (1974)	Portsmouth, England	100	15 (15%)
Beskow (1979)	Stockholm	271	60 (22.1%)
Chynoweth, Tonge, & Armstrong (1980)	Brisbane, Australia	135	23 (17.0%)

Note. Total n for all suicides = 748; n and % for suicides with primary diagnosis of alcoholism = 158 (21.1%).

TABLE 8-4. Sex Distribution among Alcoholic Suicides

Study	Men	Women
E. Robins *et al.* (1959)	27	4
Kessel & Grossman (1961)	13	0
Tashiro & Lipscomb (1964)	6	0
Ritson (1968)	6	2
Gillis (1969)	10	1
Virkkunen (1971)	43	7
Schmidt & deLint (1972)	47	4
Nicholls *et al.* (1974)	39	7
Barraclough *et al.* (1974)	12	3
Murphy, Armstrong, Hermele, Fischer, & Clendenin (1979)	43	7
Chynoweth *et al.* (1980)	18	12
Berglund (1984)	85	3

Note. Total n's: men, 349; women, 50.

alone at home, and thus the proportion of women losing jobs because of alcoholism is lower. Also, in general, women's alcoholism causes less frequent and less severe disruptions in ongoing social and family relationships.

Age at Suicide

The mean age of the 134 alcoholic suicide victims in the five studies that recorded age was 46.8 years (Table 8-5). E. Robins, Murphy, Wilkinson, Gassner, and Kayes (1959) found that suicide occurred infrequently in the early stages of alcoholism and that the alcoholic suicide victims in their series committed suicide after years of alcoholism. Those in the series of Barraclough, Bunch, Nelson, and Sainsbury (1974) had a mean duration of alcoholism of 25 years. Barraclough *et al.* compared

TABLE 8-5. Age at Time of Suicide among Alcoholic Suicides

Study	Number of alcoholic suicides	Mean age in years at suicide
E. Robins *et al.* (1959)	31	46.6
Ritson (1968)	8	43
Barraclough *et al.* (1974)	15	51.3
Murphy *et al.* (1979)	50	47.9
Chynoweth *et al.* (1980)	30	45.1

Note. Total n = 134; mean age for all studies = 46.8.

their alcoholic suicide victims with alcoholics identified in a comprehensive survey of alcoholism in Cambridgeshire, England. They found that the male alcoholics in the survey were significantly younger than the male alcoholic suicide victims (44.8 ± 14.3 vs. 50.9 ± 9.4 years; $p < .01$). Virkkunen (1971) found that among the 50 alcoholic suicide victims in his study, "the majority were between 35 and 40 years of age."

Goodwin (1973) has advanced two reasons why alcoholism contributes to suicide chiefly in middle age. First, alcoholics have an excess of mortality from other causes secondary to their alcoholism, and thus the number of alcoholics reaching old age is diminished. Second, some alcoholics recover or respond to treatment by the time they reach old age, and are not replaced by new cases of elderly alcoholics. Thus, there is a lower proportion of alcoholics among the old than among the middle-aged. Also, losses due to alcoholism tend to occur in middle age, while elderly alcoholics have probably already sustained the losses that their alcoholism was likely to cause.

Marital Status

Murphy and Robins (1967) observed that a substantially smaller proportion of the alcoholic suicides in their study were married than individuals in the general population (58% vs. 78.3%). Barraclough et al. (1974) found that more of the alcoholic suicide victims in their study were divorced than the Cambridgeshire comparison alcoholics (20% vs. 6%), and that 27% of the alcoholic suicides were widowed, compared with 5% of the comparison alcoholics. They concluded that the older alcoholic has the greater suicide risk and that the "longer alcoholism persists the more likely it is to cause the adverse personal, social and health changes which may increase risk of suicide," and that the "loss of a spouse may predispose the alcoholic to suicide". Virkkunen (1971) also found "more divorced and fewer married persons" among alcoholic than other suicides.

Drinking Status and Race

Alcoholic suicide victims are usually not abstinent but currently drinking (E. Robins, 1986). More white than black alcoholics commit suicide (Goodwin, 1973, 1982; Rushing, 1968, 1969).

Previous Suicide Attempt

A previous suicide attempt is generally considered to be the best long-range indicator that an individual has an increased risk of eventually committing suicide (Sainsbury, 1978). Studies have shown that approximately 1% of individuals who make a suicide attempt subsequently commit suicide during the next year; thus, over a 10-year period, 10% die by suicide (Kreitman, 1977). Studies of suicide completers reveal that 25–50% have made a previous suicide attempt (Roy, 1982; reviewed by Roy, 1985a,c).

There are only four studies reporting mortality in alcoholics that also record the number of alcoholic suicides who have made a previous suicide attempt; three of these are general population studies. They report a total of 104 alcoholic suicides, of whom 38 (36.5%) had made a previous suicide attempt (Table 8-6). Thus, in respect to past suicidal behavior, alcoholic suicides appear to be similar to suicide victims in general.

Postdischarge Period

Studies indicate that the period after discharge from a psychiatric admission is a period of increased risk for suicide (Black, Warrack, & Winokur, 1984). For example, Temoche, Pugh, and MacMahon (1964) estimated that among psychiatric patients in general, the subsequent suicide risk is 34 times as great as the suicide risk in the general population. Nicholls *et al.* (1974) found that, after discharge from the index admission, the suicide rate among the alcoholics in their study fell from 74 per 100,000 during the first 4 years of the follow-up to 17.9 per 100,000 during the 9th and subsequent years of the follow-up—a

TABLE 8-6.   Previous Suicide Attempt among Alcoholic Suicides

Study	Number of alcoholic suicides	Number and percentage who had made a previous suicide attempt
E. Robins *et al.* (1959)	31	6 (19.4%)
Ritson (1968)	8	7 (87.5%)
Barraclough *et al.* (1974)	15	10 (66%)
Murphy *et al.* (1979)	50	15 (30%)

Note. Total *n* for all suicides = 104; *n* and % for those with a previous suicide attempt = 38 (36.5%).

decrease in the suicide rate of 76%. Also, Berglund (1984) found that among 88 alcoholic suicides, 26 (29.5%) committed suicide within 2 years of their first admission, 19 (21.6%) during the 3rd to 5th years, 24 (27.3%) during the 6th to 10th years, and 19 (21.6%) after 10 years.

There are five studies that report the number of alcoholics who committed suicide within a year of their last hospitalization (Table 8-7). The total number of alcoholic suicide victims in these studies is 114, and approximately 40% of them committed suicide within a year of discharge. Thus, the period after discharge from a hospitalization is a period of increased risk for suicide in alcoholics, and this is another characteristic in which alcoholic suicides are similar to other psychiatric patients who commit suicide. Berglund (1985) found that those who committed suicide within 5 years of their admission were significantly older than those who survived longer, and thus suggested that it is particularly the older alcoholic who is at increased risk after discharge.

Suicide among Alcoholic Women

More men than women are found among alcoholic suicides. The ratio of men to women is about 5 to 1 (see Table 8-4). This reflects both that suicide is found more among men than women (Sainsbury, 1986) and that alcoholism is found more among men than women by a ratio of 5 to 1 (Goodwin, 1973, 1982; L. Robins, Helzer, Weissman, Orvaschel, Gruenberg, Burke, & Regier, 1984). Barraclough et al. (1974) found the same sex ratio among their alcoholic suicide victims as found in a survey of alcoholics (4 to 1), and thus concluded that "the sex of an alcoholic does not, apparently, predispose to suicide" (pp. 362–363). However, both Berglund (1984) and Nicholls et al. (1974) found that male alcoholics had a suicide rate twice that of female alcoholics.

TABLE 8-7. Suicide of Alcoholics in Relation to Last Hospital Admission

Study	Number of alcoholic suicides	Number and percentage who committed suicide within a year of last hospital admission
Norvig & Nielsen (1956)	15	8 (53.3%)
E. Robins et al. (1959)	31	5 (16%)
Kessel & Grossman (1961)	9	4 (44.4%)
Ritson (1968)	8	7 (87.5%)
Schmidt & deLint (1972)	51	"Almost half"

Note. Total n for all suicides = 114; n for those committing suicide within a year of last hospitalization 38–43.

It is also noteworthy that there are many differences between men and women alcoholics. These differences include the family history of psychiatric disorder, developmental history, drinking behavior, gender-related effects of ethanol (Linnoila, Erwin, Ramm, Cleveland, & Brendle, 1980), and alcohol misuse (reviewed by Beckman, 1975). Schuckit and Morrissey (1976) have argued that some of these sex differences are partially due to the relative rates between the sexes of different subtypes of secondary alcoholism. In particular, they point to the fact that the major secondary alcoholic subtype among men is the sociopathic alcoholic subtype, which makes up about 25% of all male alcoholism, while among women alcoholics the major secondary alcoholic subtype is the affective disorder subtype, which makes up about 30% of all female alcoholism. As sociopathic personality disorder and affective disorder are associated with different motives for committing suicide, these alcoholic subtype differences may be of interest when examining differences between alcoholic men and women for reasons for suicide.

Suicide among Alcoholic Physicians

Studies have shown that alcoholism is more common among male physicians than among other social class I males (Murray, 1974, 1977). To try to understand the reasons for this, Murray (1976b) studied 41 alcoholic physicians in Scotland who had been psychiatric inpatients. Most of these physicians had started drinking heavily in their 20s and 30s, and the most common starting point was drug dependence, an occupational hazard for physicians. Often colleagues or an employer of a drug-dependent physician had suspected that the physician had been overprescribing for himself, and consequently he had switched to abusing alcohol rather than drugs. Another common reason for starting heavy drinking was a psychiatric disorder, particularly depression. Some had started drinking heavily as medical students or in the armed forces. Using the Registrar General's figures to obtain standard mortality ratios (SMRs), Murray (1983) showed that there are three important conditions from which British physicians are more likely to die than individuals in the general population, all three alcohol-related: suicide (SMR = 335%), cirrhosis (SMR = 311%), and accidents (SMR = 180%).

The three psychiatric disorders associated with suicide among physicians are alcoholism, depression, and drug dependence (Murray, 1983; reviewed by Roy, 1985b). Murray (1976b), for example, followed up 36 alcoholic physicians over a mean of 63 months after their discharge from a psychiatric hospitalization; 7 of them died, 4 by committing suicide. Blachly, Disher, and Roduner (1968) sent questionnaires to the survivors of 249 physicians whose suicides were reported in the *Journal of the American Medical Association*'s obituary columns between May 1965 and November 1967. Alcohol or drug abuse was thought to be a significant factor in about 40%. Cranshaw, Bruce, Eraker, *et al.* (1980) recently reported that during a 13-month period 8 of the 40 physicians whom the Oregon Board of Medical Examiners had on probation, or under investigation for probation, committed suicide. For 6 of these 8 suicides, it was possible to interview the closest available family member and to compile data using a 15-page protocol developed by the American Psychiatric Association Task Force on Suicide. All 6 of these physician suicides were men, and 5 were alcohol or drug abusers.

As well as physicians themselves, their wives have an increased risk of suicide—partly due to alcoholism (Sakinofsky, 1980). For example, Evans (1965) reported on 50 physicians' wives admitted to the Institute of Living in Hartford, Connecticut, between 1960 and 1963. Of these 50 wives, 7 (14%) were alcoholic. In another study, Lewis (1965) reported that 8 of 25 physicians' wives (32%) admitted to a private psychiatric hospital in Texas had serious drinking problems. Sakinofsky speculated that the high rate of suicide in physicians' wives might be due to unmet needs for dependency and caring that their doctor–husbands' career demands and personalities denied them, and that the wives turned to alcohol to fulfill their unconscious dependency needs.

Studies of Possible Predisposing Biological Factors

Cerebrospinal Fluid Studies and Suicidal Behavior

There is considerable evidence from animal studies that alcohol causes significant alterations in central indoleamine and catecholamine turnover (Badawy & Evans, 1974; Ellingboe, 1978; Mena & Herrero, 1980; Reis, 1973; Tabakoff & Boggan, 1974; Tabakoff & Ritzmann, 1975; Truitt, 1973). There are also animal studies demonstrating that serotonin plays a role in the regulation of aggression (Eichelman, 1979; reviewed by Crawley, Sutton, & Pickar, 1985). Thus, it is of interest that in recent years there have been several reports of studies of central monoamine metabolites in patients exhibiting suicidal behaviors. The first such report was that of Asberg, Traskman, and Thoren (1976), who found a bimodal distribution of levels of the serotonin metabolite 5-hydroxyindoleacetic acid (5-HIAA) in the lumbar cerebrospinal fluid (CSF) of 68 depressed patients. These investigators also found that significantly more of the depressed patients in the low CSF 5-HIAA mode had attempted suicide in comparison with those in the high CSF

5-HIAA mode, leading to the proposal that low CSF 5-HIAA levels may be associated with suicidal behaviors. Since then, other studies in personality-disordered (Brown et al., 1979, 1982; Linnoila et al., 1983), schizophrenic (Ninan, van Kammen, Scheinin, Linnoila, Bunney, & Goodwin, 1984; van Praag, 1983), and depressed (Agren, 1980; van Praag, 1982) patients have also reported an association between low levels of CSF 5-HIAA and aggressive and suicidal behaviors, though there have also been some negative reports (Roy, et al., 1985; Roy-Byrne, Post, Rubinow, Linnoila, Savard, & Davis, 1983).

There have also been several CSF monoamine metabolite studies among alcoholics. In Japan, Takahashi, Yamane, Kondo, and Tani (1974) obtained 43 CSF specimens from 30 alcoholic patients. They found no significant difference for CSF 5-HIAA levels between alcoholics studied 1 week after alcohol withdrawal and controls. However, when the alcoholics were divided into two subgroups, according to whether or not they had abstinent symptomatology, they found that it was only the subgroup with florid withdrawal symptoms that had significantly lower CSF 5-HIAA levels than controls. Repeat lumbar punctures in this subgroup 4 weeks later showed that the CSF 5-HIAA levels remained low. As low CSF 5-HIAA levels are also found in depression, Takahashi et al. speculated that abnormality of brain serotonin metabolism might be a factor causing both the psychic abstinent symptoms and the depressive mood symptoms, including suicidal ideation, that are commonly found among alcoholics.

Later, Ballenger, Goodwin, Major, and Brown (1979) studied CSF monoamine metabolite levels in alcoholic patients and compared them with CSF levels obtained from a control group of personality-disordered patients who did not have significant drinking histories. The alcoholic patients were studied twice—first, within 48 hours of being admitted to the hospital when being detoxified, and, second, after 4 weeks of abstinence. They found that CSF 5-HIAA levels were significantly lower among the alcoholics during their abstinent phase than in their postintoxication phase, or when compared to the controls. In 1981, Banki, working in Hungary, performed lumbar punctures on 36 female alcoholic patients and found a significant negative correlation between the number of days abstinent and CSF 5-HIAA levels; this confirmed the earlier observations of Ballenger et al.

The interpretation of these findings that was suggested by Ballenger et al. (1979) was that alcoholics may have pre-existing low brain serotonin levels that are transiently raised by alcohol consumption, which in turn eventually leads to further depletion of brain serotonin levels. They speculated that a pattern may become established where the alcoholic drinks repeatedly in order to pharmacologically modify a serotonin deficiency in the brain. Ballenger *et al.* reviewed the animal studies demonstrating that alcohol does, in fact, release serotonin in the brain; they also noted that the genetic strains of rats that prefer alcohol to water have low brain serotonin levels.

In another alcohol-related CSF study, Rosenthal, Davenport, Cowdry, Webster, and Goodwin (1980) examined the CSF monoamine metabolite data obtained from 69 depressed patients. Family history data was also obtained by systematic interviews with the patients and their relatives, and diagnoses were made by family history diagnostic criteria. In all patients, the lumbar puncture was performed some time after the patients' admission to the hospital, when they had been drug-free for at least 3 weeks. Patients were classified into subgroups according to family history, and those with a history of alcoholism in at least one first- or second-degree relative were compared with those without such a history. The depressed patients with a positive family history of alcoholism had significantly lower CSF levels of both 5-HIAA and the norepinephrine metabolite 3-methoxy-4-hydroxyphenylglycol (MHPG) than those without a family history of alcoholism. However, in a negative report, Lidberg, Tuck, Asberg, Scalia-Tomba, and Bertilsson (1985) found that alcoholic homicide offenders had significantly higher CSF 5-HIAA levels than nonalcoholic murderers.

Postmortem Studies in Alcoholic Suicides

Postmortem studies examining serotonin metabolite levels and receptors in the brains of suicide victims have also provided evidence suggesting a relationship between decreased brain serotonin metabolism and suicidal behavior (reviewed by Asberg, 1986). In a postmortem study of brains from alcoholic suicide victims, Gottfries, Oreland, Wiberg, and Winblad (1975) measured the activity of monoamine oxidase (MAO)—an enzyme involved in serotonin metabolism. They compared 8 alcoholic suicide victims with 20 normal controls and found significantly decreased MAO activity among the alcoholic suicide victims in all 13 parts of the brain that they studied. However, Cochran, Robins, and Grote (1976) found no significant differences for levels of serotonin in any of 33 brain areas when they compared 6 alcoholic suicides with 6 depressed suicide victims and 6 normal controls. Further postmortem studies are needed.

Thus, the overall results of these CSF and postmortem studies using a central strategy to examine brain serotonin and its metabolism suggest that there may be a subgroup of alcoholics who exhibit suicidal behavior and who have decreased serotonin turnover.

Neuroendocrine Studies and Suicidal and Aggressive Behavior

Peripheral neuroendocrine abnormalities in psychiatric patients may be useful biological correlates of changes in the central monoamine neurotransmitters that control the release of hormones into the blood. The first suggestion of a possible biological correlate for suicide was made by Bunney and colleagues (Bunney & Fawcett, 1965; Bunney, Fawcett, Davis, & Gifford, 1969), who observed high levels of urinary 17-hydroxycorticosteroids in suicidal depressed patients. Subsequent studies have also found dysregulation of the control of plasma cortisol levels to be associated with suicidal behavior. Banki and colleagues (Banki & Arato, 1983; Banki, Arato, Papp, & Kurcz, 1984) found among 141 female psychiatric patients suffering from depression, schizophrenia, alcoholism, or adjustment disorder that not only were levels of CSF 5-HIAA significantly lower in violent suicide attempters in all four diagnostic categories, but that nonsuppression of postdexamethasone plasma cortisol levels on the dexamethasone suppression test (DST) occurred significantly more often among those who had attempted suicide than in nonattempters. Also, Agren (1983) found among 110 depressed patients that hyperactivity of the hypothalamic–pituitary–adrenal axis (as indicated by the DST) and low CSF levels of the dopamine metabolite homovanillic acid (HVA) retrospectively "predicted" patients who had made earlier dangerous suicide attempts. We have recently shown among 27 depressed patients that the combination of nonsuppression on the DST with (1) low CSF HVA levels or (2) a low ratio of CSF HVA to CSF 5-HIAA was associated with the depressed patients who had attempted suicide or who eventually committed suicide (Roy et al. 1986).

Several groups have also investigated the hypothalamic–pituitary–thyroid axis and found that the thyrotropin-releasing hormone (TRH) test reveals a blunted response of the thyrotropin-stimulating hormone (TSH) in up to 40% of depressed patients. This has also been observed in alcoholic patients as well as in other diagnostic groups (reviewed by Extein, Pottash, Gold, & Cowdry, 1984). Recently, Linkowski, van Wettere, Kerkhofs, Brauman, & Mendlewicz (1983) investigated the past history of suicidal behavior in 51 depressed women in whom the TSH response to TRH was studied. They found that patients with a history of violent suicide attempts had a reduced TSH response to TRH when compared either to depressed patients with a history of nonviolent suicide attempts or to depressed patients with no history of suicidal behavior. A 5-year follow-up study revealed that the four patients who had died by committing suicide had an absence of TSH response to TRH. Also, Gold, Goodwin, Wehr, and Rebar (1977) reported that the TSH response to TRH was negatively correlated with CSF 5-HIAA levels. These studies are of interest and need to be replicated among alcoholic patients who have made suicide attempts—particularly among alcoholic men, as violent suicide attempts occur more among men than women (Roy, 1985c), and as the ratio of men to women alcoholic suicide victims is 5 to 1.

Glucose Metabolism and Aggressive Behavior

Virkkunen (1982, 1983, 1984) has investigated abnormal glucose metabolism and insulin secretion among habitually violent and impulsive offenders. He has reported that the great majority of them were under the influence of alcohol when they committed the acts of violence with which they were charged. He found that during a glucose tolerance test the blood glucose of these personality-disordered offenders fell significantly more than that of normal controls, and that the reactive hypoglycemic level was related to whether the relatives reported that the individuals were quarrelsome and aggressive under the influence of alcohol. Also, the mean peak values of insulin secretion were significantly higher among the violent offenders with an early onset of alcohol abuse than among those without such a history. Further studies on glucoregulation among alcoholics who have attempted suicide are indicated.

Blood Platelet MAO

The enzyme MAO is involved in the metabolism of biogenic amines and is found both in the brain and in other bodily organs. There has been a great deal of interest in the strategy of measuring MAO levels in blood platelets as a possible indicator of catecholamine metabolism in the brain. Several studies have found low platelet MAO levels both in alcoholics and in their blood relatives (Pandey, Dorus, Shaughnessy, Gaviria, Val, & Davis, 1980; Sullivan, Stanfield, Maltbie, Hammett, & Cavenar, 1978; Sullivan, Stanfield, Schanberg, & Cavenar, 1978). Takahashi, Tani, and Yamane (1976) studied MAO activity in the blood platelets of 50 alcoholics and reported a rebound of low platelet MAO levels in the weeks after alcohol withdrawal that was more pronounced among the patients with delirium tremens than among patients who had exhibited no marked withdrawal symptomatology. Interestingly, they interpreted these findings as evidence that alcoholics who develop psychiatric symptoms may have impaired brain serotonin metabolism, which they speculated might possibly be due to MAO inhibition caused by the excessive alcohol intake itself. Other workers have, in fact, demonstrated that alcohol does have a direct effect in decreasing MAO activity.

In relation to suicidal behavior, Buchsbaum, Coursey, and Murphy (1976) reported that college students with low platelet MAO levels, compared with those with high levels, were more likely to have a family member who had made an attempt at suicide. Similarly, some studies have reported that alcoholics with low platelet MAO levels were more likely to have a relative who had attempted suicide (Major & Murphy, 1978; Sullivan, Cavenoy, Maltbie, Lister, & Zung, 1979).

However, the initial enthusiasm for studies of platelet MAO levels as a possible marker either for alcoholism or for suicidal behavior has decreased with the recognition that MAO type B is found in platelets, while the brain contains both MAO type A and type B, though serotonin neurons have a high concentration of MAO-B. Also, low levels of platelet MAO have been found in other groups of psychiatric patients, particularly schizophrenics (Wyatt, Potkin, & Murphy, 1979). Moreover, alcohol itself (as well as other drugs) affects platelet MAO activity, as does abstinence from alcohol (Takahashi et al., 1976). A recent review concludes that there are probably both genetic and environmental determinants of peripheral MAO activity, and that low MAO levels in blood platelets or skin fibroblasts, while probably not reflecting brain catecholamine metabolism, may still be a biological correlate of vulnerability to psychopathology (Giller, 1984).

Depression among Alcoholic Suicides

Depression occurs commonly among alcoholics. In various studies, the incidence of depression among alcoholics, using differing diagnostic criteria for depression, has ranged from 28% to 59% (Cadoret & Winokur, 1974; Weissman & Myers, 1980; Weissman, Pottenger, Kleber, Ruben, Williams, & Thompson, 1977; Winokur, 1972; Woodruff, Guze, Clayton, Carr, 1973; reviewed by Keeler, 1982). Family history data show that depression is overrepresented among the relatives of alcoholics and that alcoholism is common in the relatives of depressives (Goodwin, 1973). Furthermore, alcoholism itself produces depressive symptoms (Goodwin, 1973). However, the relative contribution of the various factors associated with depression among alcoholics—be they social, genetic, environmental, personality, or biological factors—is at present poorly understood. It is noteworthy that Vaillant (1983), after reviewing the evidence, suggests that depressive syndromes in alcoholics are probably mainly caused by the consequences of the alcoholism itself.

Bleuler (1911/1951) attributed some suicide in alcoholics to depression:

Not very rarely alcoholics suffer from depressive conditions which cannot be distinguished symptomatologically from a melancholia of manic depressive insanity, even though the delusions usually remain merely rudimentary. But they do not last so long, only about two weeks. Perhaps still briefer attacks are not so rare but they naturally hardly come to the notice of the physician. Some of the suicides of alcoholics may be attributed to this depression. (p. 354)

Beck and colleagues (Beck, Steer, & McElroy, 1982; Beck, Weissman, & Kovacs, 1976) demonstrated the association of hopelessness to suicide attempts among alcoholics.

How often alcoholic suicide victims have developed an associated depressive syndrome during which they commit suicide has been little studied. Among the total of 111 alcoholic suicides in the four studies that examined this, 63 (56.8%) were assessed as having an associated depressive syndrome (Table 8-8).

Among the 15 alcoholic suicides reported by Barraclough et al. (1974), "many depressive symptoms were recorded . . . so extensive were the symptoms of depression that 9 of the 15 were also diagnosed depressive illness" (p. 386). Chynoweth, Tonge, and Armstrong (1980) found that 13 of the 27 alcoholic suicide victims (48.1%) in their series had a depressive syndrome; in 12 of them there was also an associated physical problem, presumably secondary to the alcoholism. Of the 50 alcoholic suicide victims reported by Murphy, Armstrong, Hermele, (1979), 39 (78%) had an associated affective disorder. Almost two-thirds of these alcoholic suicides (32, or 64%) received a retrospective diagnosis of definite or probable secondary affective disorder just prior to their committing suicide. Murphy et al. were surprised that not all of their alcoholic suicides were depressed. However, although the methodology of their study was rigorous, there was only one informant per suicide victim, who may not always have had close contact with the suicide

TABLE 8-8.   Alcoholic Suicides Assessed for Whether Individuals Had an Associated Depressive Syndrome Just Prior to Committing Suicide

Study	Number of alcoholic suicides	Number and percentage who were depressed
Virkkunen (1971)	19	9 (47%)
Barraclough et al. (1974)	15	9 (60%)
Murphy et al. (1979)	50	32 (64%)
Chynoweth et al. (1980)	27	13 (48.1%)

Note. Total n for all suicides = 111; n and % for those depressed = 63 (56.8%).

TABLE 8-9. Clinical and Sociopsychiatric Symptoms in Virkkunen's (1971) Study during Period Prior to Suicide among Patients Receiving Psychiatric Treatment

Symptoms	Alcoholic suicides under psychiatric care ($n = 19$)		Nonalcoholic suicides under psychiatric care ($n = 21$)	
	Number	%	Number	%
Angst	10	53	15	71
Marked depression	9	47	15	71
Paranoid features	5	26	8	38
Hysterical features	—	—	2	10
Phobias	1	5	3	14
Marked psychosomatic symptoms	3	16	5	24
Aggressiveness	9	47	6	29
Marked outwardly directed aggressiveness	6	32	1	5
Violent behavior toward others	5	26	2	10
Addiction to prescription drugs	6	32	6	29
Epilepsy	2	11	2	10

Note. From Virkkunen (1971). Reprinted by permission of Editor of *Psychiatrica Fennica.*

victim during the last few weeks of his or her life and thus may not always have been aware of the onset of depressive symptoms.

The similarity of the percentages of alcoholic suicide and depressive suicide victims for many of the affective symptoms was striking in the study of Barraclough *et al.* (1974). In an earlier study, Virkkunen (1971) observed similar results (Table 8-9). His alcoholic suicide victims had also shown more aggressiveness and violent behavior than the other suicide victims.

Berglund (1984) reported that significantly more of the alcoholics who at follow-up had committed suicide, when compared with those who had not, had been rated at their first admission as having slight depression (47% vs. 33%, $p < .05$); as showing irritability, dysphoria, or aggressiveness (30% vs. 21%, $p < .05$); as showing lability of affect, explosiveness, or affective incontinence (31% vs. 11%, $p < .01$); or as being brittle and sensitive (16% vs. 8 %, $p < .05$). He calculated that, in his total sample, the risk for suicide was 7% during the follow-up period, but that this increased to 9% if depression or dysphoria had been present at the first admission.

Further evidence that alcoholics who exhibit suicidal behaviors also suffer from depression comes from a recent study by Whitters, Cadoret, and Widmer (1985). Among a consecutive series of 117 alcoholic inpatients, they found that significantly more of those who had attempted suicide had a lifetime diagnosis of major depression (22.5% vs. 6.0%, $p < .05$). The alcoholics who had and had not attempted suicide at some time were also compared for individual affective symptoms that occurred over a 2-week period. Significantly more of those who had attempted suicide reported dysphoria, sleep disturbance, fatigue, psychomotor retardation or agitation, worthlessness, poor concentration, slow thinking, thinking about death, wanting to die, frequent crying spells, and the feeling that life was hopeless (Table 8-10).

Life Events

The relationship of recent life events to the etiology of completed suicide has been little studied. Dorpat and Ripley (1960) found that 32 individuals in their series of 114 suicide victims in Seattle—in which the largest subgroup, 27%, was alcoholic—had lost a love object (as defined as the loss of a family member by death, separation, or divorce) in the year preceding the suicide. In another 18 of the suicide victims, a grief reaction had begun more than a year before the suicide. Dorpat and Ripley noted that a number of the suicides had taken place shortly

TABLE 8-10. Depressive Symptoms among Alcohol Abusers Who Had and Had Not Attempted Suicide

Depressive symptoms	No suicide attempt ($n = 83$)	Suicide attempt ($n = 31$)	$p <$
Dysphoria 2 years	12.0%	42.0%	.01
Dysphoria 2 wks	38.6%	64.5%	.05
Lost appetite 2 wks	32.9%	35.5%	N.S.
Lost weight 2 wks	24.1%	35.5%	N.S.
Gained weight 2 wks	19.3%	29.0%	N.S.
Insomnia 2 wks	30.1%	58.1%	.05
Hypersomnia 2 wks	22.9%	25.8%	.01
Fatigue 2 wks	33.7%	58.0%	.05
Psychomotor retardation 2 wks	16.9%	29.0%	.05
Psychomotor agitation 2 wks	16.9%	38.7%	.05
Worthlessness 2 wks	26.5%	64.5%	.001
Thought about death 2 wks	30.1%	61.3%	.001
Wanted to die	6.0%	54.8%	.0001
Suicide ideation	24.1%	100.0%	.0001
Frequent crying spells	14.5%	48.4%	.001
Felt life hopeless	45.8%	80.7%	.01
Told physician "depressed"	6.05	25.8%	.01

Note. From Whitters, Cadoret, & Widmer (1985). Reprinted by permission of Editor of *Journal of Affective Disorders.*

TABLE 8-11.   Interpersonal Loss among Alcoholic Suicides in the Studies by Murphy
and Colleagues

Type of loss	1979 study (n = 31)		1967 Study (n = 50)	
	Within 1 year	Within 6 weeks	Within 1 year	Within 6 weeks
Separated	9	7	15	9
Divorced	1	0	3	0
Widowed	1	0	0	0
Bereaved	1	0	10	3
Apart (others)	3	3	3	2
Total	15	10	25	13

Note. Adapted from Murphy *et al.* (1979). Used by permission of the Editor of *Archives of General Psychiatry.* In both studies, the number affected within 6 weeks of suicide exceeded the number expected ($p < .01$).

after divorce or separation, and they illustrated this by mentioning a male chronic alcoholic who committed suicide 2 days after his wife left him and filed for divorce. In other studies, Bunch (1972) found that the incidence of suicide was increased among those in the general population who were recently bereaved, and Fernando and Storm (1984) found that significantly more of a diagnostically heterogeneous group of 22 psychiatric patient suicides, compared to psychiatric patient controls, had experienced a loss during the previous year (57% vs. 24%). Bolin, Wright, Wilkinson, *et al.* (1968) reported that two-thirds of a series of psychiatric patients who committed suicide while on home leave had experienced actual or threatened loss in the preceding 6 months.

Murphy and colleagues (Murphy *et al.*, 1979; Murphy & Robins, 1967) have carried out two studies in alcoholics, examining the relationship of specific life events involving the loss of a close interpersonal relationship to suicide. Life events were systematically inquired about during an interview with the nearest available relative, usually the spouse. In the 1979 study, among 31 alcoholic suicides, 48% had experienced a close interpersonal loss during the year before they committed suicide, and 32% had experienced such a loss during their last 6 weeks. The results in the 1967 study were strikingly similar: Among 50 alcoholic suicides, 50% had experienced the loss of an affectionate relationship in the year before they committed suicide, and 26% had experienced such a loss during their last 6 weeks of life (Table 8-11). Virkkunen (1971) was unable to replicate the results of the 1967 study by Murphy and Robins, but this may be because he only used data obtained from official records.

Murphy and colleagues have, to date, reported only specific life events involving losses of close interpersonal relationships before alcoholics committed suicide. They used strict definitions of "interpersonal loss" and only counted losses that had actually occurred. Threatened or impending losses were not considered. However, Murphy et al. (1979; see also Murphy, 1986) have commented that in both the 1967 and 1979 studies, others of the alcoholic suicides had experienced other types of loss events, as well as other distressing life events involving health, money, and legal problems—many of which were the consequences of their alcoholism.

Life Events and Depression

The two studies by Murphy and colleagues of life events preceding suicide in alcoholics are of great interest. The role of recent loss in the etiology of depression has long been recognized (Bowlby, 1980; Freud, 1917/1957). Paykel, Myers, Dienelt, Klerman, Lindenthal, and Pepper (1969) were the first to demonstrate that adverse life events, and particularly loss events, were found significantly more often among depressed patients in the 6 months before the onset of depression than in normal controls. This finding has now been replicated several times (Benjaminsen, 1981; Brown & Harris, 1978; Fava, Munari, Pavan, & Kellner, 1981; Perris, 1984; Roy, Breier, Doran, & Pickar, 1985). Also Overall, Reilly, Kelley, and Hollister (1985) recently reported that depression among alcoholics was significantly related to disruption in close personal relationships.

Thus, the most parsimonious explanation of the finding that alcoholic suicide victims have experienced life events involving loss in the period before they committed suicide is that the life events may have precipitated a depressive syndrome. The suicide literature supports this possibility (Roy, 1986). Dorpat and Ripley (1960) noted that "in six subjects the death of a family member precipitated a severe depression which led to suicide" (p. 352); among their alcoholic suicide victims, Barraclough et al. (1974) noted that "the most obvious clinical features were the combination of severe alcohol addiction and depression occurring in a recently disturbed domestic and social setting" (p. 363).

Thus, it was not unexpected that Murphy et al. (1979) would examine the relationship between recent loss and depression among the alcoholic suicides in their series. They were surprised, however, to find "little relationship between affectional loss and the presence or absence of a secondary depression" (p. 363). They found that in fact 45% of the alcoholic suicides without known depression had experienced a loss during their last 6 weeks of life, compared with 21% of the alcoholic suicides known to have developed a depressive episode. However, it should be noted that the types of affectional loss studied (separation, divorce, bereavement, etc.) might have led to a suicide victim's being largely out of contact during the last few weeks of his or her life with the one informant interviewed (usually the spouse). Thus the possibility remains that some of the 11 alcoholic suicides without known depression who had experienced a loss in their last 6 weeks might have developed a depressive syndrome without the study's one informant per suicide being aware of it.

Personality Disorder and Suicide

Many authors have also commented on the relationship of an associated personality disorder to the eventual suicide of alcoholic patients. In fact, Menninger (1939) referred to alcoholism as "chronic suicide." Wallinga (1949) noted that "an underlying personality disturbance which finally was brought to medical attention through an attempt at self-destruction has been previously evidenced for a prolonged length of time by the refuge in alcohol". Schmidt and deLint (1972) noted that suicides shortly after discharge "were usually attributed to predisposing social and personality factors and social isolation resulting from the common interpersonal difficulties in the alcoholics' way of life." Kendell and Staton (1966), reviewing alcoholics' reasons for suicide, thought "it probable that the social isolation of the longstanding alcoholic is the most important single factor. Four of the five suicides in this study were alone and friendless at the time of their deaths." Berglund (1984) has calculated that, among the alcoholics in his study, the risk for suicide during the follow-up period increased from 7% to 13% if a patient was rated at first admission as brittle or sensitive, and increased to 18% if the patient had a history of a peptic ulcer. He notes that Hagnell and Wretmark (1957) demonstrated that alcoholics with ulcers, compared to other alcoholics, were significantly more unable to relax, overambitious, worried, and nervous.

Risk Predictor Variables

Motto (1980) addressed the issue of whether risk factors could be identified among alcohol abusers that would differentiate those who were most likely to subsequently commit suicide from those who were not. He studied 978 subjects with alcohol abuse who were admitted to hospitals because of a depressive or suicidal state. Over a mean 2-year follow-up, 53 of these patients had committed suicide. From 184 psychosocial variables, rated at the admission interview, stepwise linear discriminant and linear logistic regression analyses resulted in the selection of the 11 suicide risk predictor variables shown in Table 8-12.

Motto noted that most of the high-risk predictors selected were of a sociological nature, that two variables reflected prior and current suicidal behavior, and that one reflected a family history of emotional disorder. Unfortunately, the validation study led to the prediction of too many "false negatives" and "false positives" to be clinically useful—a general problem in studies on the prediction of suicide (Murphy, 1983; Pokorny, 1983). Thus, Motto cautioned that these factors constitute an attempt to identify the highest-risk group within a known high-risk population, and that they do not replace the need for clinical skills in the assessment of an individual alcoholic patient.

TABLE 8-12. Alcohol Abuse: Suicide Risk Predictor Variables

Variable	High-risk category	n	Suicides	p value
1. Prior suicide attempts	More than two	119	15 (12.6%)	.001
2. Seriousness of present attempt—intent	Unequivocally or ambivalently weighted toward death	142	16 (11.3%)	.003
3. Attitude toward interviewer	Negative or mixed	270	24 (8.9%)	.005
4. Financial resources	Over $1,000[a]	107	10 (9.4%)	.008
5. Type of residence	Small/medium hotel or large apartment house or no stable residence	241	21 (8.7%)	.01
6. Intelligence	High intelligence[a]	160	13 (8.1%)	.02
7. Emotional disorder in family	Parent—opposite sex	98	10 (10.2%)	.04
8. Present state of health (subject's view)	Other than "good"	458	32 (7.0%)	.04
9. Physical health—past year	Minor impairment, getting worse	50	6 (12.0%)	.06
10. Number of moves— past year	None	96	9 (9.4%)	.09
11. Job stability—past 2 years	Any change[a]	486	31 (6.4%)	.08

Note. From Motto (1980). Reprinted by permission of Editor of Suicide and Life-Threatening Behavior.
[a]Continuous variable. Risk increases as high-risk variable increases.

Conclusion

Alcoholism is associated with an increased risk of suicide (Lonnquist & Achte, 1971; Pokorny & Kaplan, 1976; Evenson, Wood, Nuttall & Cho, 1982). Up to 20% of all suicides are alcoholics, and up to 18% of alcoholics end their lives by commiting suicide. However, surprisingly little is known about the factors associated with suicide in alcoholism. Suicide is a multidetermined act, and the available evidence suggests that this is probably also the case for suicide among alcoholics. The alcoholic suicide victim tends to be male, white, middle-aged, and unmarried; to have made a previous suicide attempt; to have had a hospitalization during the preceding year; to have experienced a recent loss or other adverse life event; and to be depressed. These features are also often associated with nonalcoholic suicide victims, and thus the alcoholic suicide victim may have much in common with suicide victims in general.

Many suicides among alcoholics are preventable. E. Robins *et al.* (1959) reported that 77% of their alcoholic suicides had communicated their suicidal ideas and that 61% had stated that they intended to kill themselves. They concluded that "the high frequency of suicidal communication in . . . alcoholics suggests that public education concerning the seriousness of this behavior . . . may be helpful in reducing the suicide rate" (p. 897).

There is a great need for further research into the determinants of suicide among alcoholics. Retrospective studies could gather information about family history of both psychiatric disorder and suicidal behavior (Roy, 1983) as well as the history of the alcoholics themselves (social factors, past suicidal behavior, personality disorder and other psychiatric factors, recent life events, the mental state at the time of suicide, and the history of the alcoholism and associated problems). Careful postmortem studies could investigate neurochemical levels and receptor numbers, particularly in those areas of the brain known to be involved in the regulation of mood and aggression. Prospective studies could compare alcoholics who had made previous suicide attempts with those who had not, as well as with normal controls, on biological measures — CSF catecholamine levels, neuroendocrine challenge test responses, and results of other tests examining for abnormality in the biological substrates thought to be involved with aggressive and suicidal behaviors. Alcoholics at high risk for further suicidal behavior because of their past history and/or test abnormality could be followed prospectively, with the eventual aim of testing psychopharmacological and psychosocial interventions that might diminish this risk.

References

Agren, H. Symptom patterns in unipolar and bipolar depression correlating with mono-amine metabolites in the cerebrospinal fluid: II. Suicide. *Psychiatry Research*, 1980, *3*, 225–236.

Agren, H. Life at risk. Markers of suicidality in depression. *Psychiatric Developments*, 1983, *1*, 87–104.

Asberg, M. Biological factors in suicide. In A. Roy (Ed.), *Suicide*. Baltimore: Williams & Wilkins, 1986.

Asberg, M., Traskman, L., & Thoren, P. 5-HIAA in the cerebrospinal fluid: A biochemical suicide predictor. *Archives of General Psychiatry*, 1976, *33*, 93–97.

Badawy, A., & Evans, M. Alcohol and tryptophan metabolism. *Journal of Alcoholism*, 1974, *9*, 97–116.

Ballenger, J., Goodwin, F., Major, L., & Brown, G. Alcohol and central serotonin metabolism in man. *Archives of General Psychiatry*, 1979, *36*, 224–227.

Banki, C. Factors influencing monoamine metabolites and tryphophan in patients with alcohol dependence. *Journal of Neural Transmission*, 1981, *50*, 98–101.

Banki, C., & Arato, M. Amine metabolites and neuroendocrine responses related to depression and suicide. *Journal of Affective Disorders*, 1983, *5*, 223–232.

Banki, C., Arato, M., Papp, Z., & Kurcz, M. Biochemical markers in suicidal patients: Investigations with cerebrospinal fluid amine metabolites and neuroendocrine tests. *Journal of Affective Disorders*, 1984, *6*, 341–350.

Barraclough, B., Bunch, J., Nelson, B., & Sainsbury, P. A hundred cases of suicide: Clinical aspects. *British Journal of Psychiatry*, 1974, *125*, 355–373.

Battegay, R. Selbstmordprophylaxe Gei Suchtigen. *Praventivmedicine*, 1965, *10*, 440–454.

Beck, A. T., Steer, R. A., & McElroy, M. G. Relationship of hopelessness, depression and previous suicide attempts to suicidal ideation in alcoholics. *Journal of Studies on Alcohol*, 1982, *43*, 1042–1046.

Beck, A. T., Weissman, A., & Kovacs, M. Alcoholism, hopelessness and suicidal behavior. *Journal of Studies on Alcohol*, 1976, *37*, 66–77.

Beckman, L. Women alcoholics: A review of social and psychological studies. *Journal Studies on Alcoholism*, 1976, *36*, 797–824.

Benjaminsen, S. Stressful life events preceding the onset of neurotic depression. *Psychological Medicine*, 1981, *11*, 369–378.

Berglund, M. Suicide in alcoholism—A prospective study of 88 alcoholics: The multi-dimensional diagnosis at first admission. *Archives of General Psychiatry*, 1984, *41*, 888–891.

Beskow, J. Suicide and mental disorders in Swedish men. *Acta Psychiatria Scandanavia Supplement*, 1979, *277*, 5–138.

Blachly, P., Disher, W., & Roduner, G. Suicide by physicians. *Bulletin of Suiciodology*, 1968, *1*, 1–18.

Black, D., Warrack, G., & Winokur, G. The Iowa Record-Linkage Study: I. Suicides and accidental deaths among psychiatric patients. *Archives of General Psychiatry*, 1984, *42*, 71–75.

Bleuler, E. *Textbook of psychiatry* (A. Brill, Trans.). New York: Dover, 1951. (Originally published, 1911.)

Bolin, R., Wright, R., Wilkinson, M., Lindner, C. Survey of suicide among patients on home leave from a mental hospital. *Psychiatric Quarterly*, 1968, *42*, 81–89.

Bowlby, J. *Attachment and loss* (Vol. 3, *Loss: Sadness and depression*). New York: Basic Books, 1980.

Brown, G., Ebert, M., Goyer, P., Jimerson, D. C., Klein, W. J., Bunney, W. E., & Goodwin, F. K. Aggression, suicide, and serotonin: Relationships to CSF amine metabolites. *American Journal of Psychiatry*, 1982, *139*, 741–746.

Brown, G., Goodwin, F., Ballenger, J., Goyer, P. F., & Major, L. F. Aggressions in humans correlates with cerebrospinal fluid amine metabolites. *Psychiatry Research*, 1979, *1*, 131–139.

Brown, G., & Harris, T. *Social Origins of Depression*. London: Tavistock, 1978.

Buchsbaum, M., Coursey, R., & Murphy, D. The biochemical high-risk paradigm: Behavioral and familial correlates of low platelet monoamine oxidase activity. *Science*, 1976, *194*, 339–341.

Bunch, J. Recent bereavement in relation to suicide. *Journal of Psychosomatic Research*, 1972, *16*, 361–366.

Bunney, W. E., Jr., & Fawcett, J. Possibility of a biochemical test for suicidal potential. *Archives of General Psychiatry*, 1965, *12*, 232–239.

Bunney, W. E., Jr., Fawcett, J. A., Davis, J. M., & Gifford, S. Further evaluation of urinary 17-hydroxycorticosteroids in suicidal patients. *Archives of General Psychiatry*, 1969, *21*, 128–150.

Cadoret, R., & Winokur, G. Depression in alcoholism. *Annals of the New York Academy of Sciences*, 1974, *233*, 34–39.

Chynoweth, R., Tonge, J., & Armstrong, J. Suicide in Brisbane—a retrospective psychosocial study. *Australia and New Zealand Journal of Psychiatry*, 1980, *14*, 37–45.

Cochran, E., Robins, E., & Grote, S. Regional serotonin levels in brain: A comparison of depressive and alcoholic suicides with controls. *Biological Psychiatry*, 1976, *11*, 283–294.

Cranshaw, R., Bruce, J., Eraker, P., Greenbaum, M., Lindemann, J. Schmidt, D. An epidemic of suicide among physicians on probation. *Journal of the American Medical Association*, 1980, *243*, 1915–1917.

Crawley, J., Sutton, M., & Pickar, D. Animal models of self-destructive behavior and suicide. *Psychiatric Clinics of North America*, 1985, *8*, 299–310.

Dahlgren, K. *Suicide and Attempted Suicide, Lund, Sweden*. World Health Organization, Lindstedts, 1945. Public Health paper 35.

Dorpat, T., & Ripley, H. A study of suicide in the Seattle area. *Comprehensive Psychiatry*, 1960, *1*, 349–359.

Efron, V., Keller, M., & Gurioli, C. *Statistics on consumption of alcohol and on alcoholism*. New Brunswick, N.J.: Rutgers University Center of Alcohol Studies, 1972.

Eichelman, B. Role of biogenic amines in aggressive behaviors. In M. Sandler (Ed.), *Psycholopharmacology of aggression*. New York: Raven Press, 1979.

Ellingboe, J. Effects of alcohol on neurochemical processes. In M. Lipton, A. DiMascio, & K. Killman (Eds.), *Psychopharmacology: A generation of progress*. New York: Raven Press, 1978.

Evans, J. Psychiatric illness in the physician's wife. *American Journal of Psychiatry*, 1965, *122*, 159–163.

Evenson, R., Wood, J., Nuttall, E., & Cho, D. Suicide rates among public mental health patients. *Acta Psychiatrica Scandinavica*, 1982, *66*, 254–264.

Extein, A., Pottash, A., Gold, M., & Cowdry, R. Changes in TSH response to TRH in affective illness. In R. Post & J. Ballenger (Eds.), *Neurobiology of mood disorders*. Baltimore: Williams & Wilkins, 1984.

Fava, G., Munari, F., Pavan, L., & Kellner, R. Life events and depression. *Journal of Affective Disorders*, 1981, *3*, 159–165.

Fernando, S., & Storm, S. Suicide among psychiatric patients of a district general hospital. *Psychological Medicine*, 1984, *14*, 661–672.

Freud, S. Mourning and melancholia. In J. Strachey (Ed.), *The standard edition of the complete works of Sigmund Freud* (Vol. 14). London: Hogarth Press, 1957. (Originally published, 1917.)

Gabriel, E. Über die Todesursachen bei Alkoholikern. *Z. ges. Neurologica Psychiatrie*, 1935, *153*, 385–406.

Giller, E. Platelet and fibroblast monoamine oxidase in alcoholism. *Psychiatry Research*, 1984, *12*, 339–000.

Gillis, L. The mortality rate and causes of death of treated chronic alcoholics. *South*

African Medical Journal, 1969, *43,* 230–232.

Gold, P., Goodwin, F., Wehr, T., & Rebar, R. Pituitary thyrotrophin response to thyrotrophin releasing hormone in affective illness: Relationship to spinal fluid amine metabolites. *American Journal of Psychiatry,* 1977, *134,* 1028–1031.

Goodwin, D. Alcohol in suicide and homicide. *Quarterly Journal of Studies on Alcohol,* 1973, *34,* 144–156.

Goodwin, D. Alcoholism and suicide: Associated factors. In E. M. Pattison & E. Kaufman, (Eds.), *Encyclopedic handbook of alcoholism.* New York: Gardner Press, 1982.

Gorowitz, K., Bahn, A., Warther, F., Casper, M. Some epedemiological data on alcoholism in Maryland: Based on admissions to psychiatric facilities. *Quarterly Journal for Studies on Alcoholism,* 1970, *31,* 423–443.

Gottfries, C., Oreland, L., Wiberg, A., & Winblad, B. Lowered monoamine oxidase activity in brains from alcohol suicides. *Journal of Neurochemistry,* 1975, *25,* 667–673.

Hagnell, O., & Wretmark, G. Peptic ulcer and alcoholism: A statistical study in frequency, behavior, personality traits and family occurrence. *Journal of Psychosomatic Research,* 1957, *2,* 35–44.

Hastings, D. Follow-up results in psychiatric illness. *American Journal of Psychiatry,* 1958, *114,* 105–106.

Helgason, T. Epidemiology of mental disorders in Iceland. *Acta Psychiatria Scandanavia Supplement,* 1964, *174,* 1–258.

Keeler, M. Alcoholism and affective disorder. In E. M. Pattison & E. Kaufman (Eds.), *Encyclopedic handbook of alcoholism.* New York: Gardner Press, 1982.

Kendell, R., & Staton, M. The fate of untreated alcoholics. *Quarterly Journal of Studies on Alcohol,* 1966, *27,* 30–41.

Kessel, N., & Grossman, G. Suicide in alcoholics. *British Medical Journal* 1961, *2,* 1671–1672.

Kreitman, N. *Parasuicide.* Chichester, England: Wiley, 1977.

Lemere, F. What happens to alcoholics. *American Journal of Psychiatry, 1953, 109,* 674–676.

Lewis, J. The doctor and his marriage. *Texas State Journal of Medicine,* 1965, *61,* 615–619.

Lidberg, L., Tuck, J., Asberg, M., Scalia-Tomba, G., & Bertilsson, L. Homicide, suicide and CSF 5-HIAA. *Acta Psychiatria Scandinavica,* 1985, *71,* 230–236.

Linkowski, P., van Wettere, J., Kerkhofs, M., Brauman, H., & Mendlewicz, J. Thyrotrophin response to thyreostimulin in affectively ill women: Relationship to suicidal behaviour. *British Journal of Psychiatry,* 1983, *143,* 401–405.

Linnoila, M., Erwin, C., Ramm, D., Cleveland, P., & Brendle, A. Effects of alcohol on psychomotor performance of women: Interaction with menstrual cycle. *Alcoholism: Clinical and Experimental Research,* 1980, *4,* 302–305.

Linnoila, M., Virkkunen, M., Scheinin, M., Nuutila, A., Rimon, R., & Goodwin, F. K. Low cerebrospinal fluid 5-hydroxyindoleacetic acid concentration differentiates impulsive from nonimpulsive violent behavior. *Life Sciences,* 1983, *33,* 2609–2614.

Lonnquist, J., Achte, K. Excessive drinking in psychiatric patients who later committed suicide. *Psychiatrica Fennica,* 1971, *00,* 209–213.

Major, F., & Murphy, D. Platelet and plasma amino-oxidase activity in alcoholic individuals. *British Journal of Psychiatry,* 1978, *132,* 548–554.

Mena, M., & Herrero, E. Monoamine metabolism in rat brain regions following long term alcohol treatment. *Journal of Neural Transmission,* 1980, *47,* 227–236.

Meir, J., Breyinova, V., & Vondracek, V. The causes of death in alcoholics. *Quarterly Journal of Studies on Alcohol,* 1956, *17,* 633–642.

Menninger, K. *Man against himself.* New York: Harcourt, Brace & World, 1938.

Miles, C. Conditions predisposing to suicide: A review. *Journal of Nervous and Mental Disease,* 1977, *164,* 231–246.

Motto, J. Suicide risk factors in alcohol abuse. *Suicide and Life-Threatening Behavior,* 1980, *10,* 230–238.

Murphy, G. E. On suicide prediction and prevention. *Archives of General Psychiatry,* 1983, *40,* 343–344.

Murphy, G. E. Suicide in alcoholism. *In A. Roy (Ed.), Suicide*. Baltimore: Williams & Wilkins, 1986.
Murphy, G. E., Armstrong, J., Hermele, S., Fisher, J., & Clendenin, W. Suicide and alcoholism. *Archives of General Psychiatry*, 1979, *36*, 65–69.
Murphy, G. E., & Robins, E. Social factors in suicide. *Journal of the American Medical Association*, 1967, *199*, 303–308.
Murray, R. Psychiatric illness in doctors. *Lancet*, 1974, *1*, 1211–1213.
Murray, R. Alcoholism amongst male doctors in Scotland. *Lancet*, 1976, *1*, 1326–1328. (a)
Murray, R. Characteristics and prognosis of alcoholic doctors. *British Medical Journal*, 1976, *2*, 1537–1539. (b)
Murray, R. Psychiatric illness in male doctors and controls: an analysis of Scottish hospital inpatient data. *British Journal of Psychiatry*, 1977, *131*, 1–10.
Murray, R. The mentally ill doctor. *Practitioner*, 1983, *227*, 65–75.
Nicholls, P., Edwards, G., & Kyle, E. A study of alcoholics admitted to four hospitals: II. General and cause-specific mortality during follow-up. *Quarterly Journal of Studies on Alcohol*, 1974, *35*, 841–855.
Ninan, P., van Kammen, D., Scheinin, M., Linnoila, M., Bunney, W. E., & Goodwin, F. K. Cerebrospinal fluid 5-HIAA in suicidal schizophrenic patients. *American Journal of Psychiatry* 1984, *141*, 566–569.
Norvig, J., & Nielsen, B. A follow-up study of 221 alcoholic addicts in Denmark. *Quarterly Journal of Studies on Alcohol*, 1956, *17*, 633–642.
Overall, J., Reilly, E., Kelley, J., & Hollister, L. Persistence of depression in detoxified alcoholics. *Alcoholism: Clinical and Experimental Research*, 1985, *9*, 331–333.
Pandey, G., Dorus, E., Shaughnessy, R., Gaviria, M., Val, E., & Davis, J. Reduced platelet MAO activity and vulnerability to psychiatric disorders. *Psychiatry Research*, 1980, *2*, 315–321.
Paykel, E., Myers, J., Dienelt, M., Klerman, G., Lindenthal, J., & Pepper, M. Life events and depression. *Archives of General Psychiatry*, 1969, *21*, 753–760.
Pell, S., & D'Alonzo, C. A five year mortality study of alcoholics. *Journal of Occupational Medicine*, 1973, *15*, 120–125.
Perris, H. Life events and depression: Part 2. Results in diagnostic subgroups and in relation to the recurrence of depression. *Journal of Affective Disorders*, 1984, *7*, 25–36.
Pokorny, A. Prediction of suicide in psychiatric patients. *Archives of General Psychiatry*, 1983, *40*, 249–257.
Pokorny, A., & Kaplan, H. Suicide following psychiatric hospitalization. *Journal of Nervous and Mental Disease*, 1976, *162*, 119–125.
Polich, J., Armor, D., & Braiker, H. *The course of alcoholism*. New York: Wiley, 1981.
Reis, J. A possible role of central noradenergic neurons in withdrawal states from alcohol. *Annals of the New York Academy of Sciences*, 1973, *215*, 249–252.
Ritson, E. Suicide amongst alcoholics. *British Journal of Medical Psychology*, 1968, *41*, 235–242.
Robins, E. Completed suicide. In A. Roy (Ed.), *Suicide*. Baltimore: Williams & Wilkins, 1986.
Robins, E., Murphy, G. E., Wilkinson, R. H., Jr., Gassner, S., & Kayes, J. Some clinical considerations in the prevention of suicide based on a study of 134 suicides. *American Journal of Public Health*, 1959, *49*, 888–899.
Robins, L., Helzer, J., Weissman, M., Orvaschel, H., Gruenberg, E., Burke, J., & Regier, D. Lifetime prevalence of specific psychiatric disorders in three sites. *Archives of General Psychiatry*, 1984, *41*, 949–958.
Rosenthal, N., Davenport, Y., Cowdry, R., Webster, M., & Goodwin, F. Monoamine metabolites in cerebrospinal fluid of depressive subgroups. *Psychiatry Research*, 1980, *2*, 113–119.
Roy, A. Risk factors for suicide in psychiatric patients. *Archives of General Psychiatry*, 1982, *39*, 1089–1095.
Roy, A. Family history of suicide. *Archives of General Psychiatry*, 1983, *40*, 971–974.

Roy, A. Suicide: A multidetermined act. *Psychiatric Clinics of North America*, 1985, *8*, 243–250. (a)

Roy, A. Suicide in doctors. *Psychiatric Clinics of North America*, 1985, *8*, 377–387. (b)

Roy, A. Suicide and psychiatric patients. *Psychiatric Clinics of North America*, 1985, *8*, 227–241. (c)

Roy, A. *Recent loss and suicide in patients with recurrent affective disorder.* Manuscript in preparation, 1986.

Roy, A., Agren, H., Pickar, D., Linnoila, M., Doran, A., Cutler, N., & Paul, S. M. Reduced cerebrospinal fluid concentrations of homovanillic acid and homovanillic acid to 5-hydroxyindoleacetic ratios in depressed patients: Relationship to suicidality and dexamethasone nonsuppression. *American Journal of Psychiatry*, 1986.

Roy, S., Breier, A., Doran, A., & Pickar, D. Life events in depression: Relationship to subtypes. *Journal of Affective Disorders*, 1985, *9*, 143–148.

Roy, A., Ninan, P., Mazonson, A., Pickar, D., van Kammen, D., Linnoila, M., & Paul, S. CSF monoamine metabolites in chronic schizophrenic patients who attempt suicide. *Psychological Medicine*, 1985, *15*, 335–340.

Roy-Byrne, P., Post, R., Rubinow, D., Linnoila, M., Savard, R., & Davis, D. CSF 5-HIAA and personal and family history of suicide in affectively ill patients: A negative study. *Psychiatry Research*, 1983, *10*, 263–274.

Rushing, W. Alcohol and suicide rates by status set and occupation. *Quarterly Journal of Studies on Alcohol*, 1968, *29*, 399–412.

Rushing, W. Suicide and the interaction of alcoholism (liver cirrhosis) with the social situation. *Quarterly Journal of Studies on Alcohol*, 1969, *30*, 93–103.

Sainsbury, P. Clinical aspects of suicide and its prevention. *British Journal of Hospital Medicine*, 1978, *19*, 156–164.

Sainsbury, P. The epidemiology of suicide. In A. Roy (Ed.), *Suicide.* Baltimore: Williams & Wilkins, 1986.

Sakinofsky, I. Suicide in doctors and wives of doctors. *Canadian Family Physician*, 1980, *26*, 837–844.

Schmidt, W., & deLint, J. Causes of death of alcoholics. *Quarterly Journal of Studies on Alcohol*, 1972, *33*, 171–185.

Schuckit, M., & Gunderson, E. Deaths among young alcoholics in the U.S. Naval Service. *Quarterly Journal of Studies on Alcohol*, 1974, *35*, 856–862.

Schuckit, M., & Morrissey, E. Alcoholism in women: Some clinical and social perspectives with an emphasis on possible subtypes. In M. Greenblatt & M. Schuckit (Eds.), *Alcoholism problems in women and children.* New York: Grune & Stratton, 1976.

Sullivan, J., Cavenoy, J., Maltbie, A., Lister, P., & Zung, W. Familial, biochemical and clinical correlates of alcoholics with low platelet monoamine oxidase activity. *Biological Psychiatry*, 1979, *14*, 385–394.

Sullivan, J., Stanfield, C., Maltbie, A., Hammett, E., & Cavenar, J. Stability of low blood platelet monoamine oxidase activity in human alcoholics. *Biological Psychiatry*, 1978, *13*, 391–397.

Sullivan, J., Stanfield, C., Schanberg, A., & Cavenar, J. Platelet monoamine oxidase and serum dopamine-B-hydroxylase activity in chronic alcoholics. *Archives of General Psychiatry*, 1978, *35*, 1209–1212.

Sundby, P. *Alcoholism and mortality* (National Institute for Alcohol Research, Publ. No. 6). Oslo: Universitetforlaget, 1967.

Tabakoff, B., & Boggan, W. Effects of ethanol on serotonin metabolism in brain. *Journal of Neurochemistry*, 1974, *22*, 759–764.

Tabakoff, B., & Ritzmann, R. Inhibition of the transport of 5-hydroxyindoleacetic acid from brain by ethanol. *Journal of Neurochemistry*, 1975, *24*, 1043–1051.

Takahashi, S., Tani, N., & Yamane, H. MAO activity in blood platelets in alcoholics. *Folia Psychiatrica Neurologica Japan*, 1976, *30*, 455–462.

Takahashi, S., Yamane, H., Kondo, H., & Tani, N. CSF monoamine metabolites in alcoholism: A comparative study with depression. *Folia Psychiatrica Neurologica Japan*, 1974, *28*, 347–354.

Tashiro, M., & Lipscomb, W. Mortality experiences of alcoholics. *Quarterly Journal of*

Studies on Alcohol, 1964, *24*, 203–212.

Temoche, A., Pugh, T., & MacMahon, B. Suicide rates amongst current and former mental institution patients. *Journal of Nervous and Mental Disease*, 1964, *138*, 124–130.

Truitt, E. A biogenic amine hypothesis for alcohol tolerance. *Annals of the New York Academy of Sciences*, 1973, *215*, 177–182.

Vaillant, G. *The natural history of alcoholism*. Cambridge, Mass.: Harvard University Press, 1983.

van Praag, H. Depression, suicide and metabolism of serotonin in the brain. *Journal of Affective Disorders*, 1982, *4*, 275–290.

van Praag, H. CSF 5-HIAA and suicide in non-depressed schizophrenics. *Lancet*, 1983, *2*, 977–978.

Virkkunen, M. Alcoholism and suicides in Helsinki. *Psychiatrica Fennica*, 1971, 201–207.

Virkkunen, M. Reactive hypoglycemic tendency among habitually violent offenders: A further study by means of the glucose tolerance test. *Neuropsychobiology*, 1982, *18*, 35–40.

Virkkunen, M. Insulin secretion during the glucose tolerance test in antisocial personality. *British Journal of Psychiatry*, 1983, *142*, 598–604.

Virkkunen, M. Reactive hypoglycemic tendency among arsonists. *Acta Psychiatria Scandinavica*, 1984, *69*, 445–452.

Wallinga, J. Attempted suicide: A ten year survey. *Diseases of the Nervous System*, 1949, *10*, 15–20.

Weissman, M., & Myers, J. Clinical depression in alcoholism. *American Journal of Psychiatry*, 1980, *137*, 372–373.

Weissman, M., Pottenger, M., Kleber, H., Ruben H., Williams, D., & Thompson, D. Symptom patterns in primary and secondary depression: A comparison of primary depressives with depressed opiate addicts, alcoholics and schizophrenics. *Archives of General Psychiatry*, 1977, *34*, 854–862.

Whitters, A., Cadoret, R., & Widmer, R. Factors associated with suicide attempts in alcohol abusers. *Journal of Affective Disorders*, 1985, *9*, 19–23.

Winokur, G. Family history studies: VIII. Secondary depression is alive and well. *Diseases of the Nervous System*, 1972, *33*, 94–99.

Woodruff, R., Guze, S., Clayton, P., Carr, D. Alcoholism and depression. *Archives of General Psychiatry*, 1973, *28*, 97–100.

Wyatt, R. J., Potkin, S. G., & Murphy, D. L. Platelet monoamine oxidase activity in schizophrenia: A review of the data. *American Journal of Psychiatry*, 1979, *136*, 377–385.

CHAPTER 9

Genetics, Twin Studies, and Suicide

David Lester, PhD

Department of Psychology, Richard Stockton State College

The nature–nurture controversy in psychology has a long history. In almost every topic of study, the debate about the role of heredity and the role of experiences has arisen. Perception, aggression, and intelligence have all been the focus of (often acrimonious) debate. This debate has led to a wide variety of methodologies to tease out the relative importance of heredity and environment, most of which are methodologically unsound. Only two methodologically sound techniques for study have been identified: studies of monozygotic and dizygotic twins, and cross-fostering studies.

In this review of genetic influence on suicide, these various methodologies for studying the nature–nurture issue are briefly reviewed first, and their applicability to the study of suicide is examined. Second, the research from the methodologically sound strategies is reviewed. Third, work by Uematsu using an approach different from any of the conventional methodologies is examined. Finally, the findings are discussed.

Methodologically Unsound Studies

The Study of Animals

The ethologists have long argued that, if a large number of different species of animals show a behavior, then the behavior is probably innately determined. This argument has been used recently for aggression (e.g., Lorenz, 1966). This argument by analogy (Lorenz, 1974) has often been criticized; for example, J. Goldstein (1975) has said that because we can behave in the same way as animals does not mean that we do.

A number of investigators have explored whether animals can commit suicide. Certainly, some animals do die under circumstances such that a suicidal death would be suspected if the animals were human. The most famous anecdotal example, of course, is that of Norwegian lemmings, who migrate twice every year between their winter habitat and their summer habitat. This migration, coupled with the fact that the lemming population goes through drastic changes in numbers, has led to tales (largely unsubstantiated) of lemming migrations in which, rather than turn from their path, the lemmings cross rivers and drown or jump off cliffs to their deaths.

In the past, the debate has usually been decided by opinion backed up by the writer's professional reputation. K. Goldstein (1940), for example, asserted that animals do not commit suicide. Suicide, for Goldstein, is a conscious and rational act. Suicides willingly choose death as a solution to their problems. Animals, according to this author, are clearly not capable of conscious and rational choices, and so cannot kill themselves. Neither, for that matter, can humans with severe brain injuries commit suicide, except during rare lucid moments. If animals die, no matter how closely the death resembles human suicidal actions, the death is a mere accident.

Of course, Goldstein's use of the term "suicide" here is very narrow. It does not admit of unconscious suicidal impulses, and such a limited definition of suicide is perhaps not heuristic. Furthermore, such a viewpoint easily allows psychologists to make the logical error of inferring the motivation of organisms from their acts and then explaining the acts from the inferred motivation. If a brain-injured patient commits suicide, then he or she must have been in a transition state. Thus, the act was a voluntary one. Such an analysis is scientifically untenable.

On the other hand, Menninger (1938) asserted that animals *can* commit suicide. Menninger felt that suicidal motivation can operate at an unconscious level, and he saw many self-destructive behaviors as partially determined by suicidal motivation, such as alcoholism and self-mutilation. Certainly these kinds of behaviors are found in animals. Masserman (1943) has described alcoholism in cats, and self-mutilation has been observed in caged monkeys (Harlow, 1962; Tinklepaugh, 1928). Harlow raised baby monkeys in isolation for about 1 year. The resulting monkeys were autistic, quiet, and indifferent; however, they would show violent frenzies of rage when, for example, humans approached the cage. Then they would often mutilate themselves. A parallel can perhaps be drawn between the effect of isolation in producing self-mutilation in monkeys and the high incidence of suicidal behavior in people who have experienced early loss. Amory (1970) reported anecdotal cases of dolphins dying in a suicide-like manner after loss. Einsidler and Hankoff (1979) assumed that suicide does take place in animals and suggested that suicide can result from pain, loss of companions, and overcrowding. However, anecdotal evidence will not do; it can never convince the skeptic. In the same way, *ex cathedra* statements from people (however famous) will not suffice, either. What is needed is a method of proving that animals can kill themselves.

There has been one approach to this problem that does have potential for future research. Schaefer (1967) first identified the basic issues involved in deciding whether an animal can commit suicide: (1) Can an animal discriminate between life and death, or, to be more specific, between a live animal and a dead animal? (2) Can an animal discriminate between a lethal and a nonlethal environment? (3) Under what circumstances will an animal choose to enter a lethal environment?

Schaefer, as yet, has only demonstrated how these questions might be answered. To demonstrate that animals can discriminate a dead animal from a live one, Schaefer used an operant technique in which one lever in a Skinner box produced food when a live mouse was the stimulus, and a second lever produced food when a dead mouse was the stimulus. Experimental mice learned this discrimination.

To demonstrate that mice can discriminate between a lethal chamber and a nonlethal chamber, Schaefer allowed mice to choose to enter one of two chambers. In one chamber they were electrocuted, while in the other they were allowed to live. The behavior of these mice was the stimulus for the experimental mice. As long as the observed mouse was alive, one lever produced food; when the observed mouse was dead, a second lever produced food. The experimental mice learned this discrimination. After learning the discrimination, the experimental mice were allowed to enter either chamber. On five trials, the experimental mice entered the nonlethal chamber.[1] If these demonstrations could be replicated, it would be possible to investigate under what circumstances an animal might choose to enter the lethal chamber.

In his demonstrations, however, Schaefer failed to include controls for several factors. For example, would the experimental mice have responded differently if, instead of observing mice killed, they had observed mice waking from sleep? Perhaps it was change in the state of a mouse that led the experimental mice to avoid the "lethal" chamber, rather than mice being killed. Many other methodological problems can be raised about these demonstrations. Schaefer's demonstrations

---

[1] A second demonstration was not successful.

clearly do not yet provide adequate evidence. Even though his refor-
mulation of the problem is a great advance over the original formulation,
the existence of suicide in animals remains unproven.

Other animal studies that may throw light on the nature–nurture
issue (such as strain differences and breeding for a particular trait)
are not possible, since suicide in animals has not been demonstrated
conclusively.

Behavior Genetic Analysis

In a behavior genetic analysis, a single gene defect is identified and
its consequences explored by cross-breeding, as in the study of audiogenic
seizures in mice. This, of course, has not been done with suicide in
humans, since no single gene defect has been identified that leads to
suicide. However, an example can be drawn from the study of self-
mutilation. Self-mutilation is a behavior with resemblances to the self-
destructive behavior of suicide (Lester, 1972a). There is a genetically
caused syndrome, the Lesch–Nyhan syndrome (the result of a sex-
linked recessive inborn error in purine metabolism), which is characterized by stunting of growth, mental and motor retardation, and
compulsive self-mutilation of the tongue, lips, and fingers, primarily
by biting (Berman, Balis, & Dancis, 1969).

The Study of Infants

Study of behaviors in infants has been used in an endeavor to minimize
the effects of experience and maximize the effects of heredity. However,
suicide is not believed possible in children, since they do not possess
a mature concept of death. Thus, this technique is not possible for the
study of suicide. Elsewhere (Lester, 1969), I have discussed a report of
a fetus supposedly completing suicide and speculated as to how Goldstein
and Menninger would view such a phenomenon.

Family Trees

To show that a behavior runs in families does not enable us to dis-
tinguish between nature and nurture. However, in earlier times, studies
of family trees were thought to suggest the effects of heredity. Several
studies appeared (e.g., Shapiro, 1935) that detailed multiple suicides
in particular families. It should be noted that modern studies of family

trees can be used to provide evidence suggestive of hereditary influences; for example, Karlsson (1968) has done this for schizophrenia in Icelandic families over seven generations.

Comparison of Cultures

A study of cultures around the world, to show that a behavior has a great variability from culture to culture, has been used to argue against hereditary influences. If one culture shows a behavior while another does not, this suggests environmental influences on the behavior, assuming that there are similar gene pools in the two cultures (e.g., Mead, 1963). Again, this method is nothing more than suggestive.

Two studies have rated nonliterate cultures around the world for the incidence of suicide (Naroll, 1962; Palmer, 1965). Palmer did find a wide variation in the suicide incidence in various cultures as rated from anthropological writings on the topic; he assigned some cultures scores of zero, indicating an absence of suicidal behavior (e.g., the Andamese, Lapp, Yungar, and Zuni).

Family Studies

In family studies, the incidence of the target behavior in relatives with various degrees of genetic similarity to the patient is studied. For example, the incidence of schizophrenia among relatives of schizo-phrenics—parents, full siblings, children, half-siblings, uncles and aunts, nephews and nieces, grandchildren, and so on—has been studied (Shields, 1976).

There have been comments on the incidence of suicide in the relatives of suicides overall, but no detailed study of incidence according to the degree of relationship to the patient. Six reports indicate that suicidal people have had more relatives or friends who showed suicidal behavior (Corder, Page, & Corder, 1974; Diekstra, 1974; Garfinkel, Froese, & Golombek, 1979; Hauschild, 1968; Murphy, Wetzel, Swallow, & McClure, 1969; Woodruff, Clayton, & Guze, 1972). On the other hand, eight studies have reported no excess of such relatives and friends (Doroff, 1969; Finlay, 1970; Hill, 1969; Johnson & Hunt, 1979; Pokorny, 1960; Rorsman, 1973; Rosen, 1970; Tucker & Reinhardt, 1966).

Pollack (1938) compared suicide attempters with suicide completers and found a greater incidence of completed suicide in families of the suicide completers. Ettlinger (1964) compared suicide attempters who subsequently killed themselves with those who did not and found no significant differences in the incidence of completed suicide in the family members.

Sletten, Evenson, and Brown (1973) found an excess of attempted suicides (but not completed suicides) among the relatives of suicide attempters and an excess of completed suicides among the relatives of suicide completers. Although this result is quite tidy, the inconsistencies found by the other researchers must make us skeptical until it is replicated.

It is clear that a few studies have found an association between suicidal behavior in individuals and a history of suicidal behavior in their relatives. However, more research is needed to specify the association more exactly.

Methodologically Sound Studies

Cross-Fostering

In cross-fostering studies, the offspring of mothers with the target behavior are taken away and raised by other mothers. If the adopted offspring develop the target behavior, then genetic influences can be proven. This has been done for behaviors such as schizophrenia (Heston, 1966), but not for suicide.

Studies of Identical Twins

Identical twin studies require a comparison of identical (monozygotic) twins, orphaned at birth and raised by different sets of adoptive parents. Then, if the separated identical twins show the same target behavior, the role of heredity is proven.

Weaker versions of this methodology exist. The criterion for separation at birth is often relaxed, since such an occurrence is rare; usually, identical twins are raised by the same set of parents. Thus identical twins raised by parents (natural or adoptive) are compared with nonidentical twins raised by parents. Since identical twins are treated differently by parents than are nonidentical twins (Wilson, 1931), this is not a sound method. However, the strict methodology becomes extremely difficult to apply in the case of a rare behavior. Slater (1968) could find only 15 cases of monozygotic twins raised apart for some period of time, of whom one had schizophrenia, in all of the previous research reported.

For suicide, only the less strict methodology has been employed. Kallman (1953) reviewed the literature and collected together all reported cases of the suicidal death of at least one member of a twin pair; he was able to add to these data suicidal twin pairs that he had identified in his examination of suicidal deaths. He reported that of the 18 monozygotic twin pairs, 1 was concordant and 3 were possibly concordant. Of the 21 dizygotic twin pairs, none of the pairs were concordant.[2] Kallman concluded that suicide was probably not dependent upon inherited factors, and other writers have followed his conclusion (Fuller & Thompson, 1960).

Kallman advanced three reasons for his failure to find concordant twin pairs:

1. The suicide of one member of a twin pair could immunize the partner against yielding to self-destructive urges. Kallman thought that this was unlikely, since in many cases the suicide of the member of the twin pair occurred after the death of the other member from natural causes. Furthermore, such an explanation would have to be limited to twins, for in general it appears that experience of a suicide in a family increases the likelihood of other family members' committing suicide.

2. Suicide has a very complex etiology, and thus duplication of factors, even in twins, is very unlikely.

3. Suicide is more likely to occur when sibling rivalry is present. If one of a pair of twins completes suicide, the sibling rivalry will be eliminated (or at least reduced), and the surviving twin will be less likely to complete suicide. Kallman argued that if this were true, then suicide in only children should be rarer than in children with siblings. He examined a sample of suicide completers and found that there were no significant differences between the proportion of only children in the general population and in the sample of suicide completers (Kallman, De Porte, De Porte, & Feingold, 1949).

It would appear, therefore, that the available evidence does not support points 1 and 3, and that point 2 is the only remaining possibility as an explanation of Kallman's failure to find concordant twin pairs.

Elsewhere (Lester, 1968), I noted that, if Kallman's data were analyzed using an appropriate statistical test, then there would be significantly more concordant pairs in the monozygotic sample than in the dizygotic sample. This is what would be expected if inherited factors were at work in the determination of suicidal tendencies. However, I noted

---

[2] A "concordant pair" here means that both twins of the pair completed suicide.

several methodological inadequacies in Kallman's study. First, the sample was inadequate in size. Assuming a suicide rate of 10 per 100,000 per year, then the number of concordant pairs one would expect to find in a sample the size of Kallman's would be less than 1 pair. Second, Kallman's sample was not a random sample, since it included isolated cases reported by different investigators.[3]

Juel-Nielsen and Videbech (1970) studied twin pairs born in Denmark from 1870 to 1920. They found 77 pairs in which one twin had completed suicide; 4 of the 19 monozygotic pairs and none of the 58 dizygotic pairs were concordant for suicide. This difference was significant on a Fisher's exact test ($p = .0021$). The same sample was also surveyed by Harvald and Hauge (1965), who reported similar findings.

Haberlandt (1967) reviewed all prior studies, including those by Kallman and by Harvald and Hauge, and reported a concordance rate of 0% for 98 dizygotic twin pairs and a concordance rate of 18% for 51 monozygotic twin pairs. Blath, McClure, and Wetzel (1973) and Tsuang (1977) have also reviewed this literature; Blath *et al.* reported one monozygotic twin pair concordant for attempted suicide.

Overall, it may be concluded that monozygotic twin pairs have a greater concordance for completed suicide than dizygotic twin pairs. However, no studies have been reported of monozygotic twin pairs raised apart, and so we must be cautious in our conclusions until such a study is reported.

Uematsu's Cohort Technique

Uematsu (1961; see also Lester, 1970, 1973) proposed a different approach to the study of genetic factors in suicide. Consider those people born in a given year. If genetic factors cause the occurrence of suicide, then some proportion (p) of this cohort will die from suicide. If the gene pool of the population is sufficiently varied and distributed, there is no reason to suppose that the individuals born in one year will differ in their genetic constitution from those born in a subsequent year. Thus, this proportion p should remain constant from year to year. Suicide occurs mainly among people who are past childbearing age. They will therefore have had an opportunity to pass on their suicidogenic genes to offspring, assuming that suicidal people are as likely to marry and have children as nonsuicidal people.

---

[3] Stengel (1967) noted that Kallman did not establish the monozygosity of his twin pairs beyond doubt.

It is known that nations have reasonably constant suicide rates over time (Lester, 1972b). To test the prediction, however, we need to know the proportion of the people born each year who eventually die of suicide as compared to some other cause of death, and we need to know this proportion for a succession of years.

A second prediction that can be made for a cohort is that if the cohort has a high incidence of suicide when the cohort is young, then most of those genetically predisposed to suicide will have been removed from the cohort while it is young. Thus, the incidence of suicide in the cohort will be low when the cohort is old. This prediction has received some support from Uematsu, whose Japanese data are summarized in Table 9-1.

I have attempted to test this hypothesis in the United States (Lester, 1984); I confirmed the pattern reported by Uematsu for females, but not for males. I also noted that the presence of World War II during the time period studied could have interfered with the pattern for males.

Discussion

The only methodologically sound procedure utilized thus far for the study of the role of heredity in suicide is that of monozygotic versus dizygotic twins. Even in this methodology, no study has yet compared monozygotic twin pairs raised apart with those raised together. When this is borne in mind, it is clear that the concordance rate for completed suicide is higher in monozygotic twin pairs raised together than in dizygotic twin pairs raised together. This suggests a genetic effect for suicide.

TABLE 9-1. Correlations between the Suicide Rate of a Cohort in Japan aged 15–19 and the Suicide Rate of the Cohort in Later Years

Later ages	Males	Females
20–24	−.45	−.48
25–29	−.31	−.04
30–34	−.53	−.35
35–39	+.58	−.34
40–44	−.24	−.50
45–49	−.55	−.32

Note. Data from Uematsu (1961).

In addition, the cohort technique suggested by Uematsu does lend some partial support to the notion that a cohort of the population with a high suicide rate at one point in its life will have a low suicide rate at other points in its life. This suggests that a cohort contains only a limited number of potential suicides, a number perhaps determined in part by genetic factors. However, the technique only suggests this and by no means proves it.

It has been found that suicide is more common in those with psychiatric illness (Lester, 1972b). As Tsuang (1977) has pointed out, there is good evidence for a genetic component in the etiology of schizophrenia, affective disorder, and alcoholism. Tsuang reviewed the evidence from twin studies and cross-fostering studies for each of these three disorders. Thus, the evidence for a genetic component in the etiology of suicide may result from the genetic component in the etiology of psychiatric illness. What is needed is a study that disentangles the two outcomes—suicide and psychiatric illness.

None of the twin studies of suicide to date have made formal psychiatric diagnoses of the twins. However, even if the twins were to be diagnosed, it is hard to imagine a methodology that would test the two rival hypotheses genes → suicide, and genes → psychiatric illness → suicide. The role of genes in the etiology of suicide may, therefore, remain speculative.

References

Amory, C. After living with a man, a dolphin may commit suicide. *Holiday*, May 1970, pp. 16–18.

Berman, P., Balis, M., & Dancis, J. Congenital hyperuricemia. *Archives of Neurology*, 1969, *20*, 44–53.

Blath, R., McClure, J., & Wetzel, R. Familial factors in suicide. *Diseases of the Nervous System*, 1973, *34*, 90–93.

Corder, B., Page, P., & Corder, R. Parental history, family communication and interaction patterns in adolescent suicide. *Family Therapy*, 1974, *1*, 285–290.

Diekstra, R. A social learning theory approach to the prediction of suicidal behavior. In *Proceedings of the 7th International Congress for Suicide Prevention*. Amsterdam: Swets & Zeitlinger, 1974.

Doroff, D. Attempted and gestured suicide in adolescent girls. *Dissertation Abstracts International*, 1969, *27*, 2631B.

Einsidler, B., & Hankoff, L. Self-injury in animals. In L. Hankoff & B. Einsidler (Eds.), *Suicide*. Littleton, Mass.: PSG, 1979.

Ettlinger, R. Suicide in a group of patients who had previously attempted suicide. *Acta Psychiatrica Scandinavica*, 1964, *40*, 364–378.

Finlay, S. Suicide and self-injury in Leeds University students. In *Proceedings of the 5th International Congress for Suicide Prevention*. Vienna: International Association for Suicide Prevention, 1970.

Fuller, J., & Thompson, W. *Behavior genetics*. New York: Wiley, 1960.

202   SUICIDE AND LIFE-THREATENING BEHAVIOR

Garfinkel, B., Froese, A., & Golombek, H. Suicidal behavior in a paediatric population. In *Proceedings of the 10th International Congress for Suicide Prevention*. Ottawa: International Association for Suicide Prevention, 1979.

Goldstein, J. *Aggression and crimes of violence*. New York: Oxford University Press, 1975.

Goldstein, K. *Human nature in the light of psychopathology*. Cambridge, Mass.: Harvard University Press, 1940.

Haberlandt, W. Aportacion a la genetica del suicidio. *Folia Clinica Internacional*, 1967, *17*, 319–322.

Harlow, H. The heterosexual affectional system in monkeys. *American Psychologist*, 1962, *17*, 1–19.

Harvald, B., & Hauge, M. Hereditary factors elucidated by twin studies. In J. Neel, M. Shaw, & J. Schull (Eds.), *Genetics and the epidemiology of chronic disease*. Washington, D.C.: U.S. Government Printing Office, 1965.

Hauschild, T. Suicidal population of a military psychiatric center. *Military Medicine*, 1968, *133*, 425–437.

Heston, L. Psychiatric disorders in foster-home reared children of schizophrenic mothers. *British Journal of Psychiatry*, 1966, *112*, 819–825.

Hill, O. The association of childhood bereavement with suicide in depressive illnesses. *British Journal of Psychiatry*, 1969, *115*, 301–304.

Johson, G., & Hunt, G. Suicidal behavior in bipolar manic–depressive patients and their families. *Comprehensive Psychiatry*, 1979, *20*, 159–164.

Juel-Nielsen, N., & Videbech, T. A twin study of suicide. *Acta Geneticae Medicae et Gemellologiae*, 1970, *19*, 307–310.

Kallman, F. *Heredity in health and mental disease*. New York: Norton, 1953.

Kallman, F., De Porte, J., De Porte, E., & Feingold, L. Suicide in twins and only children. *American Journal of Human Genetics*, 1949, *1*, 113–126.

Karlsson, J. Genealogic studies of schizophrenia. In D. Rosenthal & S. Kety (Eds.), *The transmission of schizophrenia*. Oxford: Pergamon Press, 1968.

Lester, D. Note on the inheritance of suicide. *Psychological Reports*, 1968, *22*, 320.

Lester, D. Fetal suicide. *Journal of the American Medical Association*, 1969, *209*, 1367.

Lester, D. Suicidal tendencies. *Crisis Intervention*, 1970, *2*, 16–18.

Lester, D. Self-mutilating behavior. *Psychological Bulletin*, 1972, *78*, 119–128. (a)

Lester, D. *Why people kill themselves*. Springfield, Ill.: Charles C Thomas, 1972. (b)

Lester, D. The study of the inheritance of rare behaviors. *Behavior Genetics*, 1973, *3*, 197–198.

Lester, D. Suicide risk by birth cohort. *Suicide and Life-Threatening Behavior*, 1984, *14*, 132–136.

Lorenz, K. *On aggression*. New York: Harcourt, Brace & World, 1966.

Lorenz, K. Analogy as a source of knowledge. *Science*, 1974, *185*, 229–234.

Masserman, J. *Behavior and neurosis*. Chicago: University of Chicago Press, 1943.

Mead, M. *Sex and temperament in three primitive societies*. New York: Morrow, 1963.

Menninger, K. *Man against himself*. New York: Harcourt, Brace & World, 1938.

Murphy, G., Wetzel, R., Swallow, C., & McClure, J. Who calls the suicide prevention center? *American Journal of Psychiatry*, 1969, *126*, 314–324.

Naroll, R. *Data quality control*. Glencoe, Ill.: Free Press, 1962.

Palmer, S. Murder and suicide in 40 nonliterate societies. *Journal of Criminal Law, Criminology and Police Science*, 1965, *56*, 320–324.

Pokorny, A. Characteristics of 44 patients who subsequently committed suicide. *Archives of General Psychiatry*, 1960, *2*, 314–323.

Pollack, B. A study of the problem of suicide. *Psychiatric Quarterly*, 1938, *12*, 306–330.

Rorsman, B. Suicide in psychiatric patients. *Social Psychiatry*, 1973, *8*, 55–66.

Rosen, D. The serious suicide attempt. *American Journal of Psychiatry*, 1970, *127*, 764–770.

Schaefer, H. Can a mouse commit suicide? In E. S. Shneidman (Ed.), *Essays in self-destruction*. New York: Science House, 1967.

Shapiro, L. Suicide. *Journal of Nervous and Mental Disease*, 1935, *81*, 547–553.

Shields, J. Genetics in schizophrenia. In D. Kemali, G. Bartholini, & D. Richter (Eds.), *Schizophrenia today*. New York: Pergamon Press, 1976.

Slater, E. A review of earlier evidence on genetic factors in schizophrenia. In D. Rosenthal & S. Kety (Eds.), *The transmission of schizophrenia*. Oxford: Pergamon Press, 1968.

Sletten, I., Evenson, R., & Brown, M. Some results from an automated statewide comparison among attempted, committed and nonsuicidal patients. *Suicide and Life-Threatening Behavior*, 1973, *13*, 191–197.

Stengel, E. Genetic and social influences in the causation of suicide. *Eugenic Society Symposium*, 1967, *3*, 122–129.

Tinklepaugh, O. The self-mutilation of a male macacus rhesus monkey. *Journal of Mammalology*, 1928, *9*, 293–300.

Tsuang, M. Genetic factors in suicide. *Diseases of the Nervous System*, 1977, *38*, 498–501.

Tucker, G., & Reinhardt, R. *Suicide attempts* (Publication No. NAM 1-975). Washington, DC: U.S. Naval Aerospace Medical Institute, 1966.

Uematsu, M. A statistic approach to the host factor of suicide in adolescence *Acta Medica et Biologica*, 1961, *8*, 279–286.

Wilson, P. T. A study of twins with special reference to heredity as a factor determining differences in environment. Human Biology, 1931, *6*, 324–354.

Woodruff, R. A., Clayton, P. J., & Guze, S. B. Suicide attempts and psychiatric diagnosis. *Diseases of the Nervous System*, 1972, *33*, 617–621.

CHAPTER 10

Neurochemical Findings in Suicide Completers and Suicide Attempters

Michael Stanley, PhD, Barbara Stanley, PhD
Department of Psychiatry Columbia University
Lil Traskman-Bendz, MD, PhD
Stockholm, Sweden
J. John Mann, MD
Department of Psychiatry, Cornell Medical College
Elaine Meyendorff, MD
Lafayette Clinic, Detroit

Loss of human life through suicide is a major health problem in the United States, and in some groups it is on the rise. Suicide is currently ranked as the second or third major cause of death in adolescents ("Recent Trends in Suicide," 1976; U.S. Public Health Service, 1979). Although records indicate that more than 25,000 people commit suicide annually, it is estimated that suicide is grossly underreported and that the actual figure is two to three times higher (Resnick, 1980). In recognition of the magnitude of this problem, research efforts have been directed at identifying potential suicide victims, and many suicide prevention centers have been established (Borg & Stahl, 1982; G. Murphy, 1983). Most research on suicide prediction has focused on demographic, psychosocial, and personality factors (Goldney, 1982; Monk, 1975; Perlin & Schmitt, 1975). This work has identified several variables that correlate significantly with suicide, and has found several factors that are associated with being "at risk" for suicide. However, the correlations between these variables and suicide are too weak to be of practical clinical utility. Furthermore, these indicators tend to overpredict suicide potential, thus falsely identifying many individuals as suicide risks.

While the literature on biochemical factors involved in mental illness has burgeoned over the past 30 years, only a small portion of this literature is devoted to the biochemistry of suicide. Recently, biochemical studies have found serotonergic abnormalities in suicide attempters and suicide victims. These findings, combined with psychological studies, appear promising and may improve the identification and treatment of suicidal individuals.

Several studies have reported biochemical changes consistent with reduced serotonergic activity, such as lowered levels of 5-hydroxyindoleacetic acid (5-HIAA) in cerebrospinal fluid (CSF) of individuals who have attempted suicide (Asberg, Thoren, Traskman, Bertilsson, & Ringverger, 1976; Brown, Ebert, Goyer, Jimerson, Klein, Bunney, & Goodwin, 1982; van Praag, 1983). A number of postmortem studies have found reduced levels of serotonin (5-HT) and 5-HIAA in the brains of individuals who have committed suicide (Bourne, Bunney, Colburn, Davis, Shaw, & Coppen, 1968; Pare, Yeung, Price, & Stacey, 1969; Shaw, Camps, & Eccleston, 1967). Recent investigations have examined receptor alterations and have found significant differences between 5-HT-related binding parameters in suicide victims and controls that are also consistent with reduced serotonergic function in suicide victims (Paul, Rehavi, Skolnick, & Goodwin, 1984; Perry, Marshall, Blessed, Tomlinson, & Perry, 1983; Stanley, Virgilio, & Gershon, 1982). Finally, studies of suicide attempters with a variety of psychiatric diagnoses indicate that in the case of suicide, the behavior may be more closely related than the diagnosis to the biochemical changes observed.

Postmortem Findings in Suicide

There are several lines of evidence suggesting an association between 5-HT and suicidal behavior. The original postmortem suicide studies measured 5-HT and 5-HIAA in brain stem areas, particularly the raphe nuclei, where 5-HT cell bodies are concentrated. These studies found small decreases of 10–20% in levels of either 5-HT or 5-HIAA compared to controls.

It is noteworthy that in studies where information on diagnosis was available, approximately 50% of the suicide victims were endogenously depressed. The remaining cases had diagnoses of alcoholism, reactive depression, schizophrenia, or personality disorder. This suggests that the altered 5-HT and 5-HIAA levels were primarily associated with suicidal behavior, rather than with depression alone.

A total of seven studies from the 1960s through the 1980s investigated the levels of 5-HT, 5-HIAA, or both in suicide victims. Significant reductions in 5-HT levels were reported in three of these studies. Lloyd, Farley, Deck, and Hornykiewicz (1974) measured 5-HT and 5-HIAA in raphe nuclei of five suicides and five controls. Three of the five suicides died by drug overdose. They found no significant difference in 5-HIAA levels between the two groups. There was, however, a significant reduction in 5-HT levels for the suicide group. Pare et al. (1969) determined norepinephrine (NE), dopamine (DA), 5-HT, and 5-HIAA levels in suicide victims who had died by carbon monoxide poisoning. They found no significant difference between the two groups for NE, DA, and 5-HIAA. They did report a significant reduction in brain stem levels of 5-HT for the suicide group. However, when age effects were partialed out, no significant reduction was noted. Shaw et al. (1967) found lower brain stem levels of 5-HT in suicide victims compared to controls, a statistically significant difference. About half of the suicide group died by barbiturate overdose, and the other half died by carbon monoxide poisoning.

Two out of seven studies have reported significant reductions in the levels of 5-HIAA in suicide victims. Bourne et al. (1968) measured NE, 5-HT, and 5-HIAA in the hindbrains of suicides and found significantly lower levels only for 5-HIAA. Beskow, Gottfries, Roos, and Winblad (1976) reported a significant decrease in 5-HIAA levels in a group of suicide victims compared with controls. However, this effect may have been related to the difference in postmortem interval between the two groups.

More recently, studies by Owens, Cross, Crow, Deakin, Ferrier, Lofthouse, and Poulter (1983), as well as those conducted by Stanley, McIntyre, and Gershon (1983), have not observed significant reductions in the concentrations of 5-HT or 5-HIAA in the frontal cortices of suicide victims.

In many of the studies just mentioned, factors such as death by drug overdose or carbon monoxide poisoning, extensive postmortem delay, and lack of an age-matched control group may have confounded the results, and may partly account for the lack of uniformity in results. In addition, there are other uncontrollable sources of error. The levels of monoamines and their metabolites are known to be influenced by factors such as diet, acute drug use, alcohol, and so on. These latter variables have minimal impact upon the receptor-binding characteristics of the brain, as receptor binding is not as responsive to acute influences.

Studies of receptor binding have shown that changes in the number or density of monoamine binding sites can be induced by altering the level of transmitter release, either by chronic administration of antidepressants or by lesioning experiments that deplete particular monoamines. Recently, receptor sites have been identified that appear to be associated with the presynaptic 5-HT uptake sites that are labeled by [3H]imipramine, and postsynaptic receptor sites that are labeled by 5-

HT antagonists such as [^{3}H]ketanserin. Imipramine binding sites have been characterized in platelets and various regions of brain. Some of the experimental evidence linking imipramine binding with 5-HT includes the following: (1) Autoradiographic studies of [^{3}H]imipramine binding sites show distribution similar to serotonergic terminals; (2) chemical and electrolytic lesions of the raphe nuclei cause a significant reduction in 5-HT level and in the number of imipramine binding sites; (3) the use of an irreversible ligand results in reduced [^{3}H]imipramine binding and 5-HT uptake; and (4) the potency of antidepressant drugs to inhibit 5-HT uptake is significantly correlated with their potency to inhibit [^{3}H]imipramine binding.

The clinical significance of imipramine binding was provided by the studies of Langer and coworkers, who reported decreases in the number of binding sites in the platelets of depressed patients (Langer & Raisman, 1983). The association of imipramine binding with 5-HT function, as well as the significant reduction in binding density in depression, suggests the possibility of alterations in imipramine binding in suicide victims.

Stanley *et al.* (1982) tested this hypothesis by determining imipramine binding in the brains of nine suicide victims and nine controls. There were no significant differences between the two groups with respect to age, sex, and postmortem interval. The suicide victims chosen had died in a determined manner, (e.g., gunshot, hanging, etc.) and the control group was chosen to match for sudden and violent deaths. The findings indicated a significant reduction in the number of imipramine binding sites in frontal cortex (suicides, B_{max} = 330 ± 39 fmol/mg protein; controls, B_{max} = 587 ± 75 fmol/mg protein), with no difference in binding affinity (K_d).

Since the completion of this study, three other studies have measured imipramine binding in either suicide victims or depressives dying from natural causes. Paul *et al.* (1984) reported a significant decrease in imipramine binding in hypothalamus in suicide victims, with no change in desipramine binding. The latter binding site is associated with the NE reuptake site. Perry *et al.* (1983) found decreases in imipramine binding in the brains of depressives who died from natural causes. In contrast, Meyerson, Wennogle, Abel, Coupet, Lippa, Rauh, and Beer (1982) reported increased imipramine binding in suicides.

In summary, there have been four published studies thus far that have measured imipramine binding; three of these studies have reported decreases, while one has found an increase. These results are consistent with the accumulating evidence suggesting the involvement of 5-HT in suicide. Specifically, reduced imipramine binding (associated with presynaptic terminals) may be indicative of lower-functioning 5-HT nerve terminals, and would be in agreement with those reports of reduced postmortem levels of 5-HT and 5-HIAA in the CSF of suicide attempters.

In addition to the assessment of postmortem presynaptic function of the 5-HT system in suicide, it is possible to measure postsynaptic 5-HT binding sites using 5-HT antagonists such as [3H]spiroperidol or [3H]ketanserin, which measure $5\text{-}HT_2$ receptors. $5\text{-}HT_2$ receptor binding in animals has been shown to change in response to chronic antidepressant treatment and lesioning of 5-HT nuclei.

Stanley and Mann (1983) compared postmortem $5\text{-}HT_2$ binding sites in frontal cortex in 11 suicide victims with 11 controls. Both groups were matched for age, sex, postmortem interval, and suddenness of death. A significant increase was found in the number of $5\text{-}HT_2$ binding sites, with no change in affinity in the suicide group. Some of these samples had also had imipramine binding measured. The correlation between the binding density of these two receptor populations was $-.42$ (Pearson product–moment correlation), but it was not significant ($p > .20$), perhaps owing to the small sample size ($n = 22$). Nevertheless, the trend suggests that as the 5-HT presynaptic input (estimated by imipramine binding) decreases, there is a compensatory increase in the number of postsynaptic $5\text{-}HT_2$ binding sites.

The finding of raised numbers of $5\text{-}HT_2$ (postsynaptic) binding sites in the frontal cortex of suicide victims further supports the involvement of 5-HT in suicidal behavior. Furthermore, changes in the numbers of 5-HT receptors in suicide victims appear to be restricted to $5\text{-}HT_2$ and imipramine binding, since no changes have been found in the number of $5\text{-}HT_1$ receptors in this population (Mann, Stanley, McBride, & McEwen, 1986). Owens et al. (1983) have reported no difference in $5\text{-}HT_1$ receptor binding in nonmedicated suicide victims compared to controls.

The combined findings of decreased imipramine binding and increased $5\text{-}HT_2$ binding are indicative of decreased serotonergic activity in suicide victims. The same effect was not demonstrable, however, by direct measurements of 5-HT or 5-HIAA in frontal cortex. Stanley et al. (1983) measured 5-HT and 5-HIAA in 24 suicide victims and 24 controls, in whom factors such as death by drug overdose, extensive postmortem delay, and age and sex matching did not differ significantly between the two groups. As was not the case in many of the previous postmortem studies, both 5-HT and 5-HIAA were measured in the same individuals. This allowed an estimation of turnover in this system by examining the ratio of 5-HIAA to 5-HT. The results revealed no significant difference between the two groups in 5-HT or 5-HIAA levels. There was no difference in the ratio of 5-HIAA to 5-HT. Owens et al. (1983) also noted no difference in cortical 5-HIAA levels between suicides and controls. Thus, it is possible that binding sites that may change in response to more chronic effects—in contrast to levels of 5-HT and 5-HIAA, which are more sensitive to very acute effects—may serve as better indicators of this system's steady state prior to death.

There is a significant body of data suggesting a role for the cholinergic system in affective disorders. Because the incidence of individuals diagnosed to have affective disorders who subsequently commit suicide is high, it is of interest to determine 3-quinuclidinyl benzilate (QNB) binding in the brains of suicide victims. QNB is a reversible muscarinic antagonist that has been used in several human postmortem studies to examine changes in the cholinergic system. QNB binding was assayed in 44 individuals (22 suicides and 22 controls) (Stanley, 1984). Both groups were matched for age, sex, and postmortem interval. The results indicated no significant difference between the suicide and control groups for either the number of binding sites (B_{max}) or binding affinity (K_d). A recent study by Kaufman, Gillin, O'Laughlin, and Kleinman (1984) also found no difference in QNB binding in suicides. In contrast to these findings, a preliminary study by Meyerson et al. (1982) reported increased QNB binding in suicides.

Delayed down-regulation of beta-adrenergic receptors has been reported as a common property of almost all known effective antidepressants; however, the relationship of beta-adrenergic receptors to untreated depressive disorders and suicidal behavior remains uncertain. Two laboratories have now reported an increase in the number of beta-adrenergic receptors in suicide victims compared to controls (Mann et al., 1986; Zanko & Biegon, 1983). One laboratory reported no differences in beta-adrenergic receptor binding (Meyerson et al., 1982). The finding of increased beta-adrenergic receptors would be consistent with reduced noradrenergic function, but clearly requires replication and extension by additional studies of catecholamines and metabolites, as well as biosynthetic enzymes such as tyrosine hydroxylase.

Since 5-HT is a substrate for the degradative enzyme monoamine oxidase A (MAO-A), the status of this enzyme in suicide victims has been explored. Two initial studies examined postmortem MAO activity in suicides compared to controls (Grote, Moses, Robins, Hudgens, & Croninger, 1974). A second study found reduced MAO activity in patients in whom the suicide was associated with alcoholism (Gottfries, Oreland, Wilberg, & Winblad, 1975). These studies included a significant proportion of patients who had died by carbon monoxide or drug overdose, which may have altered their neurochemistry. They also employed a single substrate concentration, a method that is less informative and less sensitive than enzyme kinetic studies.

Mann and Stanley (1984) assayed MAO-A and MAO-B in the frontal cortex of 13 suicides and 13 controls, using labeled 5-HT and phenylethylamine (PEA) as substrates for MAO-A and MAO-B, respectively.

The victims studied died by determined and violent means, (gunshot, hanging, jumping from height) with the exception of one overdose. There were no significant differences between the suicide and control group with respect to factors such as age, sex, and postmortem interval. The results of this kinetic study showed no significant difference between the groups for either substrate (5-HT or PEA). There was a significant positive correlation between age and MAO-B V_{max} for both groups. There was no correlation between postmortem interval and MAO enzyme kinetics.

The series of suicide victims described above was distinguished from those of other studies of brain MAO in suicide by the exclusion (for the most part) of those who died by overdose; the potential problem of drug effects contaminating the results was thereby avoided. Taken together with the results from our laboratory, it appears that the lowered brain MAO activity in alcoholic suicides may be related primarily to alcoholism rather than to suicidal behavior, since Gottfries et al. (1975) have suggested that MAO activity was reduced in alcoholic suicides but not in nonalcoholic suicides.

In summary, there is a growing body of evidence derived from postmortem studies linking suicide and 5-HT. Five of seven postmortem studies reported decreased levels of either 5-HT or 5-HIAA in the brain stems of suicide victims. However, caution should be exercised in the interpretation of these findings, since (1) many of the deaths were due to drug overdose and carbon monoxide poisoning; (2) there was a lack of age-matched controls; and (3) in some instances there was an extremely long postmortem interval. Two studies assessing the levels of 5-HT and 5-HIAA in the frontal cortex of suicide victims have found no differences relative to controls.

Three of the four studies measuring imipramine binding in postmortem brain samples of suicide victims or depressives have reported decreases. Two studies have measured 5-HT$_2$ receptors in suicide victims. One study found a significant increase in 5-HT$_2$ binding density in suicide victims. A second study also noted an increase in 5-HT$_2$ binding (but not a significant one) in a small sample of apparently non-drug-treated suicides. There were no significant differences in two studies of 5-HT$_1$ binding in suicide victims.

Two of three studies measuring muscarinic binding in suicide victims found no difference relative to controls. The other study reported an increase. Two of three studies reported increased beta-adrenergic binding in brain tissue from suicide victims.

No differences were found in brain MAO-A or MAO-B enzyme kinetics in suicides and controls.

These data suggest a strong association between serotonergic function and suicide—one that transcends diagnostic categories and raises the possibility of involvement of the noradrenergic system, perhaps in the role of mediating effects of more acute precipitants of suicide.

In Vivo Studies of Suicide Attempters

Several clinical studies have examined the relationship of 5-HT-related biochemical measures to suicidal behavior (for an overview, see Brown *et al.*, 1982). One of the earliest studies was conducted by Asberg and colleagues (1976), in which the CSF levels of 5-HIAA were measured in a group of depressed patients, including several who had attempted and two who later committed suicide. Analysis of 5-HIAA levels of the patients who made serious suicide attempts revealed that they had significantly lower values than the other depressed patients. This finding has since been extended not only to depressed patients, but also to patients with psychiatric diagnoses such as personality disorders or schizophrenia. Brown *et al.* (1982) found a significant reduction in 5-HIAA levels in subjects diagnosed as having personality disorders with a history of suicidal behavior.

van Praag (1983) reported significantly lower levels of CSF 5-HIAA in schizophrenic patients who had attempted suicide, compared with those who had not. Similarly, Ninan, van Kammen, Scheinin, Linnoila, Bunney, and Goodwin (1983) also found significant reductions in CSF concentrations of 5-HIAA in schizophrenics with a history of suicidal behavior, compared to those with no history of this behavior.

Low levels of CSF 5-HIAA were also found in individuals with a history of aggressive behavior (Brown *et al.*, 1982). A high incidence of suicide attempts was associated with low levels of 5-HIAA in a group of violent and impulsive murderers (Linnoila, Virkkunen, Scheinin, Nuutila, Rimon, & Goodwin, 1983). This suggests that suicidal behavior may be related to impulsivity or aggression, which in turn is associated with dysfunction of the 5-HT system.

Recently, Stanley (1984) examined 5-HIAA and homovanillic acid (HVA) in the CSF of 21 serious suicide attempters and 10 psychiatrically ill nonattempters from mixed diagnostic categories. They observed a tendency toward decreased levels of 5-HIAA in those individuals with a history of a suicide attempt, with suicide attempters having a mean CSF 5-HIAA level of 17.5 ng/ml ($SD = 5.8$) and nonattempters having a mean value of 21.5 ng/ml ($SD = 4.0$). This mean difference yielded a trend that approached significance ($t = 1.90, df = 29, p = .06$) (Figure 10-1). There was no difference in HVA levels between the two groups.

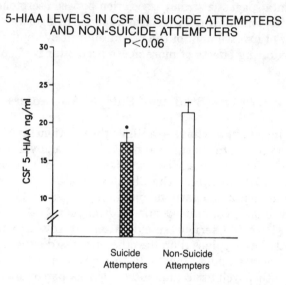

Figure 10-1. 5-HIAA levels in CSF in suicide attempters and nonattempters. (From Stanley, unpublished data, 1984.)

Together these studies consistently point to a dysfunction in the 5-HT system in suicide attempters—evidence that is consistent with the biochemical abnormalities found in postmortem studies of suicide.

Imipramine binding and 5-HT uptake in the platelet are two peripheral measures that may be related to central 5-HT function. Both have been reported to be altered in patients suffering from depression. Imipramine binding has been characterized in human platelets and shown to be associated with the platelet 5-HT uptake sites (Langer, Moret, Raisman, Dubocovich, & Briley, 1980; Rehavi, Skolnick, & Paul, 1982). Several studies have reported decreases in the number of imipramine binding sites in those diagnosed as depressed (Asarch, Shih, & Kulcsar, 1980; Paul et al., 1984; Raisman, Sechter, Briley, Zerifian, & Langer, 1981). There are a number of studies demonstrating that 5-HT uptake in the platelets is also reduced in depression (Born, Grignani, & Martin, 1980; Kaplan & Mann, 1982; Mirkin & Coppen, 1980; Tuomisto & Tukiainen, 1976). Since a large number of suicidal patients are depressed, peripheral measures may be related to suicidal behavior and to estimates of central 5-HT activity (specifically, CSF levels of 5-HIAA). Furthermore, reduced imipramine binding in the brains of suicide victims compared with control subjects (Paul et al., 1984; Stanley et al., 1982) raises the question of the relationship of reduced imipramine binding and 5-HT uptake to depression and/or suicidal behavior.

Stanley and Mann (1984) examined imipramine binding in the platelets of 33 serious suicide attempters and psychiatric diagnostic controls. These preliminary data yielded a trend toward a decreased number of imipramine binding sites, as indicated by a lower B_{max} value in those individuals with a history of suicide attempt ($\bar{x}$ = 790; *SD* = 158) compared with those who had not made an attempt ($\bar{x}$ = 862; *SD* = 131) (Figure 10-2). The direction of this preliminary data is in agreement with earlier work reported for imipramine binding in brain. However, this relationship is not significant, and additional data must be collected to determine whether this trend will continue.

In an attempt to correlate peripheral markers with CNS measures, a comparison of platelet imipramine binding (B_{max}) and CSF levels of 5-HIAA revealed no significant correlation for the two measures (r = .15). Thus, although both binding and 5-HIAA levels tend to be lower in suicide attempters, the preliminary data show that the two measures are not strongly correlated. As in the case of CSF estimates of 5-HIAA, there is neither a sufficient total number of samples nor a large enough series of diagnostic controls to permit any firm conclusions to be drawn regarding the utility of the measure in assessing suicidal behavior.

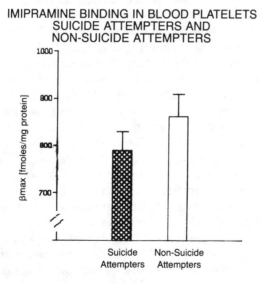

Figure 10-2. Imipramine binding in blood platelets in suicide attempters and nonattempters. (From Stanley, unpublished data, 1984.)

Platelet MAO activity has been studied extensively in both schizophrenia and depression. Platelet MAO was found to be unaltered in drug-free schizophrenics (Mann, Kaplan, Georgotas, Friedman, Branchey, & Gershon, 1981; Mann & Thomas, 1979), although one group has reported reduced platelet MAO in subgroups of schizophrenics (Wyatt, Potkin, Bridge, Phelps, & Wise, 1980). There is a greater consensus in the literature that platelet MAO activity may be lowered in bipolar depressed patients (Landowski, Lysiak, & Angielski, 1975; D. L. Murphy & Weiss, 1972) and is possibly elevated in unipolar endogenous depression (Mann, 1979; Nies, Robinson, Harris, & Lamborn, 1974).

Despite the large body of work on platelet MAO activity in depression, there have been few studies examining the relationship of platelet MAO activity and suicidal behavior. Buchsbaum and colleagues (Buchsbaum, Coursey, & Murphy, 1976; Buchsbaum, Haier, & Murphy, 1977) reported that male patients with low platelet MAO activity and augmented average evoked response had a significantly higher prevalence of suicide attempts than other patients. These findings point to a relationship between platelet MAO and suicidal behavior. However, in order to assess the strength of this relationship better, it would be necessary to directly compare diagnostically matched patient groups with and without a history of suicide attempts.

In addition to the peripheral measures of imipramine binding and 5-HT uptake, cortisol secretion may be related to suicidal behavior. While the major focus in the area of control of cortisol secretion has been depression, several findings have been reported that may implicate it in suicide. In 1965, Bunney and Fawcett reported that 3 of 36 depressed patients who subsequently committed suicide had high levels of 17-hydroxycorticosteroids in their urine. The same group reported similar findings in a follow-up study of 94 patients, 8 of whom were suicidal (Bunney, Fawcett, Davis, & Gifford, 1969). In a study of 22 diagnostically mixed patients, elevated urinary cortisol was reported for two patients who subsequently committed suicide (Ostroff, Giller, Bonese, Ebersole, Harkness, & Mason, 1982). Similar findings were also reported for plasma cortisol levels in a large group of patients (diagnosis not specified). Six patients in this group who committed suicide were found to have higher levels of plasma cortisol (Krieger, 1970).

More recently, the relationship between plasma cortisol and suicidality has been investigated using the dexamethasone suppression test (DST). Carroll, Greden, and Feinberg (1981) investigated 250 melancholic patients and found abnormal DSTs in 5 patients who committed suicide and in 11 patients who attempted suicide by violent means. There were, however, three patients who did commit suicide whose DSTs were normal. Coryell and Schlesser (1981) studied 243 depressed patients,

5 of whom subsequently committed suicide. Four of the five completed suicides had abnormal DSTs. Targum, Rosen, and Capodanno (1983) reported a significantly higher incidence of abnormal DSTs in endogenously depressed patients with a history of a suicide attempt, compared with those who had not made a suicide attempt. A similar trend was observed by another group of investigators (Banki & Arato, 1983), who noted a higher proportion of nonsuppression among those who had attempted suicide.

Thus, while there appears to be an association between either abnormal cortisol secretion or nonsuppression of the DST and suicide attempts, this relationship has been studied generally in a single diagnostic group, that of depression. In this regard, Carroll *et al.* (1981) have argued that the specificity of the DST for identifying suicide risk may be restricted to those with a diagnosis of melancholia. Further studies are necessary to ascertain whether abnormal cortisol secretion is present in suicide attempters with other diagnoses.

In summary, several measures of both central and peripheral biochemical functioning have been examined in suicidal individuals. Many investigators have noted low levels of CSF 5-HIAA, a finding consistent with evidence for serotonergic dysfunction provided by postmortem studies. Recent studies show a trend toward decreased 5-HIAA in suicidal individuals, but further work remains to be done in this area. The relationship of suicidal behavior to platelet MAO activity, imipramine binding, and 5-HT uptake remains to be clarified.

Conclusion

While biochemical research in suicide presents promising findings, the number of studies is small, and those studies that have been conducted to date suffer from methodological constraints. First, most of the biological studies of suicide attempters have relatively small sample sizes and typically investigate only one diagnostic classification. Therefore, it is problematic to generalize the results. Secondly, several studies have been post hoc analyses of chart reviews. Conclusions must be drawn with caution, and studies involving more than one diagnostic group, utilizing a range of central and peripheral measures, are required to address these questions specifically. The finding of correlations between biochemical measures and suicidality may contribute to a theoretical understanding of the pathogenesis of this behavior; it may also potentially aid in its diagnosis, in prediction of risk, and in development of new pharmacological treatments.

References

Asarch, K., Shih, J. C., & Kulcsar, A. Decreased ^{3}H-imipramine binding in depressed males and females. *Communications in Psychopharmacology*, 1980, *4*, 425–432.

Asberg, M., Thoren, P., Traskman, L., Bertilsson, L., & Ringverger, V. Serotonin depression—biochemical subgroup within the affective disorders? *Science*, 1976, *191*, 478–480.

Banki, C. M., & Arato, M. Amine metabolites and neuroendocrine responses related to depression and suicide. *Journal of Affective Disorders*, 1983, *5*, 223–232.

Beskow, J., Gottfries, C. G., Roos, B. E., & Winblad, B. Determination of monoamine and monoamine metabolites in the human brain: Post mortem studies in a group of suicides and in a control group. *Acta Psychiatrica Scandinavica*, 1976, *53*, 7–20.

Borg, S., & Stahl, M. Prediction of suicide. *Acta Psychiatrica Scandinavica*, 1982, *6S*, 221–232.

Born, G. V. R., Grignani, G., & Martin, K. Long-term effect of lithium on the uptake of 5-hydroxytryptamine in human platelets. *British Journal of Clinical Pharmacology*, 1980, *9*, 321–325.

Bourne, H. R., Bunney, W. E., Jr., Colburn, R. W., Davis, J. M., Shaw, D. M., & Coppen, A. J. Noradrenaline 5-hydroxytryptamine, and 5-hydroxyindoleacetic acid in the hindbrains of suicidal patients. *Lancet*, 1968, *12*, 805–808.

Brown, G. L., Ebert, M. H., Goyer, P. F., Jimerson, D. C., Klein, W. J., Bunney, W. E., & Goodwin, F. K. Aggression, suicide, and serotonin: Relationships to CSF amine metabolites. *American Journal of Psychiatry*, 1982, *139*(6), 741–746.

Buchsbaum, M. S., Coursey, R. D., & Murphy, D. L. The biochemical high-risk paradigm: Behavioral and familial correlates of low platelet monoamine oxidase activity. *Science*, 1976, *194*, 339–341.

Buchsbaum, M. S., Haier, R. J., & Murphy, D. L. Suicide attempts, platelet monoamine oxidase and the average evoked response. *Acta Psychiatrica Scandinavica*, 1977, *56*, 69–79.

Bunney, W. E., Jr., & Fawcett, J. A. Possibility of a biochemical test for suicidal potential. *Archives of General Psychiatry*, 1965, *13*, 232–239.

Bunney, W. E., Jr., Fawcett, J. A., Davis, J. M., & Gifford, S. Further evaluation of urinary 17-hydroxycorticosteroids in suicidal patients. *Archives of General Psychiatry*, 1969, *21*, 138–150.

Carroll, B. J., Greden, J. F., & Feinberg, M. Suicide, neuroendocrine dysfunction and CSF 5-HIAA concentrations in depression. In B. Angrist, G. D. Burrows, M. Lader, O. Lingjaerde, G. Seovall, D. Wheatley. (Eds.), *Recent advances in neuropsychopharmacology*. New York: Pergamon Press, 1981.

Coryell, W., & Schlesser, M. A. Suicide and the dexamethasone suppression test in unipolar depression. *American Journal of Psychiatry*, 1981, *138*(8), 1120–1121.

Goldney, R. Loss of control in young women who have attempted suicide. *Journal of Nervous and Mental Disease*, 1982, *4*, 198–201.

Gottfries, C. G., Oreland, L., Wilberg, A., & Winblad, G. Lowered monoamine oxidase activity in brains from alcoholic suicides. *Journal of Neurochemistry*, 1975, *25* 667–673.

Grote, S. S., Moses, S. G., Robins, E., Hudgens, R. W., & Croninger, A. B. A study of selected catecholamine metabolizing enzymes: A comparison of depressive suicides and alcoholic suicides with controls. *Journal of Neurochemistry*, 1974, *23*, 791–802.

Kaplan, R. D., & Mann, J. J. Altered platelet serotonin uptake in schizophrenia and melancholia. *Life Sciences*, 1982, *31*, 583–588.

Kaufman, C. A., Gillin, J. C., O'Laughlin, T., & Kleinman, J. E. Muscarinic binding in suicides. *Psychiatry Research*, 1984, *12*, 47–55.

Krieger, G. Biochemical predictors of suicide. *Diseases of the Nervous System*, 1970, *31*, 479–482.

Landowski, J., Lysiak, W., & Angielski, S. Monoamine oxidase activity in blood platelets from patients with cyclophrenic depressive syndromes. *Biochemical Medicine*, 1975, *14*, 347–354.

Langer, S. Z., Moret, C., Raisman, R., Dubocovich, M. L., & Briley, M. High affinity ^{3}H-imipramine binding in rat hypothalamus: Association with uptake of serotonin but not of norepinephrine. *Science*, 1980, *210*, 1133–1135.

Langer, S. Z., & Raisman, R. Binding of ^{3}H-imipramine and ^{3}H-desipramine as biochemical tools for studies in depression. *Neuropharmacology*, 1983, *22*(3 Spec. No.), 407–413.

Linnoila, M., Virkkunen, M., Scheinin, M., Nuutila, A., Rimon, R., & Goodwin, F. K. Low cerebrospinal fluid 5-hydroxyindoleacetic acid concentration differentiates impulsive from nonimpulsive violent behavior. *Life Sciences*, 1983, *33*, 2609–2614.

Lloyd, K. G., Farley, I. J., Deck, J. H. N., & Hornykiewicz, O. Serotonin and 5-hydroxy-indoleacetic acid in discrete areas of the brainstem of suicide victims and control patients. *Advances in Biochemical Psychopharmacology*, 1974, *11*, 387–397.

Mann, J. J. Altered platelet monoamine activity in affective disorders. *Psychological Medicine*, 1979, *9*, 729.

Mann, J. J., Kaplan, R. D., Georgotas, A., Friedman, E., Branchey, M., & Gershon, S. Monoamine oxidase activity and enzyme kinetics in three subpopulations of density-fractionated platelets in chronic paranoid schizophrenics. *Psychopharmacology*, 1981, *74*, 344.

Mann, J. J., & Stanley, M. Postmortem monoamine oxidase enzyme kinetics in the frontal cortex of suicide victims and controls. *Acta Psychiatrica and Scandinavica*, 1984, *69*, 135–139.

Mann, J. J., Stanley, M., McBride, P. A., & McEwen, B. *Increased serotonin and beta-adrenergic receptor binding in the frontal cortex of suicide victims.* Manuscript submitted for publication, 1986.

Mann, J. J., & Thomas, K. M. Platelet monoamine oxidase activity in schizophrenia: Relationship to disease, treatment, institutionalization and outcome. *British Journal of Psychiatry*, 1979, *134*, 366.

Meyerson, L. R., Wennogle, L. P., Abel, M. S., Coupet, J., Lippa, A. S., Rauh, C. E., & Beer, B. Human brain receptor alterations in suicide victims. *Pharmacology, Biochemistry, and Behavior*, 1982, *17*, 159–163.

Mirkin, A. M., & Coppen, A. Electrodermal activity in depression: Clinical and biochemical correlates. *British Journal of Psychiatry*, 1980, *137*, 93–97.

Monk, M. Epidemiology. In S. Perlin (Ed.), *A handbook for the study of suicide.* New York: Oxford University Press, 1975.

Murphy, D. L., & Weiss, R. Reduced monoamine oxidase activity in blood platelets from bipolar depressed patients. *American Journal of Psychiatry*, 1972, *128*, 35–41.

Murphy, G. On suicide prediction and prevention. *Archives of General Psychiatry*, 1983, *40*, 343–344.

Nies, A., Robinson, D. S., Harris, L. S., & Lamborn, K. R. Comparison of monoamine oxidase substrate activities in twins, schizophrenics, depressives and controls. *Advances in Biochemical Psychopharmacology*, 1974, *12*, 59.

Ninan, P. B., van Kammen, D., Scheinin, M., Linnoila, M., Bunney, W., & Goodwin, F. CSF 5-HIAA levels in suicidal schizophrenic patients. *American Journal of Psychiatry*, 1984, *141*, 566–569.

Ostroff, R., Giller, E., Bonese, K., Ebersole, E., Harkness, L., & Mason, J. Neuroendocrine factors of suicidal behavior. *American Journal of Psychiatry*, 1982, *139*(10), 1323–1325.

Owens, F., Cross, A. J., Crow, T. J., Deakin, J. F. W., Ferrier, I. N., Lofthouse, R., & Poulter, M. Brain 5-HT$_2$ receptors and suicide. *Lancet*, 1983, *i*, 1256.

Pare, C. M. B., Yeung, D. P. H., Price, K., & Stacey, R. S. 5-hydroxytryptamine, noradrenaline, and dopamine in brainstem, hypothalamus, and caudate nucleus of controls and of patients commiting suicide by coal-gas poisoning. *Lancet*, 1969, *ii*, 133–135.

Paul, S. M., Rehavi, M., Skolnick, P., & Goodwin, F. K. High affinity binding of antidepressants to a biogenic amine transport site in human brain and platelet: Studies in depression. In R. Post & J. C. Ballenger (Eds.), *Neurobiology of mood disorders.* Baltimore: Williams & Wilkins, 1984.

Perlin, S., & Schmitt, S. Psychiatry. In S. Perlin (Ed.), *A handbook for the study of suicide.* New York: Oxford University Press, 1975.

Perry, E. K., Marshall, E. L. F., Blessed, G., Tomlinson, B. E., & Perry, R. H. Decreased
    imipramine binding in the brains of patients with depressive illness. *British Journal
    of Psychiatry*, 1983, *1412*, 188–192.
Raisman, R., Sechter, D., Briley, M. S., Zerifian, J., & Langer, S. Z. High affinity ³H-
    imipramine binding in platelets from untreated and treated depressed patients
    compared to healthy volunteers. *Psychopharmacology*, 1981, *75*, 368–371.
Recent trends in suicide. *Statistical Bulletin*, 1976, *57*, 5–7.
Rehavi, M., Skolnick, P., & Paul, S. M. Solubilization and partial purification of the
    high affinity ³H-imipramine binding site from human platelets. *Federation of European
    Biochemical Societies Letters*, 1982, *150*(2), 514–518.
Resnick, H. L. P. Psychiatric emergencies. In H. I. Kaplan, A. M. Freedman, B. J. Sadock.
    et al. (Eds.), *Comprehensive textbook of psychiatry III*. Baltimore: Williams & Wilkins,
    1980.
Shaw, D. M., Camps, F. E., & Eccleston, E. G. 5-Hydroxytryptamine in the hind-brain
    of depressive suicides. *British Journal of Psychiatry*, 1967, *113*, 1407–1411.
Stanley, M. Cholinergic receptor binding in the frontal cortex of suicide victims. *American
    Journal of Psychiatry*, 1984, *141*, 1432–1436.
Stanley, M., & Mann, J. J. Increased serotonin-2 binding sites in frontal cortex of suicide
    victims. *Lancet*, 1983, *ii*, 214–216.
Stanley, M., Unpublished data, 1984.
Stanley, M., McIntyre, E., & Gershon, S. *Postmortem serotonin metabolism in suicide
    victims*. Paper presented at American College of Neuropsychopharmacology, 1983.
Stanley, M., Virgilio, J., & Gershon, S. Tritiated imipramine binding sites are decreased
    in the frontal cortex of suicides. *Science*, 1982, *216*, 1337–1339.
Targum, D. S., Rosen, L., & Capodanno, A. E. The dexamethasone suppression test in
    suicidal patients with unipolar depression. *American Journal of Psychiatry*, 1983,
    140(7), 877–879.
Tuomisto, J., & Tukiainen, E. Decreased uptake of 5-hydroxytryptamine in blood platelets
    from depressed patients. *Nature*, 1976, *262*, 596–598.
U.S. Public Health Service. *Facts of life and death* (DHEW Publication No. (PHS 79-
    1222). Washington, D.C.: U.S. Government Printing Office, 1979.
van Praag, H. M. CSF 5-HIAA and suicide in non-depressed schizophrenics. *Lancet*,
    1983, *ii*, 977–978.
Wyatt, J. R., Potkin, S. G., Bridge, T. P., Phelps, B. H., & Wise, C. D. Monoamine oxidase
    in schizophrenia: An overview. *Schizophrenia Bulletin*, 1980, *6*, 199.
Zanko, M. T., & Biegon, A. Increased β-adrenergic receptor binding in human frontal
    cortex of suicide victims. *Society for Neuroscience Abstracts*, 1983, Part 1, 210.

CHAPTER 11

Endocrinology and Suicide

Charles L. Rich, MD
Department of Psychiatry, University of California at San Diego

An association between endocrine gland pathology and psychiatric symptomatology has been recognized for over 200 years (Parry, 1940). This obviously occurred before the hormones could be measured, before replacement hormones could be manufactured, and before any notion of the complex relationships with central nervous system (CNS) neurohormones had been formulated. It seemed clear fairly early that the major mental changes were related to "organicity" (i.e., deterioration of intellectual functioning, plus or minus psychosis). Depressive-like symptoms of apathy, stupor, and low mood were also common. Although endocrine underactivity more commonly produced depressive-like symptoms, overactivity of the glands did not do the opposite. For example, while hyperthyroid patients were noted to be anxious and insomniac, they were also observed to be weak and fatigued. The possibility of undiagnosed (and possibly reversible) endocrine disease being responsible for vast numbers of mental hospital patients did not materialize, however.

The appearance of replacement hormones changed the picture somewhat. Patients given exogenous adrenal corticosteroids, for example, became euphoric and occasionally developed a manic-like psychosis. This observation sparked continued curiosity about the relationship between endocrine glands and the psyche.

While gigantic strides were being made in endocrine research, interest in suicide among research psychiatrists was also growing. It was clear that most psychiatric patients did not die by suicide (Miles, 1977). On the other hand, two independent studies of suicide (Dorpat & Ripley, 1960; Robins, Murphy, Wilkinson, Gassner, & Kayes, 1959) found that most (90 + %) of the victims were psychiatrically ill. This finding has been replicated several times in different countries over the ensuing years (Barraclough, Bunch, Nelson, & Sainsbury, 1974; Chynoweth, Tonge, & Armstrong, 1980; Ovenstone, 1973; Rich, Young, & Fowler, in press; Seager & Flood, 1965). Depression, alcoholism, and, more recently, drug abuse have been found most frequently. Many of the alcohol and drug abusers have had prominent depressive symptoms as well.

A variety of physiological abnormalities have been described in depressed patients. They suggest biological concomitants if not causes for some depressions. Some of these involve not only endocrine glands, but also their links to the brain. A major stumbling block in studying the relationship of these abnormalities to suicide, though, was the inevitable reality that it is impossible to do such studies in the post-mortem state. Some studies have used suicide attempters, but the difficulties attendant on that strategy have been thoroughly elucidated (K. Smith & Maris, 1985). Various clinical research units for the study of affective disorders began accumulating a few subjects who eventually committed suicide. This provided some prospectively gathered data. Fortunately, such suicides occurred infrequently. Unfortunately, rapid changes in technology made older cases hard to compare to more recent ones.

In spite of the difficulties described here, the story on endocrine function and suicide is far from over. The teasing leads remain. The increasing number of clinical research units dedicated to the study of affective disorders assures that more systematically collected prospective data (psychosocial as well as physiological) will become available when suicides unfortunately occur in this extremely high-risk group. It is important, then, to summarize progress to date in the area, so that clinicians have an idea of what may be available now or in the future to assist in the assessment of suicide risk. It is also important for researchers to attempt to formulate strategies for data collection now, knowing that they may not bear fruit for some time.

The Endocrine System(s)

The endocrine system is not as clearly defined as was once thought. The simple concept of a gland such as the thyroid being either "overactive" or "underactive" has given way to descriptions of multiple substances (hormones), some of which may be produced by more than one gland. Each hormone, then, in essence constitutes its own system. It acts in concert with the various target organs it affects, as well as the controls exerted on it by the CNS. This chapter deals with two systems whose relationship to depression and suicide have been extensively studied. They are the thyroid hormones and the adrenal hormone cortisol. Other systems have been related to mental changes as well, but they are not considered here. In particular, these include the parathyroid and sex hormones.

Depressive-like symptoms have been described in conjunction with both excesses and deficiencies of parathyroid hormone. These changes have been directly related to either high or low blood calcium levels, which resulted from either lower or higher parathyroid hormone levels. Petersen (1968) mentioned "suicidal tendencies" in some of his hyperparathyroid patients, but did not report any actual suicides (or even attempts). The mental changes cleared with correction of the calcium abnormalities, so it appears that they are more likely to have been related to the calcium levels than to the parathyroid hormone itself. Some interest in calcium metabolism and affective disorders persists (Carman & Wyatt, 1979), but it is removed from the realm of the parathyroid gland.

The female sex hormones have attracted a great deal of attention in relation to depression and suicide. The male sex hormones have been suggested to be related to problems associated with aggressiveness, but not depression or suicide.

Finally, it is not within the purview of this chapter to delve into relationships that doubtless exist between peripheral endocrine glands and CNS neurotransmitters and receptors. The chain from hormone to neurohormone to neurotransmitter to suicide may exist, but many connecting links are undoubtedly missing. The future may bring clarification of the chain, but for the time being the issue of neurotransmitters and receptors is covered in other chapters of this volume.

The Thyroid System

The thyroid gland was probably the first endocrine gland to be associated with mental disorders. The prominent location of this gland in the front of the neck permits easy, direct access to physical examination. This access allowed clinicians to diagnose thyroid disease in living subjects even before corrective surgery was possible.

The term "myxedematous madness" (Asher, 1949) was coined to describe what was apparently the most common complication of prolonged hypothyroidism—a dementia with psychosis (Jellinek, 1962). Depressive symptoms were also common. In 1961, Pitts and Guze reported three cases in which the depression remained after correction of the thyroid deficiency. Two of those subsequently improved further with electro-convulsive therapy (ECT), suggesting the possibility of concurrent af-fective and thyroid disorders in these patients.

Hyperthyroidism has been associated with a wider range of mental status changes, from subtle anxiety to profound psychosis (Bursten, 1961; Clower, Young, & Kepas, 1969). Difficulty has been repeatedly found in distinguishing symptoms of hyperthyroidism from those that might have been present prior to occurrence of the thyroid disease. Nonetheless, depressive symptoms play a prominent role.

Even though depressive symptoms occur frequently in both hypothy-roid and hyperthyroid patients, the disease states are not found at all frequently in psychiatric patient populations (Nicholson, Liebling, & Hall, 1976). In fact, a study by McLarty, Ratcliffe, Ratcliffe, Shimmins, and Goldberg (1978) found that the frequency of hypo- or hyperthyroidism in mental hospital patients may be no higher than the population at large, and in their sample thyroid disease was not related to psychiatric diagnosis (when corrected for age). Also, Cohen and Swigar (1979) showed that a considerable number of people with either low or elevated thyroid hormone levels on admission to a hospital reverted to normal spontaneously within 2 weeks. Finally, Checkley (1978) reported that episodes of thyrotoxicosis (hyperthyroidism) in five patients with manic-depressive illness did not affect the course of the psychiatric disorder. All in all, it would not seem that a connection between thyroid disease and other psychiatric disorders has been established.

Nonetheless, depressive symptoms do indeed complicate the treatment of some thyroid disease patients. There do not seem to be, however, any reports of suicide occurring in hypo- or hyperthyroid patients. This is not to say that they have not occurred, but rather that, if they have, they have not been reported.

Two other approaches to the intriguing thyroid story have been ex-tensively investigated. Thyroid hormones had failed when used on their own for treating depression. The development of tricyclic anti-depressant medication, however, opened a potential new avenue for their use. Prange's group from North Carolina found that both thyroid hormone and thyroid-stimulating hormone (thyrotropin, or TSH—the pituitary gland hormone that stimulates the thyroid gland) would speed the antidepressant effect of the drug imipramine (Prange, Wilson, Knox, McClane, & Lipton, 1970; Prange, Wilson, Rabon, & Lipton, 1969; Wilson, Prange, McClane, Rabon, & Lipton, 1970). The overall final improvement was not greater, but it occurred faster. The same phe-nomenon was reported by Wheatley (1972) with thyroid hormone and amitriptyline, another tricyclic antidepressant drug.

The search for the answer to this mystery continued deeper into the brain. A substance called thyrotropin-releasing hormone (TRH), which stimulates the release of TSH, was discovered in the hypothalamus (the area just above the pituitary). Soon, TRH was being given to depressed patients by Prange's group. They initially described an anti-depressant effect of TRH injections (Prange, Lara, Wilson, Alltop, & Breese, 1972). This finding did not hold up in repeat studies elsewhere (Coppen, Peet, Montgomery, Bailey, Marks, & Woods, 1974; Mountjoy, Weller, Hall, Price, Hunter, & Dewar, 1974). More importantly, however, Prange's group described a low response of TSH to the TRH injections in the depressed patients (Prange *et al.*, 1972). This finding was sub-sequently replicated in many experiments, including ones that showed the abnormality to be present even when the persons were not depressed (Loosen & Prange, 1982). This suggests that, while the abnormality may be a marker for the disease (a trait variable), it may not be helpful in determining when people are depressed (a state variable).

Throughout this line of investigation, no mention was made of suicide until a report by Linkowski, van Wettere, Kerkhofs, Brauman, and Mendlewicz (1983). In a 5-year follow-up of 51 hospitalized depressed women, they found that 4 had died by suicide. All 4 had had low TSH response to TRH injections during their index hospitalization. While the subjects were all women, and not all of the subjects with low TSH responses committed suicide, all the cases who did die by suicide had low responses. Admittedly, this is a very early finding in a small number of cases, but it certainly brings the thyroid system clearly back into prominence in the endocrinology of suicide.

It is far too early to close the book on the thyroid system. It appears that excesses or deficiencies of thyroid hormones are responsible mainly for "organic" mental dysfunctions. There does not seem to be any direct relationship between thyroid hormones and suicide. On the other hand, the upper end of the thyroid system—the TRH–TSH connection—bears further watching and investigation. The blunted TSH response occurs in too many people with affective (and other psychiatric) disorders at this time to be of immediate clinical use in suicide prevention, though.

The Adrenal Cortical (Cortisol) System

The adrenal glands are situated at the top of each kidney. A variety of steroid hormones are produced by the outer layer (cortex) of these glands. The most predominant hormone (and the one that has commanded the most interest in relation to depression and suicide) is cortisol. It was recognized early that overactivity or underactivity of the adrenal cortex could be caused either by primary disease of the adrenal cortex itself or by disease of the pituitary gland. The pituitary hormone that controls the secretion of cortisol by the adrenals is adrenocorticotrophic hormone (ACTH).

Cushing's syndrome is the condition associated with overproduction of adrenal cortical hormones. The physical changes resulting from excess cortisol are the same as when patients are given synthetic corticosteroids or ACTH. Surprisingly, though, the attendant mental symptoms are different. Patients with Cushing's syndrome are typically anxious and depressed, with psychomotor slowing (Starkman, Schteingart, & Schork, 1981). In an extensive review of reported cases, Spillane (1951) noted, in fact, several reports of suicide among Cushing's syndrome patients. It is hard to tell what, if any, direct relationship existed in these cases between the adrenal disease and suicide. A more recent report of 35 cases of Cushing's syndrome described depressive symptoms in most, but they tended to be short-lived and associated with other mental changes. This suggests more similarity to an organic depressive syndrome. The authors noted that 2 of the patients had made suicide attempts after the onset of the Cushing's syndrome, but neither was successful.

Synthetic substitutes for cortisol, on the other hand, are most notorious for their association with euphoria (Taylor, Ayer, & Morris, 1956). There is some speculation that this euphoric response results from the clinical improvement in the diseases being treated with these substances, but most clinicians believe it goes beyond that. Regardless, depression occurs only in a small proportion of patients taking adrenal steroids (or ACTH), and suicide has not been reported as a complication. It seems unlikely that no one taking adrenal steroids has ever committed suicide; again, however, if they have, it has not been reported.

Mental symptoms occur in as many as 70% of persons with adrenal cortical insufficiency (Addison's disease) (Sorkin, 1949). The metabolic abnormalities resulting from this disease are widespread and may account for the more "organic" nature of the mental changes. Again, in spite of the depressive quality of many of these patients, suicide has not been reported as a concomitant.

Somewhat unlike the situation with the thyroid, then, there have been intimations of a relationship between adrenal cortex hyperactivity and suicide. The relationship has been explored even more thoroughly in studies of adrenal cortical function in depressed patients without apparent adrenal disease.

The development of inpatient research units has made accurate longitudinal observations of many behavioral and physiological variables possible. In 1965, Bunney and Fawcett reported three suicides who had been studied on a research ward prior to their deaths. Among other things, the investigators had measured 17-hydroxycorticosteroids (17-OHCS) in the urine of all their research subjects. This substance is the metabolic breakdown product of cortisol. They discovered that the three suicide victims had high 24-hour 17-OHCS urine levels, but, during the same time, had low scores for suicidal behavior. They suggested the possibility that the 17-OHCS measurement could be used as a test for identifying depressed patients with a high risk for suicide even if they were not admitting to being depressed. Results from subsequent studies of urinary 17-OHCS were not as clearly positive, but a lack of standardization of methodology was evident (Bunney, Fawcett, Davis, & Gifford, 1969; Fink & Carpenter, 1976; Krieger, 1970; Levy & Hansen, 1969). Cortisol itself was then measured in blood plasma (Krieger, 1974), cerebrospinal fluid (Traskman, Tybring, Asberg, Bertilsson, Lantto, & Schalling, 1980), and urine (Ostroff, Giller, Bonese, Ebersole, Harkness, & Mason, 1982). Elevations of cortisol were fairly uniformly described, but the really small numbers of actual suicides involved in these reports have made conclusions most difficult to reach. It has also been argued that the high-arousal state of persons on the verge of suicide could also account for the cortisol elevations (if any), and they would thus not be related directly to the cause of the depression.

While interest in direct measurement of cortisol has been fading from the scene, other discoveries related to hyperactivity of the cortisol system have commanded a great deal of attention. Normally, when a person is given a dose of a synthetic corticosteroid (e.g., dexamethasone), the pituitary stops its production of ACTH in order to tell the adrenal that the system has enough cortisol. Cortisol levels in the blood will stay very low for 18 hours or so after a dose of 1 mg of dexamethasone. This has been called the "dexamethasone suppression test" (DST). It has been shown that a sizable number of depressed persons do not respond normally and continue producing cortisol (perhaps even at high levels) in the face of a dexamethasone challenge (Carroll, Feinberg, Greden, et al., 1981). Also, unlike the TRH–TSH abnormality mentioned above, the abnormal DST seems to occur mostly when people are depressed (state variable). This again suggests that the cortisol system abnormalities are not directly related to a biological cause (if any) of depression. There is also a great deal of debate as to whether the DST is specific enough to diagnose depression (i.e., does it occur in too many other circumstances?) (Pitts, 1984). On the other hand, the DST might offer clinical usefulness in correlating with depressive episodes that could have a high suicide risk.

In 1981, Coryell and Schlesser reported 5 suicides out of 243 patients who had had DSTs during their index hospitalization. Of the 243 patients, 205 had primary depression, and 96 of those had abnormal DSTs. Four of the suicides occurred among the 96 with abnormal DSTs. While tantalizing, this result did not reach statistical significance (when compared to the 109 who did not have abnormal DSTs, none of whom had committed suicide at the time of follow-up). Also, the fifth suicide was committed by a person with secondary depression who had a normal DST. For the time being, it would seem clinically judicious to continue to worry just as much about potential suicide in depressed patients with normal DSTs and/or secondary depressions as about possible suicide in the primary unipolar depressives with abnormal DSTs.

The trail of abnormal cortisol secretion in depressed patients has extended beyond the pituitary. Meltzer, Perline, Tricou, Lowry, and Robertson (1984) have reported that oral doses of 5-hydroxytryptophan (a precursor of the neurotransmitter serotonin) were more likely to stimulate cortisol secretion in patients with affective disorders than in normal controls. The cortisol levels were even higher in the patients who had histories of suicide attempts. The problems of considering attempters have been mentioned above. Nonetheless, this line of investigation suggests the possibility that the endocrine abnormalities seen in depressives, suicidal persons, and even suicide completers may be a result of abnormalities in higher areas of the brain. These putative abnormalities are discussed in Chapter 10.

These findings do point to the need to continue to gather data. The DST is easily performed and well standardized at this point, so the data obtainable from regular clinical treatment settings should be reasonably valid. Again, the problem will be one of accumulating enough systematically studied subjects who have actually committed suicide. Until then, clinical caution must prevail. It can be hoped, at least, that this abnormality in the cortisol system may become a useful adjunct in assessing immediate suicidal potential.

Combined Thyroid–Cortisol Abnormalities

The use of several tests in combination is, of course, common medical practice. The possibility that the results of testing both the thyroid and cortisol systems could be more powerful than either alone has been the subject of study for some time (Lieber & Newbury, 1985; Targum, 1984). The TRH–TSH test might identify those with the depressive trait, and the DST might tell when they are in serious depressive states. No reports of subjects who have received both tests and subsequently committed suicide have appeared yet, however. Because of the greater complexity in performing the TRH–TSH test and the infrequency of suicides, it seems likely that information on the test combination will accumulate much more slowly than data for just the DST.

Summary

The data accumulated so far suggest several tentative conclusions. First, thyroid and adrenal gland disease unquestionably can produce severe mental disturbances. Most of these are "organic" in nature, but depressive symptoms are common as well. A connection between these diseases and suicide has not been established, however. Research cannot really address this possibility adequately, since these studies are difficult, if not impossible, to do in the postmortem state at this time. Ways should continue to be sought to overcome this problem. Clinically, it seems advisable to treat all depressed, suicidal persons with the same caution, whether they have diseases of these endocrine systems or not.

The differences in responsiveness of the thyroid and adrenocortical systems among depressed and perhaps truly suicidal persons are of greater theoretical as well as practical clinical interest. The TRH–TSH test and the DST may not be as specific as once thought. Nonetheless, the abnormalities do occur with regularity in specific subgroups of depressed patients. It is far too early to stop research on the DST or the TRH–TSH test. Clinically, however, it is premature to make important management decisions about suicidal patients based on these test results. At this time, we really have no means of pinpointing the persons who will eventually suicide. The hope that they may someday provide valid data for assessing real suicide potential is there, and clinicians should stay informed in this arena. Until that day comes, though, we must continue to exercise caution regarding our clinical judgments and to live with their uncertainties.

References

Asher, R. Myxedoematous madness. *British Medical Journal*, 1949, *2*, 555–562.
Barraclough, B., Bunch, J., Nelson, B., & Sainsbury, P. A hundred cases of suicide: Clinical aspects. *British Journal of Psychiatry*, 1974, *125*, 355–373.
Bunney, W. E., Jr., & Fawcett, J. A. Possibility of a biochemical test for suicidal potential. *Archives of General Psychiatry*, 1965, *13*, 232–239.
Bunney, W. E., Jr., Fawcett, J. A., Davis, J. M., & Gifford, S. Further evaluation of

228 SUICIDE AND LIFE-THREATENING BEHAVIOR

urinary 17-hydroxycorticosteroids in suicidal patients. *Archives of General Psychiatry*, 1969, *21*, 138–150.

Bursten, B. Psychoses associated with thyrotoxicosis. *Archives of General Psychiatry*, 1961, *4*, 267–273.

Carman, J. S., & Wyatt, R. J. Calcium: Bivalent cation in the bivalent psychoses. *Biological Psychiatry*, 1979, *14*, 295–336.

Carroll, B. J., Feinberg, M., Greden, J. F., Tarika, J., Albala, A. A., Haskett, R. F., James, N. M., Kronfol, Z., Lohr, N., Steiner, M., de Vigne, J. P., Young, E. A specific laboratory test for the diagnosis of melancholia. *Archives of General Psychiatry*, 1981, *38*, 15–22.

Checkley, S. A. Thyrotoxicosis and the course of manic–depressive illness. *British Journal of Psychiatry*, 1978, *133*, 219–223.

Chynoweth, R., Tonge, J. I., & Armstrong, J. Suicide in Brisbane—A retrospective psychosocial study. *Australia and New Zealand Journal of Psychiatry*, 1980, *14*, 37–45.

Clower, C. G., Young, A. J., & Kepas, D. Psychotic states resulting from disorders of thyroid function. *Johns Hopkins Medical Journal*, 1969, *124*, 305–310.

Cohen, K. L., & Swigar, M. E. Thyroid function screening in psychiatric patients. *Journal of the American Medical Association*, 1979, *242*, 254–257.

Coppen, A., Peet, M., Montgomery, S., Bailey, J., Marks, V. & Woods, P. Thyrotrophin-releasing hormone in the treatment of depression. *Lancet*, August 24, 1974, 433–435.

Coryell, W., & Schlesser, M. A. Suicide and the dexamethasone suppression test in unipolar depression. *American Journal of Psychiatry*, 1981, *138*, 1120–1121.

Dorpat, T. L., & Ripley, H. S. A study of suicide in the Seattle area. *Comprehensive Psychiatry*, 1960, *1*, 349–359.

Fink, E. B., & Carpenter, W. T., Jr. Further examination of a biochemical test for suicide potential. *Diseases of the Nervous System*, 1976, *37*, 341–343.

Jellinek, E. H. Fits, faints, coma, and dementia in myxoedema. *Lancet*, November 17, 1962, 1010–1012.

Krieger, G. Biochemical predictors of suicide. *Diseases of the Nervous System*, 1970, *31*, 478–482.

Krieger, G. The plasma level of cortisol as a predictor of suicide. *Diseases of the Nervous System*, 1974, *35*, 237–240.

Levy, B., & Hansen, E. Failure of the urinary test for suicide potential: Analysis of urinary 17-OHCS steroid findings prior to suicide in two patients. *Archives of General Psychiatry*, 1969, *20*, 415–418.

Lieber, A. L., & Newbury, N. Use of biologic markers in a general hospital affective disorders program. *Journal of Clinical Psychiatry*, 1985, *46*, 217–221.

Linkowski, P., van Wettere, J. P., Kerkhofs, M., Brauman, H., & Mendlewicz, J. Thyrotrophin response to thyreostimulin in affectively ill women: Relationship to suicidal behavior. *British Journal of Psychiatry*, 1983, *143*, 401–405.

Loosen, P. T., & Prange, A. J., Jr. Serum thyrotropin response to thyrotropin-releasing hormone in psychiatric patients: A review. *American Journal of Psychiatry*, 1982, *139*, 405–416.

McLarty, D. G., Ratcliffe, W. A., Ratcliffe, J. G., Shimmins, J. G., & Goldberg, A. *British Journal of Psychiatry*, 1978, *133*, 211–218.

Meltzer, H. Y., Perline, R., Tricou, B. J., Lowry, M., & Robertson, A. Effect of 5-hydroxytryptophan on serum cortisol levels in major affective disorders: II. Relation to suicide, psychosis, and depressive symptoms. *Archives of General Psychiatry*, 1984, *41*, 379–387.

Michael, R. P., & Gibbons, J. L. Interrelationships between the endocrine system and neuropsychiatry. In C. C. Pfeiffer & J. R. Smythies (Eds.), *International review of neurobiology* (Vol. 5). New York: Academic Press, 1963.

Miles, C. P. Conditions predisposing to suicide: A review. *Journal of Nervous and Mental Disease*, 1977, *164*, 231–246.

Mountjoy, C. Q., Weller, M., Hall, R., Price, J. S., Hunter, P., & Dewar, J. H. A double-blind crossover sequential trial of oral thyrotrophin-releasing hormone in depression. *Lancet*, May 18, 1974, 958–960.

Nicholson, G., Liebling, L. I., & Hall, R. A. Thyroid dysfunction in female psychiatric patients. *British Journal of Psychiatry*, 1976, *129*, 236–238.

Ostroff, R., Giller, E. Bonese, K., Ebersole, E., Harkness, L., & Mason, J. Neuroendocrine risk factors of suicidal behavior. *American Journal of Psychiatry*, 1982, *139*, 1323–1325.

Ovenstone, I. M. K. Spectrum of suicidal behaviours in Edinburgh. *British Journal of Preventive and Social Medicine*, 1973, *27*, 27–35.

Parry, C. H. Diseases of the heart. *Medical Classics*, 1940, *5*, 8–20.

Petersen, P. Psychiatric disorders in primary hyperparathyroidism. *Journal of Clinical Endocrinology*, 1968, *28*, 1491–1495.

Pitts, F. N., Jr. Recent research on the DST: Editorial. *Journal of Clinical Psychiatry*, 1984, *45*, 380–381.

Pitts, F. N., Jr., & Guze, S. B. Psychiatric disorders and myxedema. *American Journal of Psychiatry*, 1961, *118*, 142–147.

Prange, A. J., Jr., Lara, P. P., Wilson, I. C., Alltop, L. B., & Breese, G. R. Effects of thyrotropin-releasing hormone in depression. *Lancet*, November 11, 1972, 999–1002.

Prange, A. J., Jr., Wilson, I. C., Knox, A., McClane, T. K., & Lipton, M. A. Enhancement of imipramine by thyroid stimulating hormone: Clinical and theoretical implications. *American Journal of Psychiatry*, 1970, *127*, 191–199.

Prange, A. J., Jr., Wilson, I. C., Rabon, A. M., & Lipton, M. A. Enhancement of imipramine antidepressant activity by thyroid hormone. *American Journal of Psychiatry*, 1969, *126*, 457–469.

Rich, C. L., Young, D., & Fowler, R. C. San Diego suicide study: I. Young versus old cases. *Archives of General Psychiatry*, in press.

Robins, E., Murphy, G. E., Wilkinson, R. H., Gassner, S., & Kayes, J. Some clinical considerations in the prevention of suicide based on a study of 134 successful suicides. *American Journal of Public Health*, 1959, *49*, 888–899.

Seager, C. P., & Flood, R. A. Suicide in Bristol. *British Journal of Psychiatry*, 1965, *111*, 919–932.

Smith, C. K., Barish, J., Correa, J., & Williams, R. H. Psychiatric disturbance in endocrinologic disease. *Psychosomatic Medicine*, 1972, *34*, 69–86.

Smith, K., & Maris, R. *Suggested recommendations for the study of suicide and other life-threatening behaviors*. Paper presented at the meeting of the American Association of Suicidology, Toronto, 1985.

Sorkin, S. Z.: Addison's disease. *Medicine,* 1949, *28*, 371–425.

Spillane, J. D. Nervous and mental disorders in Cushing's syndrome. *Brain*, 1951, *74*, 72–94.

Starkman, M. N., Schteingart, D. E., & Schork, M. A. Depressed mood and other psychiatric manifestations of Cushing's syndrome: Relationship to hormone levels. *Psychosomatic Medicine*, 1981, *43*, 3–18.

Targum, S. D. Persistent neuroendocrine dysregulation in major depressive disorder: A marker for early relapse. *Biological Psychiatry*, 1984, *19*, 305–318.

Taylor, S. G., III, Ayer, J. P., & Morris, R. S., Jr. Cortical steroids in treatment of cancer. *Journal of the American Medical Association*, 1956, *144*, 1058–1064.

Traskman, L., Tybring, G., Asberg, M., Bertilsson, L., Lantto, O., & Schalling, D. Cortisol in the CSF of depressed and suicidal patients. *Archives of General Psychiatry*, 1980, *37*, 761–767.

Wheatley, D. Potentiation of amitriptyline by thyroid hormone. *Archives of General Psychiatry*, 1972, *26*, 229–233.

Wilson, I. C., Prange, A. J., Jr., McClane, T. K., Rabon, A. M., Lipton, M. A. Thyroid-hormone enhancement of imipramine in nonretarded depressions. *New England Journal of Medicine*, 1970, *282*, 1063–1067.

Subject Index

230

F

S